D0230050

P o w y s

50-51
Builth Wells
A470

48-49

46-47
Aberaeron

Cardigan

38-39
D y f e d
Carmarthen

36-37
Fishguard
A40

25-27
Milford Haven
Pembroke

44-45
M50
Monmouth
A40

42-43
Brecon
A40

40-41
Llandovery
A482

34-35
Gwent
Newport
M4

32-33
Merthyr Tydfil

30-31
West Glamorgan

28-29
Swansea
A48
M4

24-25
CARDIFF
A48

22-23
A470
A48
South Glamorgan
M4

20-21
Port Talbot

Llanelli

Mid Glamorgan

Bristol Channel

Scale 12.5 miles to 1 inch approx.

0   40   80 Kilometre

0   50 Miles

Contents

How to use The Leisure Atlas

The Hamlyn Leisure Atlas of Wales has been designed to be both comprehensive and flexible - there are a great many ways of using it.

First and foremost, it offers a superb atlas of Wales, on an ideal scale of about 1·6 miles to the inch. The maps are detailed enough to show almost every tarmac road, however narrow, and a great many lesser tracks as well. With this atlas, there is no excuse for sitting in a main road traffic jam when attractive country lanes offer a more enjoyable and much less frustrating alternative.

Bartholomew's unique colour-coded height presentation provides a graphic picture of the geography of the region, while the maps show both natural and man-made features in remarkable detail. Careful interpretation of the maps themselves will do much to enhance any visit to Wales.

Superimposed on these outstanding maps, however, are over 2000 symbols covering a range of 27 leisure activities and facilities, details of which can be found in the gazetteer section after the maps. The information represented by these symbols can also be used in many ways.

There are two basic ways of undertaking any holiday trip: you can plan every detail in advance, or you can simply turn up and find out what is available on arrival. This atlas works equally well in both cases.

For those who prefer to plan their holidays in advance, a brief perusal of the maps will quickly reveal those areas most richly endowed with one's favourite activities. Or one can browse through the gazetteer pages dealing with a particular pastime and thereby identify the map pages on which that pastime is best catered for.

The Atlas works just as well, of course, for the many people who prefer to take pot luck: after helping one reach the chosen destination, the appropriate map will reveal the full range of leisure activities available in that area.

Finding the Information

Each map page is divided into six squares, marked with red grid lines. Each of these squares is identified throughout this Atlas by its page number and a letter between a and i: the key to these letters appears at the top of each page.

To find out about any chosen symbol, therefore, one must first work out the map reference of that symbol. The reference of the Castle in the example shown here is 25c and details about it can be found in the section on Castles which can be found on pages 93 and 95.

In addition to its map reference, each symbol is usually identified in the gazetteer by a name in bold type corresponding to the name found at or near the symbol on the map. This is particularly helpful when several identical symbols appear in one map square.

Wherever possible, each symbol appear exactly on its actual location. In some cases, such as in towns, this has proved impossible and the address or some other description of the actual location has therefore been included in the gazetteer.

There are also some locations with so many activities that it proved impossible to fix all the symbols onto the site. In such cases, the symbols have been grouped together in a box. Each box has the name of the town printed above it; or it is placed adjacent to the town's name printed on the map; or the box is linked by a short line to the actual location.

Where maps overlap, the extent of the duplication can be seen on the small diagrams at the top of each page. Where maps do overlap, some symbols will obviously appear on more than one map: when this occurs, the later entry is cross-referenced to the earlier one.

Finally, don't forget that events which occur only occasionally are not marked on the map, but appear (with their map references) in the Calendar of Events.

Using the Gazetteer

Each entry usually includes details of its opening hours and of other facilities available at the same site: these are shown by symbols after each entry, indicating that further information can be obtained in the relevant section of the gazetteer, except for 🍽 which means that refreshments are available (although not necessarily throughout the stated opening period) and ⼏ which simply indicates a picnic site, for which no details are given.

Where opening times are given, they apply throughout the specified period unless otherwise stated. If no dates are given, the site is open all year; however, it has been assumed that all sites will be closed on days such as Christmas and New Year's Day and anyone planning a visit at such a time should telephone first.

Telephone numbers have been supplied wherever possible, together with the appropriate STD codes: where the exchange name differs from the location given for the activity, the name of the exchange is also given, so that local calls can be made.

Many sites, particularly such non-commercial ones as prehistoric earthworks, scenic walks, nature trails, etc., will be free of charge even when this is not specified in the gazetteer. *Free* is only included when we have definite information to that effect and users must be prepared to pay for any activity not marked as *Free*.

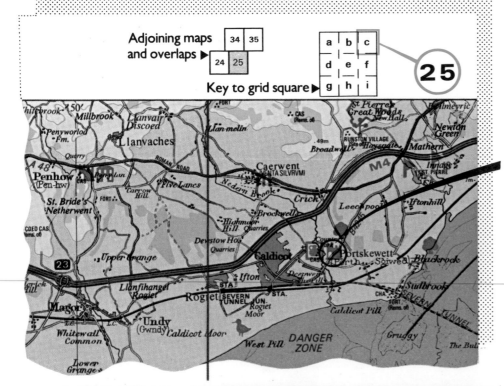

Adjoining maps and overlaps ▶ | 34 | 35 |
24 | 25 |

Key to grid square ▶ | a | b | c |
d | e | f |
g | h | i |

25

Castles

additions include the 15th century great hall. Magnificent views from ramparts. Now being fully restored. Guided tours. *Good Friday to September, Wednesday to Sunday 1000-1800.* ⼏

25c Caldicot Castle (tel. 0291 420241). Started by the Normans in 1100, it was completed by Thomas Woodstock, sixth son of Edward III, in 1396. Features from throughout those years remain, notably the 14th century great gateway, whose towers have been restored. Used by Prince Hal (later Henry V) when he was Lord of Monmouth. The castle now supplies an appropriate setting for Welsh mediaeval banquets. *March to October: castle open daily PM; banquets Monday to Saturday evenings* (tel. 0291 421425) 🍽 ▣ ⼏

27f Carew Castle. One of the most attractive castles in Wales, the present structure was begun in 1270, replacing an earlier Norman fort. It was enlarged by the Tudors in the 15th century, was the scene of a great tournament in 1507, but was badly

Introducing Wales

Wales, within easy reach of most of Britain's largest cities, is a world of a difference in many respects. A small country, a mere 200 miles from north to south, it is positively crammed with all kinds of scenery. It's also a land with its own special personality, rich in heritage and with a language thought to be the oldest in Europe. Yet it's just on your doorstep.

Getting to Wales is both easy and fast, with good inter-city train services and a network of major trunk roads connected to the main motorway system. Further extensions of the M4 motorway and the contruction of the North Wales Expressway will make the coast of Wales even more accessible from the east.

Along the 750 mile coastline popular seaside resorts, like Llandudno, Aberystwyth and Tenby, provide plenty of holiday entertainment for all the family. Smaller coastal towns and fishing villages will appeal to those who prefer a quieter style of holiday. And for those who want to get completely away from it all there are remote sheltered coves, spacious sandy beaches and rocks peninsulas. The Pembrokeshire coast, one of Wales's national parks, offers such a base and is best explored on foot along the waymarked footpath which runs its entire length.

Walkers are not confined, however, to this coastal path: behind most of Wales' coast is a wonderful hinterland, with hidden valleys, silent hills and rugged mountains. You don't have to be an experienced hill-walker or mountaineer to enjoy their beauty - hundreds of waymarked walks, through forests, over hills, beside rivers, have been specially designed to appeal to a wide audience, including families with young children. If you still prefer others to do the walking, why not explore the mountains on a pony: throughout Wales now there are dozens of pony trekking and riding centres offering treks on a daily or half-day basis. Narrow-gauge railways will also take you at a leisurely pace through some superb countryside, much of which·is inaccesssible by road. If you have a head for heights you can even take the mountain railway - Britain's only rack and pinion railway - to the 3560ft summit of Snowdon. Canal cruising is another undemanding way of exploring parts of the country, through undulating hills and valleys in the Brecon Beacons National Park or in the Vale of Llangollen in North Wales. The range of holiday activities for the more adventurous is just as extensive, including canoeing down rapid white-water courses, hang-gliding and parascending.

Sightseeing and touring, of course, form part of most people's visit to Wales. High on the priorty list of attractions not to be missed are the castles of Wales, including such mighty mediaeval fortresses as Conwy, Caernarfon, Harlech and Caerphilly, as well as the lesser known, dramatically sited ruins, like Castell Carreg Cennen, near Llandeilo. Then there are cathedrals and abbeys, cromlechs, Celtic crosses and Roman remains - all with an enthralling tale to tell. History is interpreted for you in the museums of Wales in a lively and entertaining manner. You can enter a simulated coal mine at Cymer, near Port Talbot, or the National Museum of Wales in Cardiff, and learn how coal has been extracted through the ages. Better still, take a ride into a real slate mine at Blaenau Ffestiniog, where Victorian mining conditions have been recreated. Much can be learnt of the rural history of Wales in the Welsh Folk Museum, at St Fagan's near Cardiff, where centuries-old cottages and farmhouses have been reconstructed stone by stone in the wooded grounds of a Tudor mansion. Here, as in craft workshops scattered throughout rural Wales, there are demonstrations of traditional crafts, which are again an inherent part of this country's past.

Time, however, has not stood still. Cardiff, the capital of Wales, has all the assets one would expect to find in a modern city - theatres, cinemas, shoppping precincts and sporting facilities. (Don't forget, Cardiff is also the mecca for Welsh rugby!) What is more it is only an hour's drive from the Brecon Beacons, the Usk and Wye valleys. Swansea, its near neighbour and Wales' second largest city, is just as fortunate, being at the gateway to the Gower Peninsula, a designated area of outstanding beauty. For a glimpse of modern Swansea's unmistakably Welsh character step inside its indoor market: although housed in a modern complex, many of the stalls, manned by Welsh-speaking women, sell fresh, local produce, including cockles, laverbread and Welsh cakes.

In the rural market towns you need not look far for their true Welsh characteristics. On narrow streets, after the weekly mart, or in the pub you'll hear local farmers discussing the day's events in their own distinctive language. You may even come across some impromptu singing. Wales, after all, is known as the land of song. Nowhere is this more obvious than in the South Wales valleys, where the male voice choir tradition is still as strong as ever.

Tourist Information

There are over 70 tourist information centres in Wales run in accordance with standards laid down by the Wales Tourist Board. The staff at these centres can give advice on a wide range of subjects, from accommodation and travel to local events and attractions. All these offices, together with a few centres run by other organisations (the National Trust, National Parks, etc.) are listed on page 122.

The Wales Tourist Board also organise a number of schemes deigned to help the traveller: these include the Dragon Award, displayed by static caravan sites guaranteeing high standards; the Tourist Menu, displayed by hundreds of restaurants, hotels and inns which undertake to serve a 3-course meal at a totally inclusive price which is clearly stated before ordering; the Book a Bed service, displayed at Tourist Information Centres which can arrange accommodation locally and/or further afield; A Taste of Wales, displayed by any establishment offering a range of traditional and contemporary Welsh food; and the Wales Farmhouse Awards, given to those establishments which meet certain standards set by the Tourist Board. The appropriate signs for all these schemes are shown on this page.

History and Legend

From Prehistoric to Roman times

Man's story in Wales begins at least 50, 000 years ago, a period which archaeologists call the Palaeolithic and Mesolithic Ages. At that time, when the massive glaciers of the Ice Age were retreating, he was a cave-dweller and a huntsman, whose quarry included the wild horse, woolly rhinoceros, mammoth and hyena. Much evidence of his existence has been found in rock shelters and small caves, such as the Goat's Hole at Paviland (map 20h),on the Gower Peninsula, and the more recently excavated Bone Cave, part of the Dan-yr-ogof Caves complex in the Upper Swansea Valley (map 31b).

His successors of the Neolithic Age left even more substantial visual remains - massive, impressive burial chambers, known as cromlechs, examples of which can be seen in many parts of Wales: Pentre Ifan, near Newport, Dyfed (map 38a), is one of the finest in Britain, with a 16½ ft long capstone balancing on three giant uprights. These Neolithic people came from France and possibly Spain, and unlike their cave-dwelling predecessors, lived a relatively settled life in wooden huts, working the land and rearing animals.

The Celts followed, bringing with them even greater skills and a language, Ancient British, from which all the Celtic languages -Welsh, Cornish, Breton, Manx, Scots and Irish Gaelic - were to develop. To defend themselves against marauders and other natives they built their forts on hilltops, an initiative which was to prove worthwhile when the Romans first invaded Britain in 43 AD.

Within four years most of south-east England had been seized by the Romans, but the natives in the western part, which is now Wales, resisted their attacks. Despite the fierce opposition and the heroic resistance, led by legendary figures such as Caractacus and Boedicea, however, the whole of Wales had fallen to Roman hands

The evocative remains of the Welsh Castell Dinas Bran (map 71e; see page 59).

by 75 AD. Two Roman legionary fortresses, each with 6000 legionaries, were established at Chester (Deva) in the north and Caerleon (Isca) in the south. Remains of the barracks blocks and a fine amphitheatre have been excavated at the latter (map 25a).

A further 24 garrisoned forts were built at strategic points, linked by a marvellous network of roads, parts of which can still be traced. Segontium, at Caernarfon (map 67b), was an important fort at the terminus of the Deva Roman road, while the chief inland forts were at Y Gaer (near Brecon, map 42f), Forden (near Welshpool, map 59h), and Caersws (map 78f). Venta Silurum, the town of the Silures tribe, was founded at Caerwent (map 25a) as part of their official policy to 'Romanize' the natives.

Nevertheless during the 300 years of Roman occupation, the natives lived much as before in their hilltop forts, just like their ancestors. However, they did benefit from their rulers' skills and knowledge. They emulated their building techniques; admired their artistic talents in making fine jewellery, pottery and glass; they even borrowed from their language. *Ffenestr* (window) from the Latin fenestra, *mur* (wall), *pont* (bridge), and *porth* (gate) are all legacies of the Roman occupation.

But just as Irish raiders, Picts and Saxons made menacing attacks on the Roman Empire in Britain, so other parts were threatened too. The Empire was breaking up and by about 380 AD Roman control had more or less ceased in Wales.

Early Christianity

Even before the Romans had left, Christianity had made its presence felt in Wales; by the 6th century, the foundations of the Age of Saints were firmly laid. St David, later to become the patron saint of Wales, did as many religious men of his time and established a monastery in a remote corner of the country, where he could live the simple life of self-denial. His shrine, at the heart of the splendid St David's Cathedral, has been a place of pilgrimage for centuries. Earlier, at Llantwit Major, St Illtud founded one of the most important educational institutions of the

Celtic Church, which was gradually absorbed into the Roman Church.

During the Age of Saints, Wales entered a period of stability and heroic confidence. Literature flourished, providing the basis for a poetic tradition which was to last for centuries. Warriors became heroic legendary figures, eulogised by the poets and giving birth to such tales as the Arthurian legend, so that over the centuries it has become hard to separate truth from legend. One thing is certain, however: by the 6th century the Celtic people were confined to the west. Border battles followed between Saxons and Celts, and these were not settled until Offa, King of Mercia, built his dyke to separate the two territories in 790 AD.

The Invaders
Peace did not prevail for long, however, as Wales was subjected to even greater threats. Early in the 9th century, Wales faced the first savage attacks by the Vikings; 200 years later they were still as ruthless as ever. Churches and monasteries were prime targets for these pillaging pagan raiders, attracted by their prized booty. Despite this trail of destruction, however, they succeded in getting only a few footholds on the Welsh coast, thanks to the defence of Rhodri Mawr (Rhodri the Great) - when he died in 876, Rhodri ruled two-thirds of the country, and was acknowledged as overlord by the native Welsh princes.

Hywel Dda (Howell the Good), his grandson, became one of the most notable Welsh kings. Like Rhodri he united and ruled most of Wales, and spent much of his life defending his territories against attacks by the Danes. Yet he is remembered chiefly not as a warrior but as the founder of a legal code based on the ancient laws which then existed in Wales. This unified legal code was applied throughout the country, replacing the various tribal laws and customs; with it came a greater sense of unity and stability. Hywel's justice, however, became a political weakness after his death, when his sons squabbled over land tenure - a problem Hywel had sought to eliminate with his laws. In the resulting state of disunity, Wales was again exposed to the invading Saxons and Danes.

During the 11th century, Wales faced a new enemy, the Normans, who built a network of defensive strongholds around the country to confirm their authority and power. Many of them were ingenious examples of military cunning: Caerphilly Castle in South Wales, for instance, has the finest system of water defences in Britain. The natives, undeterred, withstood their attacks in many parts of Wales. and as the 12th century drew to a close, much of the country was still ruled by native Welsh princes, the most powerful and influential being Lord Rhys of Deheubarth.

Llewelyn II, the last of the native Welsh princes, died in 1282, effectively ending the strong Welsh resistance to the Anglo-Normans under Edward I. Like his grandfather, Llywelyn Fawr, he had won the allegiance of the petty princes and aquired the role of overlord in the matters of national importance. His death, at the hand of a young English trooper, was a shattering blow to Wales. Fearing that another leader of Llywelyn's stature might unite the Welsh in outright rebellion against the English Crown, Edward immediately embarked upon his ambitious castle building programme, which included the masterpieces at Beaumaris, Caernarfon, Harlech and Conwy.

That 'other Llywelyn' feared by Edward did eventually come to power over 100 years later: his name was Owain Glyndwr.

Owain's Revolt
Less than 20 years after the Peasant's Revolt in England, a group of Welsh rebels gathered outside the town of Ruthin, in north Wales, and proclaimed Owain Glyndwr Prince of Wales. A born leader, Glyndwr possessed all the attributes of a true blooded prince of traditional stock, being direct descended from the princes of Powys. He was educated at Gray's Inn and was later described by William Shakespeare as "a worthy gentleman exceedingly well read."

As his influence spread, it became obvious that Glyndwr's revolt was more than a peasants' uprising - it grew into a national war which raged for 10 years. It was a war which symbolised the Welsh people's opposition to the rule and oppression of the English throne; a war of national identity. By 1403, Glyndwr ruled the whole of Wales, apart from Pembrokeshire, which he took by force with 10,000 troops in 1405, assisted by allied French armies. Wales was now declared a completely independent state, and Glyndwr proclaimed himself Prince of Wales. His achievements, although short-lived, were considerable: he established Wales' own civil and diplomatic service, a parliament and treasury, armed forces and a legal system. He even planned two Welsh universities, but these were never realised. By 1408 the tide had turned, as the castles at Aberystwyth and Harlech reverted to English hands and in 1410 he was outlawed, after fighting his last battle at Shrewsbury. Within a few years he disappeared, never to be seen or heard from again, except in the poets' lines. To the bards he personified the spirit of national consciousness, a spirit which was to haunt them for a long time.

The Act of Union
Inspired by Glyndwr's rebellion, a spirit of pride and self-confidence prevailed throughout the 15th century, and this was reflected in the poetry of the period. During the middle years of the Wars of the Roses, Wales was equally divided between the parties of York and Lancaster. The eastern parts were predominantly Yorkist, supported by William Herbert (later the Earl of Pembroke) at Raglan Castle, while the west, as well as large areas of south Wales, were held by the Lancastrians. When Henry Tudor, of Welsh origin, returned from exile, supported by the Lancastrians, he landed at Dale, on the Pembrokeshire coast, and mustered Welsh troops on his way to Bosworth Field, where he overwhelmingly defeated Richard III. This victory in 1485 marked the end of the Wars of the Roses, and the beginning of the Royal House of Tudor, as Henry ascended to the throne.

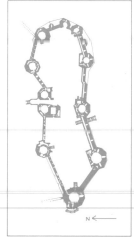

Caernarfon Castle
(map 67b; see page 94)

The figure-eight shape of this sophisticated fortress was dictated by the shape of the rock on which it stands. In addition to the conventional land entrances, it could be supplied by sea via the water gate in the Eagle Tower, the large tower at the bottom of both illustrations.

N ←

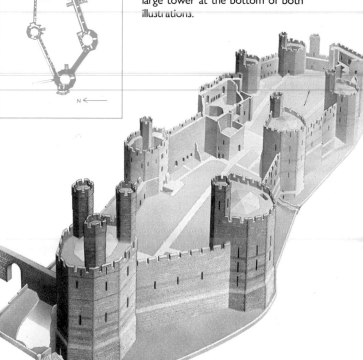

Welsh poets celebrated this English king, and their patrons, the gentry, sought favour in his Royal courts. He was looked upon as the 'saviour' and 'deliverer' of Wales, a suitable successor for Glyndwr. Little did they realise that his reign would also signify the end of their long battle for independence. By 1536, his son, Henry VIII, had passed the Act of Union which stated that "Wales shall be, stand and continue for ever and henceforth incorporated, united and annexed to and with this Realm of England."

The Industrial Revolution

Small ironworks were established in the south-eastern corner of Wales as early as the second half of the 16th century. But is was about 200 years later, after Abraham Darby had perfected his iron-making process at Coalbrookdale, using coal instead of charcoal for smelting, that there began an ironmaking boom which was to change the whole face of this part of Wales. Ironmasters from the Midlands chose the north-eastern edge of the coalfield for their works, for supplies of iron ore, coal for coke making, and limestone were plentiful here. At Merthyr Tydfil in 1759 John Guest established the Dowlais Ironworks, which by 1840 became the world's largest with 18 blast furnaces employing 10,000 people. In the same immediate area, Crawshay's Cyfarthfa Works opened in 1765, followed by the Hill's Plymouth Works in 1767 and Homfray's Penydarren Works, all contributing to the massive output which made Merthyr Tydfil the largest iron-manufacturing centre in the world.

Until the 1830's, coal was the hand-maiden of iron; now it became an industry in its own right, demanding railways to replace the tramroads and canal networks. Green valleys, such as those at Rhondda, Neath and Ogmore, were exploited for their 'black diamonds'; the ports of Barry and Penarth were built to export millions of tons of coal, making the Bristol Channel the busiest stretch of water in the world during the 19th century. The 3rd Marquess of Bute, the biggest of the coal-owners built himself a lavish home symbolising the wealth he had won at the expense of thousands who lived and worked in squalid conditions: Castell Coch at Tongwynlais is essentially an extravagant Victorian folly conceived by the Marquess and his architect, who also restored Cardiff Castle in the same whimsical style. Ironically, but perhaps appropriately, Robert Thompson Crawshay, one of Merthyr's iron kings, wrote his own epitaph asking "God, forgive me".

Conditions were certainly bad for the workers, representing the worst features of the Industrial Revolution, and were compared with "those of a newly-discovered gold-field or a plantation in tropical Africa". They bred discontent and social unrest which led to uprisings and riots heralding the first working-class movement in Wales.

In North Wales the great Quarrymen's Strike in 1874 heralded the establishment of a quarrymen's union. Major tourist attractions, including the Llechwedd Slate Caverns and Gloddfa Ganol at Blaenau Ffestiniog, now serve as monuments to these men and their once industry, which supplied the world's slate for over a century. Mining for gold, silver, lead and copper was also at its peak in the mid 19th century; mid Wales had no less than 133 lead mines, one of which has now been preserved at Ponterwyd, and Anglesey had the largest copper mine in the world. Sadly, these industries have also declined, but like the slate, iron and early coal industries they have left a rich heritage to be explored by today's visitors and archaeologists.

Myth and Legend

Wales has always been a country deeply rooted in its own traditions and its past. But through the mists of time even the most significant figures of early Welsh history have become almost legendary characters, shrouded in a world of magic and mystery. Elaborated over the years by poets and by the Celtic imagination, they have become superhuman beings, with immense powers. Even the poets themselves were, generations later, looked upon as wizards and prophets. Taliesin was a poet of the 6th century who sang the praises of king and warrior; like Merlin, he became a legendary figure with great visionary powers to whom ficticious poetry was attributed in the Middle Ages.

Artist's impression of the Furnace Ironworks at Eglwysfach (map 52c; see page 105) as it must have looked during the 18th century.

The Celtic imagination reveals itself most brilliantly in prose, especially in the Mabinogion - a mediaeval collection of folk tales considered one of the great masterpieces of European literature. It takes the reader into a world of monsters and giants, magic and mystery. King Arthur appears as the cousin of Culhwch, a young prince who falls in love with a giant's daughter. And just as there are real places associated with the legendary Arthur, so too there are places associated with the characters of the Mabinogion. Math, son of Mathonwy, was lord of Gwynedd, while Bendigeidfran, the giant, held court at Harlech. Other mythical characters are set in Snowdonia, in the Nantlle Valley and Dinas Dinlle, Maentwrog and Traeth Mawr, Ceredigion and Ardudwy.

Some legends are not so old: one of the best known and a firm favourite with young children is the tale of Gelert, the faithful hound mistakenly killed by Prince Llywelyn after it had rescued his baby son from the ravages of a wolf. Thousands of visitors each year visit the dog's grave at Beddgelert not realising that an enterprising 18th century hotelier in the village adapted an old tale to boost his trade - he raised the cairn of stones, the 'dog's grave', with the help of the parish clerk!

Another great myth is perpetuated at the Royal National Eisteddfod, an annual festival of music and poetry, drama and art, which alternates between North and South Wales. Highlights of the week's events are the rituals of the Gorsedd (company) of bards, and the crowning and chairing of the winning bards, ceremonies reputedly based on ancient druidic rites, but which were actually devised in the 18th century. Their creator was Edward Williams, generally known by his bardic title, Iolo Morgannwg. A brilliant literary forger, he declared that the bards of his native Glamorgan had maintained the old druidic tradition throughout the ages, and he produced fictitious written evidence to prove this. Thus did he create the Gorsedd of the Bards, led by an all-powerful Archdruid, who crowns and chairs the winning poets of today. Though it has long been proved that Iolo's ceremonies are merely spurious antiquarianism, the myth lives on and more and more people are invested into the honourable Gorsedd of the Bards of the Isle of Britain.

The Seven Wonders of Wales

In the gazetteer section of this guide you will find several references to the legendary 'Seven Wonders of Wales'. As a quick check list for you we include here an ancient ditty, which lists them all succinctly in rhyme:

Pistyll Rhaeadr and Wrexham steeple,
Snowdon's mountain, without its people,
Overton yew trees, Gresford bells,
Llangollen Bridge and St. Winifred's Well.

Pistyll Rhaeadr, the spectacular 169ft high waterfall near Llanrhaeadr ym Mochnant (see page 82) is still considered a major attraction, as is Snowdon - at 3560ft, the highest mountain in England and Wales. But many will argue that the other five have long been superseded by far greater wonders -outstanding engineering feats such as Thomas Telford's Pontcysyllte Aqueduct (see page 107) or more advanced technological innovations such as the Dinorwig Pumped Storage Power Station at Llanberis, which will generate 1320 megawatts of electricity in ten seconds! Look out for others during your wanderings in Wales, with the help of our leisure atlas.

Survival of a Language

Welsh is still spoken by some half a million people, about 24% of the total population of Wales. In the county of Gwynedd, in North Wales, the percentage is much higher, with three in every five people (62% in 1971) speaking the language quite unselfconsciously as their mother tongue. To them it's the language of home, school, the local pub and the office. Like all minority languages, however, it is threatened with extinction, suffocated by the stronger influences of the majority language and culture.

English has always been both the strongest influence on and the greatest threat to the Welsh language, not merely because of the close proximity of the two countries and the ease of access, but because of political and administrative legislation which made Welsh the inferior tongue. In 1536, with Henry VIII's Act of Union, English became the official language of administration, commerce and law in Wales. This would have been the death knell for the language had it not been for the efforts of a small group of Renaissance Welsh scholars and the Reformation. During the 16th century men of letters in Wales had been encouraged by the Renaissance sweeping through Europe to become more aware of their own language and culture. At the same time the Reformation emphasized that the scriptures should be made available to every man and woman in his or her own tongue, so the complete Bible and the Book of Common Prayer were translated into Welsh and made available to the people. Paradoxically, Elizabeth I had hoped that in providing a Welsh Bible the people would "by conferring both tongues together the sooner attain to the knowledge of the English tongue". Instead the translation - a significant event in the history of Wales - gave new strength and respectibility to the language and laid the foundations of modern Welsh.

Further religious revivals ensured the survival of the language into the 18th century, when interest was rekindled in Welsh scholarship and literature. Despite some industrialisation in the north and the south-east, Wales at this time was still basically an agricultural nation, with about 80% of the population of 500,000 still Welsh-speaking in 1800. This changed dramatically during the next 100 years, with the growth of the iron and coal industries in the South Wales valleys and the mass immigration which ensued. By 1901 in a typical valley town, only one in five spoke Welsh. In Mid Glamorgan today only 11% of the population are Welsh-speaking, although the establishment of Welsh-based nursery and secondary schools will probably halt any further decrease.

Education is now the key to the language's survival. In 1870 the Education Act made English the medium for compulsory primary education, and this rule was extended to the secondary system in the 1890s, denying Welshmen an education in their own tongue. Further oppression was again halted by cultural and religious revivals. Rural depopulation from the strong Welsh-speaking areas and a steady immigration of English speakers, as well as the impact of the mass media, have contributed to a continued erosion of the language over the last 20 years, but with more Welsh schools and a new generation of young Welsh speakers dedicated to its survival, its future seems assured.

Croeso i Gymru
Welcome to Wales

As you enter Wales by road, the Welsh language manifests itself immediately with the words *Croeso i Gymru* -Welcome to Wales. These are the first signs which show you are in a different country, with its own language and its own distinctive culture. Look out for others as you drive through town and country. *Maes parcio* - car park, *Llwybr cyhoeddus* -public footpath, *Canolfan Croeso* - Tourist Information Centre, *gwely a brecwast* - bed and breakfast, these are just a few examples of the many bilingual signs now in common use in Wales.

You will also come across 'dual place names' on road signs in Wales, where a town or village has an English as well as Welsh name; for example Swansea - *Abertawe*, Cardiff - *Caerdydd*, Brecon - *Aberhonddu*.

Many Welsh place names start with the word *Llan*, meaning church, the most famous being the tongue twisting - Llanfairpwllgwyngyllgogerychwyrndrobwllllantysiliogogogoch, on the Isle of Anglesey (map 75i), thankfully abbreviated to Llanfair P.G. or Llanfairpwll! A saint's name usually follows - for example: Llanberis, the Church of Saint Peris; Llandudno, the church of Saint Tudno.

Aber' meaning confluence, is another word commonly found in Welsh place names, usually followed by the name of a river - for example: Aberaeron, Aberdovey, Abersoch and Aberystwyth.

To help you understand a little more about some of the place names shown on our maps and on road signs in Wales, we have included here a brief glossary of those words which appear most frequently.

Welsh	English
abaty	abbey
aber:	confluence of river
afon:	river
allt:	hill, slope
bach, bychan:	small
ban, pl, bannau:	peak(s)
banc:	mound, bank
bedd:	grave
betws:	church, oratory
blaen, pl, blaenau	top(s), summit(s)
bod:	abode, place
bro:	vale
bryn, pl, bryniau:	hill(s)
bwlch:	opening, mountain pass
cae:	field
caer:	fortress
capel:	chapel
carreg:	stone, rock
carnedd:	cairn, mound, heap
cefn:	ridge, back
cei:	quay, harbour
ceiliog:	cockerel
celli, gelli:	grove
coch:	red
coeden, pl. coed:	tree(s)
cors:	bog, fen
craig:	rock
croes:	cross

Welsh	English
crug:	cairn, mound, heap
cwm:	valley
cwrt:	court, manor
dau(m); dwy(f):	two
derwen, pl, derw:	oak(s)
dinas:	fort, city
dôl:	meadow
du:	black
dŵr:	water
dyffryn:	valley
eglwys:	church
felin:	see *melin*
ffordd:	road, way
ffrwd:	stream
ffynnon:	well
garth:	hill, ridge, enclosure
glan:	shore, bank of river
glas:	blue, green
glyn:	valley, glen
gwaun:	moor
gwyn:	white
hafod:	summer residence
haul:	sun
hen:	old
hendre:	winter residence
heol:	street, road
is:	lower
isaf:	lowest
lan:	see *glan*

Welsh	English
llan:	church, enclosure
llannerch:	clearing
llechwedd:	wooded hillside, slope
llwyd:	grey
llyn:	lake
llys:	court, manor
maes:	field, square
maen:	rock, stone
mawr:	big, large
melin:	mill
melyn:	yellow
merthyr:	martyr
môr:	sea
morfa:	sea marsh
mynydd:	mountain
neuadd:	hall
newydd:	new
oer:	cold
ogof:	cave
pandy:	fulling mill
pant:	hollow, valley
pegwn:	peak
pen:	top, ridge, end
penrhyn:	promontory, peninsula
pentref:	village
plas:	manor
pont:	bridge
porth:	entrance, port, harbour

Welsh	English
pwll:	pool
rhaeadr:	waterfall
rhiw:	hill, slope
rhos:	moor, plain
rhyd:	ford
sain, sant, pl, saint:	saint(s)
tafarn:	inn, tavern
tal:	end, top, front
tan:	beneath, below
tomen:	mound, cairn
ton:	town
traeth:	beach
tref:	town
tri:	three
trum:	ridge, summit
twr:	tower
twyn:	hill, knoll, dune
tŷ:	house
tyddyn:	smallholding
twyni:	sea shore, sand dune
uchaf:	upper
uwch:	higher, above
y, yr:	the (article) or the relative particle
yn:	in
ynys:	island
ysbyty:	hospice, hospital
ystrad:	valley

Wales Today

Mention Wales to most people and they will immediately think of coal mines and steel-works. True, there are a few of both, but they are confined to the industrial belts of south and north-east Wales, and even these are rapidly diminishing. Apart from a few pockets of light industry, mainly centred on the larger towns, most of north and mid Wales relies almost wholly on tourism and various forms of agriculture for its livelihood.

Hill sheep farming predominates, not surprisingly in a country which has more sheep than people. Most of the land in north Wales is over 600ft high, with much of it over 1200ft. The higher pastures, where the shepherds of old built their 'hafod' (summer residence), are still used for summer grazing. The hardy Welsh sheep are most common in Snowdonia, although in mid Wales the Speckled Face ewes of Beulah, near Builth Wells, are gaining prominence. Also increasingly popular in hill farming country are the hardy Welsh Black cattle, a beef breed which also provides milk. These and other Welsh-bred stock always attract attention at the local agricultural shows and, of course, at the Royal Welsh Show in Builth Wells, which is the highlight of the farming calendar in Wales. Crops are confined to the richer, fertile valleys and to the lowlands of the Lleyn Peninsula, the Isle of Anglesey, the Gower Peninsula and the Vale of Glamorgan. The former county of Pembrokeshire, now part of Dyfed, is particularly noted for its potatoes.

Tourism is the second most important industry in Wales, attracting about 12 million visitors every year and earning (in 1979) about £360 million for the Welsh economy. Agriculture is actually being supplemented by tourism in some parts, with about 4000 farms involved in one way or another with the industry. In the rural areas there is also a growing number of craft workshops, which are helping to alleviate local unemployment. At Llanaelhaearn, there is a particularly good example of a thriving workers' co-operative initiated by the local people. The woollen industry, at its most prosperous in the 19th century, still survives, although it has to struggle in the face of cheaper textile imports.

Wales also has a long tradition of sea-fishing, although the rich catches of herring and mackerel have long since disappeared. Conwy now has a thriving mussel industry and in the Menai Strait there are profitable commercial seed oyster beds.

Heavy industry in south Wales is gradually being replaced by lighter engineering and manufacturing industries, often operated by international companies. One of the most recent successes in the industrial south has been the establishment of highly efficient Japanese electronic factories which have provided jobs in areas of high unemployment, but many thousands more will be needed, as the heavier industries are wiped out completely.

Geology

Since the days when those first intrepid travellers, the Victorians, explored the mountains of North Wales, millions have followed in their footsteps to marvel at the grandeur of that rugged landscape. Yet how many have ever paused and wondered how it was formed? Geologists - and those who have entered the Time Tunnel of Milestones at the Geological Museum of North Wales at Bwlchgwyn - will know that the answer lies beneath the surface, in the layers of rocks formed over millions of years.

On the Isle of Anglesey are some of Britain's most ancient rocks, possibly 500 million years old, of the pre-Cambrian

Useful Telephone Numbers

Motoring Information
Recorded summaries cover road conditions within 50 miles of the listed towns.

Bristol (including the M4 Severn Bridge approaches). 0272 8021
Cardiff (Glamorgan, Gwent and south Powys). 0222 8021
Liverpool (most of Clwyd). 061-246 8021

Weather Forecasts

Recorded forecasts giving the general outlook are available as follows:

Cardiff area 0222 8091
North Wales Coast (Conwy to Chester) 061-246 8093

More specific forecasts, for climbers, sailors, fishermen, etc., can be obtained from the following establishments (which operate throughout the year unless otherwise stated):

RAF Valley (Anglesey) Meteorological Office 0407 2288
Holyhead (Anglesey) Coastguard Rescue HQ 0407 2051
Royal Aircraft Establishment (Aberporth) Meteorological
Office 0239 810117
Fishguard Coastguard Rescue HQ 0348 3449
St Ann's (near Milford Haven) Coastguard Rescue HQ 064 64 218
Mumbles Coastguard Rescue HQ 0792 66534
Swansea Post Office (*summer only*) 0792 8011
Rhoose Airport (west of Cardiff) Met. Office 0446 710343
Barry Island Coastguard Rescue HQ 0446 5016

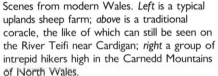

Scenes from modern Wales. *Left* is a typical uplands sheep farm; *above* is a traditional coracle, the like of which can still be seen on the River Teifi near Cardigan; *right* a group of intrepid hikers high in the Carnedd Mountains of North Wales.

period. These same rocks form the character of the landscape in the south-western corner of Wales, as far as St David's, merging with the younger Silurian rocks which dominate mid Wales. Snowdonia's range of mountains, although not as ancient as these pre-Cambrian rocks, are still amongst Europe's oldest, being of Ordovician and partly pre-Cambrian origin. They were created by volcanic eruptions, whose slow-cooling lavas became solid granite. Under extreme pressure this formed the metamorphic blue slate, so evident in the Nantlle Valley, Llanberis, Bethesda and Blaenau Ffestiniog.

Cambrian and Ordovician rocks give way to those of the Silurian period in Clwyd, where the landscape is much gentler. Beyond Llangollen, there are even younger carboniferous formations, running into the coal measures of Ruabon and Wrexham, and the limestone areas of north-east Wales, so heavily exploited in the last century.

Mid Wales was also exploited for its mineral wealth - mainly gold, silver and lead. North of the Mawddach estuary, where the Upper and Lower Cambrian rocks meet, is known as the 'Dolgellau Gold Belt', an area which has provided the gold for several Royal wedding rings.

Underlying most of the south Wales region is the Old Red Sandstone of the Ordovician period, manifesting itself in the rich red soil of the fertile valleys of Powys, Gwent and eastern Dyfed. Upon this sandstone lie layers of carboniferous rock - limestone and coal - whose exploitation during the Industrial Revolution changed the whole face of the narrow valleys of south Wales. Nowhere does it show more vividly how rocks can determine the character of a country's industry as well as its landscape.

Climate

With such a varied landscape it's no surprise that Wales has a wide variation in climate. Western coastal regions benefit from mild westerly winds, which can be to the advantage of sailing enthusiasts based at one of the many protected harbours along this coast. On the northern coast, in the rain-sheltered resorts of Clwyd, and on the Isle of Anglesey and the low-lying Lleyn Peninsula, the winters are usually mild, followed by sunny springs, making for dry periods in April and May.

In the mountains the picture is ever-changing. Snowdonia's many peaks, particularly those over 3000ft, experience some snows in winter and early spring. Although there is rarely enough to guarantee skiing on the slopes, the often icy conditions on the rock faces do attract climbers hoping to practise alpine climbing techniques. Mists come quickly to the hills and mountains: even in summer, when the lowlands and valleys are baking in the sunshine, the mountains can be shrouded in dangerous mists. If you are out walking on the hills and mountains of Snowdonia or the Brecon Beacons, watch the weather and be prepared for any sudden changes: the temperature drops 1° Fahrenheit with every 300 feet you climb, so warm clothing is essential. Rain can be heavy at times in the uplands, which explains why Wales has so many giant lakes and reservoirs supplying some of the large conurbations of England and Wales with water. Green and fertile river valleys are also the result of this preponderance of water.

One of the mildest parts of Wales is the Pembrokeshire Coast, in the south west corner, where spring comes early and is usually late to leave. Here the major resorts usually claim more sunshine hours than the rest of Wales.

Flora and fauna

Like the rest of Britain, a large portion of Wales's total land mass of 5 million acres was once covered by deciduous forests. Although most of these indigenous forests have long since disappeared, following 4000 years of agricultural activity and an Industrial Revolution, much of the country has remained relatively unspoilt. Three national parks, four areas of outstanding natural beauty, country parks and an increasing number of nature reserves are ensuring the preservation of the countryside and its natural wildlife habitats.

Snowdonia, largest of the three national parks, comprises 840 square miles of varied countryside - mountains and moorlands, divided by deep valleys, lakelands and forests, three lovely estuaries and 25 miles of coastline. Dominating this landscape is Snowdon itself, the highest point in Britain south of the Scottish Highlands, where many rare and luxuriant alpine plants grow. At Cwm Idwal, near Capel Curig - an area studied by many leading botanists, including Charles Darwin, and now the first of Wales's national nature reserves - the rare Snowdon Lily can be found. On the blustery summits of Snowdonia's craggy mountains is a wide variety of grasses and mosses, including the woolly moss. Heathers, too, are in abundance, clothing many of these mountains and their neighbouring hills in a deep purple hue. Oakwoods indigenous to Snowdon have been preserved at the Coedydd Maentwrog nature reserve and also in the Padarn Country Park at Llanberis, but in the Gwydyr, Machno, Lledr and Beddgelert Forests, which cover a combined total of 23, 463 acres, they have mainly been replaced by the sitka spruce. Other species planted by the Forestry Commission in this area since the end of World War I are the Douglas fir, the western red cedar and the lodge-pole pine. For more information about these forests and their wildlife follow some of the vast network of waymarked forest walks in Snowdonia or call in at the Forest Exhibition Centre in Gwydyr Forest (see page 80).

Successive ice ages formed Snowdonia's U-shaped valleys and lakes, which were scooped out or dammed by glacial deposits. During that period the rare gwyniad, a cold water coarse fish, was locked into two lakes - Llyn Padarn and Llyn Tegid. The rarest animals found in the park are the polecat and the pine marten; in the wooded areas the red squirrel is still in evidence, although the destructive grey variety has penetrated into most areas. Herds of wild goats can also be seen, particularly around Beddgelert and Capel Curig, but the eagle, once the symbol of Snowdonia and its princes, is now extinct. Above the 1000ft contour line now soars the ring ouzel, with peregrine falcons. kestrels and buzzards.

Across the Menai Strait from Snowdonia is the Isle of Anglesey, linked to the mainland by Telford's suspension bridge and Stephenson's adapted tubular bridge. Designated 'an area of outstanding natural beauty', the island's coastline provides a habitat for a variety of birds. On the north coast are some interesting examples of nature living close to industry - at the Penrhos Nature Reserve, on Holy Island, an area teeming with bird life; and Wylfa Head, home of sea birds, flowers and plants as well as a huge nuclear power station. In the north-eastern corner is Cemlyn Bay, a bird sanctuary and nature reserve, while to the south is Llanddwyn Island, part of the 1556 acre Newborough Warren, noted for its bird and plant life. Priestholme, as its more popular name of Puffin Island implies, is a breeding ground for puffins.

Cardigan Bay is another 'must' for ornithologists, being the nesting ground for colonies of sea birds, including the kittiwake and guillemot. On Cardigan Island, now a nature reserve, there are fulmars, black-backed gulls, oystercatchers and shags. Further north along this coast, another important reserve has been established on the Dovey Estuary, with a smaller RSPB bird sanctuary at Ynyshir, near Eglwysfach.

Mid Wales has the best example of boglands, namely Cors Goch Glan Teifi, otherwise known as Tregaron Bog, and the smaller Cors Fochno, commonly knows as Borth Bog. The former, a national nature reserve covering 1898 acres and claimed to be the largest and one of the richest in Britain, has a varied flora and fauna which includes rare plants and mosses, species of butterflies, moths and visiting birds. As is the case with many of Snowdonia's nature reserves, a special permit is required to explore this area, available from the Nature Conservancy Council at Penrhos, Bangor, Gwynedd. Unlike Tregaron, Borth Bog is an expanse of low-lying marshlands, backed by extensive dunelands, which provide a natural habitat for plants, birds and animals.

In mid Wales, the forests have also been opened up with a series of waymarked forest trails and walks. Reservoirs, man-made like the forests, are providing new breeding grounds for wildlife. To illustrate this the North Wales Naturalists' Trust has devised a scenic nature trail around Llyn Clywedog. In the same way, from their visitor centre at Cwm Rheidol, the C.E.G.B. have established a nature trail to demonstrate how they have preserved the environment during the construction of their hydro-electric power station. Nearby is Coed Rheidol, a nature and forest reserve with 115 acres of oakwood.

South Wales's Brecon Beacons National Park extends over three counties, from the northern tip of Gwent and the industrial valleys of the region, across south Powys and westwards into Dyfed. Most of its 519 square miles of mountains and open moorland are above the 1000ft line, the highest peak being

This idealised cliff shows the wide variety of species which can be seen in such locations throughout the region. The birds shown are: **A** Puffin, which prefer the grassy slopes above the cliffs, but will also nest in crevices near the top; **B** Fulmar, which favour the broad ledges near the summit; **C** Kittiwake, which prefer steep cliffs; **D** Guillemot, which nest close together along exposed sections of cliff face; **E** Cormorant, which nest among the rocks at the cliff base; **F** Black Guillemot, which use caves and/or crevices along the cliff base near the sea; **G** Razorbill, which favour rock crevices at the corners of cliff.

Penyfan (2907ft). Upland birds sighted here include the buzzard, merlin, red grouse and golden plover, while within the woodlands (25,000 acres of which are coniferous) goldcrests, woodpeckers and redstarts are most prevalent. Man made lakes, such as the Talybont and Llwyn-onn Reservoirs, above Merthyr Tydfil, are again providing new habitats for waterfowl, including waders, terns and herons. Even the much-used Llangorse Lake, the largest natural lake in south Wales, gives shelter to a wide variety of both visiting and breeding waterfowl. Of the 200 species of birds recorded in the park, it's claimed that 100 breed in the Llangorse area. Surprisingly, the lake also has a rich and fascinating flora, including many species of reeds and aquatic plants.

Surprising too is the abundance of wildlife in the industrial valleys of south Wales, once so heavily scarred by the coal and iron industries. Country Parks have been created at Aberdare, Cymmer, Margam and Pen-y-fan Pond and with the help of local authorities, official bodies and volunteers, miles of pleasant waymarked walks have been laid. There is no shortage of nature trails and forest walks in the Wye Valley, either, and although Tintern Forest is now predominantly coniferous, there are fine examples of deciduous woodland in the Wyndcliff national nature reserve.

The Gower Peninsula also escaped the Industrial Revolution through its lack of exploitable resources; instead, it became a designated 'area of outstanding beauty'. Here, the coast's spectacular limestone cliffs and grassy headlands are interspersed with salt-marshes and duneland, providing the perfect environment for a variety of wildlife and vegetation. Amongst the most notable wild flowers found along this beautiful coastline are the Yellow Whitlow-grass, the Fen orchid, the Marsh orchid and the Hoary Rock-rose. Birds colonising the Gower include large flocks of oystercatchers (many of which feed on the cockle beds of Penclawdd), razorbills, guillemots and kittiwakes. Oxwich's natural nature reserve is a breeding ground for the reed warbler.

Further west you will find the Pembrokeshire Coast National Park, whose rocky cliffs and sandy bays are so easily accessible by means of the extensive Coast Path, which runs for its entire length from St Dogmael's to Amroth. Bird life abounds on this coastline and on the offshore islands, many of which are now nature reserves. Skomer, perhaps the most famous and the most accessible (by boat from Martin's Haven), provides a refuge for guillemots, kittiwakes, razorbills, puffins, shags, cormorants and Manx shearwaters, while smaller Grassholm is inhabited almost exclusively by one of the world's largest gannet colonies. Skokholm, the third of these offshore islands, is an ornithologist's delight and was the first bird observatory established in Britain (access is still restricted). Wild flowers are a major attraction on Pembrokeshire's rocky cliffs and headlands, especially in springtime when they are ablaze with such specimens as the pink thrift, golden gorse, cowslip, sea campion and bluebell.

Country Code

In the national parks of Wales, efforts are being made to maintain a balance between the interests of those who work and those who play within their boundaries. Visitors must remember that much of the land, the mountains and the hills also provide farmers' livelihoods. So whenever *you* are out walking in Wales, please follow these simple rules:

* Guard against risk of fire
* Close all gates behind you, especially those at cattle grids, etc.
* Keep dogs under control
* Keep to the paths across farmland - you have no right of way over surrounding land
* Avoid damaging fences, hedges and walls
* Safeguard water supplies
* Protect wildlife, plants and trees - do not pick flowers, leave them for others to enjoy
* Drive carefully on country roads
* Respect the life of the countryside - and you will be welcomed

Angling

More people practise angling than any other sport in Britain. There are three main forms of angling, of which the most popular is coarse or freshwater fishing. This is followed by sea fishing, with holiday makers each year adding to the number of regular sea anglers. The third category is game fishing, traditionally with flies, but increasingly with spinners or bait, for game fish such as salmon and trout. Although a more specialised form of angling, this has rapidly become more popular in recent years. With new reservoirs being stocked with rainbow and brown trout, trout fishing is no longer the privilege of those with access to a small number of jealously guarded waters.

Coarse fishing

Angling for coarse fish is very varied, with numerous techniques. Freshwater is either flowing, as in rivers and streams, or still, as in natural lakes or man made waters such as gravel pits. A typical river might have a number of different zones, each with distinct characteristics and containing different species. A river with its source in mountains or hills will begin with a fast runnning stretch in which might be found trout. This will merge into a lower zone where in summer the water might reach 15°C, and where the beautiful grayling might be found, along with dace and gudgeon. As the river widens and runs more smoothly, the barbel zone will be reached, where chub, roach and perch will also have their territories. In the last zone in which the water remains fresh,the river is likely to meander more slowly over a wider valley and the species become more numerous: bream, tench, carp, perch, roach, rudd and the predatory pike and zander can be caught. The last distinct zone is where the water is brackish as fresh and seawater meet. Here will be found migratory fish, such as eel and flounder, and strictly sea fish such as mullet, bass and shad.

Still waters can also be roughly categorised by their height above sea level. High natural lakes are likely to contain trout, carp, pike and perch; lower, warmer waters will contain the same fish as the slow, meandering rivers mentioned above.

A fisherman buying line, hooks and floats for the first time would do well to seek advice from the local tackle shop. There are numerous techniques, the most popular being float fishing. In fast water, however, legering can be profitable: the bait is offered on the bottom, with a single large lead weight used to hold the line down. On a strange water it is good practice to watch the methods and baits the regulars are using.

Sea fishing

Many readers of this section will be coarse anglers planning to do some sea fishing on their holidays. Plenty of fishing is available, as generally speaking wherever you are allowed access to a coastline, you can fish without a permit. The variety is wide, as piers, estuaries, beaches and rocks provide differing conditions and catches; and there are opportunities for boat fishing.

The rod required will vary with the type of fishing. It will usually be of glass fibre for lightness and flexibility, but where a rod of 8ft might be suitable for boat fishing, one of around 12ft is better for long casting from the shore - a rod of about 8-10ft will enable a fisherman to try all forms of sea fishing.

Pier fishing: fishing from a pier is a good introduction to sea fishing. No great casting skill is necessary and there are usually plenty of fellow anglers around to learn from. Mullet are often caught from piers, as they feed on the algae around old pier supports. Bass, pollack and, from September onwards, whiting can also be caught. Ragworm, sand-eels or slivers of small fish caught on the spot can be used as bait. A drop net is needed for bringing up the catch.

Estuaries, beaches and rocks: food is moved around on the tide in estuaries; bait natural to the estuary, such as lugworm, ragworm, mussels and small crabs, will catch mullet, bass and flounder.

Beaches provide opportunities to practise long casting - a cast of 100 yards or more will be necessary to achieve any success. Remember, though, that commercial fishing has severely reduced fish stocks and even experienced anglers suffer many fishless days. When casting, the tackle should hang about 2ft from the tip. With (for right-handed casters) the left shoulder facing the sea and the feet apart, swing smoothly forward and overhead, releasing the line as the rod reaches the vertical. Bass are a popular species to seek from beaches, particularly after dark.

Boat fishing falls into categories of its own: fishing in harbours and tidal rivers, inshore boat fishing (i.e. within 3 miles of the shore), fishing on deep water reefs and wreck fishing. The techniques, baits and range of species to be caught are so numerous that it is impossible to deal with them all here. Most people will go out first with experienced friends, or with a skipper plying for hire, and should discuss in advance what equipment it will be necessary to bring. When booking a place on a boat with a professional skipper, check the terms of the charter. Many skippers operate a rule that the angler may keep two fish only; this often causes disappointment to anglers who catch a boatful and have not checked the terms in advance.

Game fishing

Fishing for salmon and trout is a specialised form of angling. There are three methods of catching the fish: with fly, spinners or bait. Rods vary with the method and with the depth and width of the water. Generally a fly rod is longer and more flexible than a spinning rod. The method used is not always the choice of the angler: on some rivers spinning is not allowed or is restricted to certain times of the year, forcing the angler to employ the more difficult fly fishing. There are two methods: sunk line and floating line. With the sunk line, the fly is allowed to sink slowly towards the bottom. Floating line fishing is usually used for salmon, when the water warms up and the fish are likely to be in shallow water. The flies used are dry flies, which are almost weightless and float on the surface film of the water. When casting a dry fly, the weight of the line is used to carry the fly out. Spinning is a method of catching game fish using lures, such as the ever-popular Devon Minnow, which resembles a small fish and spins through the water. These are the normal methods of fishing, but game fish are occasionally caught with natural bait such as sprats, prawns or worms.

Another difficulty, especially with salmon fishing, is its expense: the best waters are private. However, reservoirs and lakes all over England and Wales now provide excellent trout fishing, many such waters being listed on pages 113-117. It is always advisable to plan fishing visits in advance and to make enquiries about availabilty and permits in good time rather than to arrive in the hope of some immediate fishing.

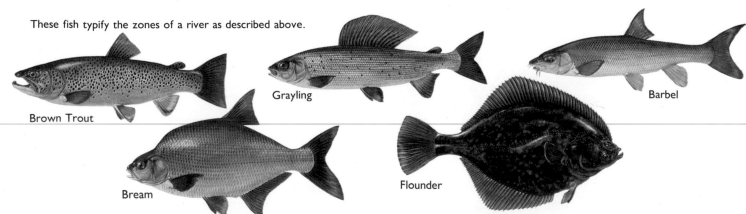

These fish typify the zones of a river as described above.

Brown Trout

Grayling

Barbel

Bream

Flounder

Food and Drink

Welsh fare is traditionally simple and economical - good homely cooking using produce from the farmland, pastures and coastline.

For many years Welsh cooking was based on oatmeal, as in so many Celtic countries. Even now oatcakes are cooked on a bakestone or planc in the same way as in Scotland. Flour is now widely used, however, and the general texture of baked foods has become more floury, as in the buttermilk scones which are now popular.

Since the heavy industrialisation of Wales and the expansion of the mining areas, less pasture has been available for grazing sheep. This has made lamb and mutton less prominent in the local diet, although they are still particularly delicious - Welsh lamb and mutton are greatly prized for their sweetness and flavour.

When the fishing industry occupied the coasts, many parts of which are now taken up with heavy industry, such foods as limpets, cockles and seaweed (laver) were more widely enjoyed. They remain a traditional part of the Welsh culinary repertoire. The cockle industry is an old one - the women used to scrape up the cockles, rinse them out in the sea then carry them home in huge baskets, often to make cockle pie, a dish sometimes augmented with local limpets.

In some shops and markets in south Wales you can find wooden tubs of smooth, fine seaweed called laver. To render this edible, the Welsh boil it for 5-6 hours until it is pulpy, then mash it with oatmeal to make a paste known as laverbread. Sometimes this is served on hot buttered toast with seasoning and lemon juice. As a breakfast dish laverbread is shaped into cakes, coated with more oatmeal, fried and served with bacon and fried bread. It is occasionally added to chowders or mutton cawl (broth) or is served with roast lamb.

The Welsh rivers and lakes are now a good source of fresh-water fish; in some districts there are now large trout fisheries, but trout, and sometimes salmon, have been traditional fare for many years in dishes such as baked trout with bacon.

Sheep are the main livestock raised in Wales, so the best meat dishes have developed around the succulent local lamb and mutton. Tatws a cig yn y popty (literally, meat and potatoes in the oven) is an Anglesey favourite in which breasts of lamb are cooked on a bed of potatoes and onions in a thickened stock. Potatoes are often used to add bulk to meat dishes - during the 19th century a Carmarthenshire miser dreamed up a truly thrifty dish which has become known as the Miser's Feast: sliced bacon, onions and potatoes are simmered together in a little water until the potatoes are tender and have absorbed all the liquid. The bacon is taken out and served as one meal and the flavoured potatoes are put aside as another meal for next day.

Local game used to be very plentiful, and hearty rabbit stews, rook pie and a dish apparently unique to Wales - salt duck - are still popular standards. To make salt duck, the Welsh cover the bird in salt for two or three days before it is cooked. It is then roasted and served with a rich cream-and-onion-sauce.

General poverty has prompted the Welsh to make good use of offal over the course of many years. Cow heel brawn and the great Welsh favourite, faggots, are typical economical dishes. Faggots can still be found bubbling in huge pans in the markets; they are served hot with peas as a take-away meal.

Economical meatless dishes are just as tasty as the meaty ones -leeks make a tasty filling for pasties which are traditionally made in the shape of a trimmed leek. Glamorgan sausages are an unusual type of croquette made in the old days with strong Glamorgan cheese. Now that this is no longer available, strong Cheddar is mixed with breadcrumbs and onion and formed into sausage shapes.

The leek, as Wales' national vegetable, is the base for a multitude of dishes: cream soup, broth, leek porridge and all sorts of hot pots. Tatws slaw, a dish of potatoes mashed with buttermilk; Welsh onion cake and Welsh cheese pudding are typical of the simple, thrifty but tasty food which is to be found in the rural areas.

A selection of traditional Welsh foods.

The most famous Welsh cheese come from Caerphilly: a mild-flavoured, crumbly white cheese, not generally used for cooking. Strong Cheddar is preferred for cooking, but Caerphilly is delicious eaten by itself or with fruit. Cheddar is used for the famous Welsh rarebit in which, traditionally, cheese is grated and mixed with milk or beer, seasoning and mustard and is then grilled on hot buttered toast.

In many cases planc or bakestone cakes double up as a pudding in a Welsh farmhouse meal, but some true puddings have become classics. Snowdon pudding, a steamed suet mixture with dried fruit is served with a sweet wine sauce; flummery, an oat porridge, sweetened and flavoured with fruit, ale or wine; and pwdin reis mamgu, a light baked rice pudding, are just some of the favourites, but a starchy trend is noticeable in most of these good hearty puddings.

Trollins were originally oat dumplings with currants, made to be served with stews. Now they are made with flour and are served as a pudding.

Wales is famous for its bread and cakes, both from the oven and from the bakestone. Originally 'bara' meant sustenance, but it is now widely used to mean bread. Bara planc is cooked on a bakestone, while bara brith, made with the same yeasted fruit mixture, is baked in the oven.

Often on baking day, part of the bread dough would be put aside and formed into small flat cakes. These would be cooked on the bakestone and served for tea, spread with plenty of butter.

Spiced potato cakes an teisen tincar (tinker's cake) are two other mixtures which are often cooked either in the oven or on the bakestone. Planc pastries, traditionally plate-sized rounds of pastry sealed together around a fruit or jam filling, are cooked on a bakestone too. These were always cooked at harvest time to sustain the men and women in the fields.

Welsh cheesecake, Welsh cakes, pikelets and crampog (buttermilk cakes) are examples of the Welsh penchant for serving small cakes hot from the bakestone with butter. Of course, there are large cakes too, such as cree (lard) cake, or Anglesey dark cake, both heavy, rich cakes - not for the Welsh are airy sponges or cream cakes!

Apart from the good beers from the local breweries and the seldom-found Welsh whisky, Wales is not noted for its beverages. The strong chapel-going faction were an abstemious lot, so alcohol has never been a particular speciality of Wales, where more emphasis is placed on solid nourishing food and good simple, tasty dishes made from local produce.

Sailing

On all but the wildest sections of coast, there are extensive facilities both for those with their own boats and for those who wish to hire. Slipways offering access to the public are also shown on the maps.

However experienced you are, the seas in this region can be treacherous and there are a number of safety precautions which must always be taken. Before setting out, always obtain a weather forecast - the local coastguard station is the best source for this; they are marked CG on the maps, or you can obtain the telephone number from the nearest Tourist Information Office (see page 122). Whenever a gale of Force 8 or above is expected within 6 hours, warning flags are hoisted at coastguard stations and at harbours and piers.

Always leave details of your trip with someone, or leave a note on the car windscreen, so that people know when you are missing and can instigate a search. The information needed is: a description of your boat (length, colour, name, type); the number of people on board; a list of any safety equipment carried; when you set sail and when you expect to return.

Carry extra clothing (especially waterproofs) even in summer, as you could be stranded or becalmed and it can become very cold at sea at any time of year. Always wear an approved design of life jacket.

Whenever a gale of Force 8 or above is expected, flags are flown from each Coastguard station indicating the wind direction.

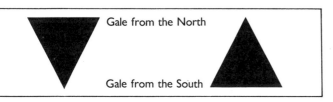

Gale from the North

Gale from the South

If you fall overboard, remove your shoes and any heavy clothing immediately, but retain the rest of your garments, as these will help keep you warm. Tread water as slowly as possible to preserve energy, although a proper life jacket will keep you afloat with no effort on your part. Recognised distress signals include: standing up with arms apart, raising and lowering them as if imitating a bird; waving a flag or any item of clothing; flying the Red Ensign (normally flown from the stern) high in the rigging or upside down. If you see any of these from the shore, dial 999 and ask for the coastguard.

Although the general rule is that steam gives way to sail, you must bear in mind that modern supertankers and the like simply cannot manoeuvre with any speed at all - it can take them a couple of miles to stop, for example! - and that in narrow or crowded sea lanes large vessels may have no choice but to maintain their course. Standard horn signals are: 1 blast "am turning to starboard", 2 blasts " am turning to port", 3 blasts "am reversing".

Racing

With over 400 different types of sailing dinghy and roughly the same number of sailing clubs, you can always be sure of seeing some racing somewhere. For the uninitiated, yacht races offer appear to be little more than confusing melees of milling boats, with a great deal of manoueuvring before the actual start. It may help the spectator to know the procedure, which is as follows: ten minutes before the start, a cannon or maroon is fired and the flag of the yacht class involved is broken from the club flagstaff; five minutes before the off, there is another bang and a Blue Peter flag appears alongside the other; the actual start is signalled by a third report and by the lowering of both flags. When yachts are actually racing, they usually fly a small, square racing flag from the masthead (rather than the usual burgee).

Wind Speed

This is normally indicated by a numerical scale of force, known as the Beaufort Scale after Sir Francis Beaufort (1774-1837), the English admiral who invented it.

Beaufort Number	Wind Speed (mph)	Description of conditions on land and sea
0	0-1	**Calm** Smoke rises vertically.
1	1-3	**Light Air** Smoke drifts.
2	4-7	**Light Breeze** Can be felt on the face.
3	8-12	**Gentle Breeze** Moves leaves and small twigs. Small waves
4	13-18	**Moderate Breeze** Raises dust and waste paper; thin branches move. Waves 4-5ft; 'White horses' form.
5	19-24	**Fresh Breeze** Small trees sway. Waves 6-8ft.
6	25-31	**Strong Wind** Large branches move; wind is distinctly audible. Waves up to 12ft; crests foaming.
7	32-38	**High Wind** Large trees move; resistance to walking against the wind. Waves up to 16ft, breaking in gusts
8	39-46	**Gale** Breaks twigs off trees; difficult to walk against wind. Waves 20-25ft; sea 'boiling' in places.
9	47-54	**Severe Gale** Tears tiles off roofs; picks up relatively large objects. Waves up to 30ft; sea foaming everywhere; poor visibility in spray.
10	55-63	**Storm** Uproots trees; damages buildings. Waves up to 40ft; difficult to see through spray.
11	64-75	**Hurricane**
12	75 plus	**Hurricane**

Moor and Mountain

Although there is no mountaineering in the Alpine sense anywhere in the region, the uplands offer a surprising diversity of activities: hill walking, scrambling, orienteering, rock climbing, and even some skiing in winter - all of which are detailed in the gazetteer.

On a fine summer's day, the high peaks look very inviting, their seemingly gentle slopes apparently quite benign. You should not be taken in: the weather can change with alarming speed and the combination of height, wind and rain can be (and often is) a killer. The effect of wind speed on temperature can be seen in the accompanying chart; but the temperature also falls by about 1°F for every 300ft you climb. This combination of height and wind is a powerful one: if the temperature at sea level is 50°F (typical of a spring day), a gentle 10mph breeze at the rather modest height of 1,000ft will produce a temperature only just above freezing point!

Nor are the slopes as gentle as they appear from the comfort of your car: it can take far longer than you think to reach your destination on foot - expect to average no more than 2mph, and allow one hour extra for each 1,500ft above sea level.

These rather alarming figures should not deter you from enjoying the spectacular scenery available; they are intended to force home the need to take elementary precautions. Always plan your route first - this atlas is ideal for that. Remember that mist and fog can descend very quickly, especially from autumn to late spring, so you must know where you are at all times. Travel in company and stick to waymarked or well established paths where possible. Wear the right clothes: woollens, stout footwear and windcheaters (ideally in a bright colour, just in case someone has to look for you). Take with you a compass, a watch, a whistle, a torch, some chocolate, a

Wind Chill
Shows the effect of wind speed (expressed on the Beaufort Scale, details of which can be seen opposite) on temperature (in degrees Fahrenheit). The temperatures listed on the top row are those which would be shown on a thermometer protected from any wind; those below are the equivalents at the various wind speeds. The area coloured blue represents the danger zone, in which there is risk of exposed flesh suffering frostbite. Remember that freezing point is +32°F.

Wind Force	Temperature							
	+50	+40	+30	+20	+10	0	—10	—20
2	+48	+37	+27	+16	+ 6	— 5	—15	—26
3	+40	+28	+16	+ 4	— 9	—21	—33	—46
4	+36	+22	+ 9	— 5	—18	—36	—45	—58
5	+32	+18	+ 4	—10	—25	—39	—53	—67
6	+29	+15	— 1	—17	—31	—46	—61	—77
7	+27	+11	— 4	—20	—35	—49	—67	—82
8+	+26	+10	— 6	—21	—37	—53	—69	—85

small first-aid kit and coins for emergency telephone calls.

If you do get into trouble, remember that six of anything is the recognised emergency signal: 6 flashes of the torch, 6 blasts on a whistle or just 6 yells.

Rock climbers, in addition to all the above, should wear safety helmets, tough boots and should always climb roped together with good quality nylon rope. Leave the heroics to the experts, many of whom you can enjoy watching at the more severe locations described in the gazetteer section on Climbing.

Calendar of Events

Events are listed by map reference, making it easy to discover what other attractions are available in any area at the same time. Remember that dates and times may vary from year to year and that you should always obtain more information before travelling by telephoning either the number supplied or the nearest Tourist Information Office (see page 122).

March
24c Newport: Drama Festival, Dolman Theatre. Performances by visiting theatre groups. *1st or 2nd week.*
40b Llanybydder: Horse Fair. *Last Thursday.*

April
24e Cardiff: Spring Exhibition, Richmond Art Centre, 181 City Road. *All month: weekdays 1030-1730, Saturdays 1000-1730.*

International Theatre Festival for Young People, based at the Sherman Theatre, Senghennyd Road (tel. 0222 371405), but with many events also held at Milford Haven (27d). Professional drama groups from all over the world take part; performances are held in Cardiff throughout the week. *1st week.*

Welsh Jazz Festival, Chapter Arts Centre, Market Road, Canton. Full programme of live music. Details from the Welsh Jazz Society, c/o New Theatre, Park Place, Cardiff. *Last week.*
27d Milford Haven: Internation Theatre Festival. *1st week.* See Cardiff.
50b Llandrindod Wells: Annual Antiques Fair. Metropole Hotel (tel. 0597 2881). *1st weekend: 1100-2000.*
56h Aberdovey: Yacht Club Handicap Races. *Easter weekend.*
59e Welshpool: Flower Festival, Trelydan Hall. *Easter weekend.*
71a Ruthin: Mediaeval Days. Townsfolk dress up in period costumes; dancing in the streets etc. *Every Wednesday.*

May
21e Swansea: Programme of Children's Events, Patti Pavilion, near the Guildhall. *Weekdays AM.*

22c Maesteg: Urdd National Eisteddfod (details: tel. Aberystwyth 0970 3744).
22f Ogmore: Annual Ogwr Tiki Raft Race down the Ogmore River. *3rd Saturday.*
22f Bridgend: Annual Maytime Festival of Drama, Bridgend Recreation Centre. Amateur dramatic societies compete for trophies. (details: tel. 0656 62141). *2nd week.*
23g Llantwit Major: Drama Week at the Town Hall (tel. 044 65 3707).
24e Cardiff: International Welsh Rally starts and finishes in the city. Rally cars travel the length and breadth of Wales to tackle many high speed 'special stages' on forestry commission, military and private property (details: British Motor Sports Association tel. London 01-235 8601). *Usually 3rd weekend.*
27a Haverfordwest: Spring Fair.
34b Llantilio Crosseney: Festival of Music and Drama in the church. *1st week.*
40b Llanybydder: Horse Fair. *Last Thursday.*
52d Aberystwyth: Aberystwyth Festival (tel. 0970 611707). Light entertainment; classical, jazz, rock and folk music; opera; films; children's events; sports; exhibitions. *1st weekend.*
56h Aberdovey: Yacht Racing. *Last week.*
67b Caernarfon: North Wales Show at Tydyn Hen. *Last week.*
71a Ruthin: Mediaeval Days, See April.
77a Llandudno: Annual Celebrity Concert, Arcadia Theatre. *2nd weekend.*
77b Colwyn Bay: Annual Drama Festival, Prince of Wales Theatre. Plays by leading amateur companies. *3rd week.*
77c Abergele: Horse Show. *3rd Saturday.*
77f Gwrych Castle: Mediaeval Jousting Tournaments. *Sunday to Friday from 1500.*

June
21e Swansea: Programme of Children's Events. See May.
24a Llandaff Cathedral: Annual Festival. Choral and orchestral music (tickets and details: tel. 044 63 2395). *2nd/3rd weeks for 10 days: performances 1930-2200. Advance booking recommended.*
24e Cardiff: Royal Salutes in Bute Park, Cardiff Castle, usually at

noon, to celebrate: the Queen's Coronation *(2nd)*, the birthday of HRH Duke of Edinburgh *(11th)*; Queen's official birthday *(16th)*.

27a Haverfordwest: River Pageant.

27d Milford Haven: Regatta.

28d Saundersfoot: Yacht Racing. Open meeting for GP14, Osprey and Mirror Dingy classes. *Last weekend.*

28g Tenby Arts Festival (tel. 0834 3297). Brass bands, orchestral and choral music, drama, etc., at various venues in the town. *Last week.*

38d Rosebush: Annual Show and Gymkhana of the Maenclochog Branch of the Royal British Legion at the New Inn. *3rd Saturday from 1000.*

40b Llanybydder: Horse Fair. *Last Thursday.*

42b Merthyr Cynog: Annual Trotting and Galloway Races. *2nd Saturday from 1430.*

56a Barmouth: Start of the Three Peaks Yacht Race. Contestants sail to and climb Snowdon, Snae Fell and Ben Nevis. *3rd Saturday.*

62a Porthmadog: Yacht Racing. Dinghies and cruisers on alternate weekends.

62c Llyn Trawsfynydd: Yacht Racing. Dinghies and cruisers on alternative weekends.

71a Ruthin: Mediaeval Days. See April.

79g Mold: North Wales Art Societies Annual Exhibition, Civic Centre. *1st week.*

July

21e Swansea: Gower Festival. Chamber and choral music, arts and crafts, drama and poetry, held in the city and at various other venues throughout the Gower peninsula (details: tel. Reynoldston 044 122 319). *Last 2 weeks*

Patti Pavilion, near the Guildhall: Programme of Children's Events *(weekdays AM);* Variety Shows *(Thursday evenings);* Concerts *(Sunday evenings).*

23g Llantwit Major: Art Exhibition in the Town Hall (tel. 044 65 3707).

24e Cardiff: Charles Street Annual Carnival. Street drama, Punch & Judy, folk and rock music, magic, juggling, sideshows, children's events, dancing, etc. (details: tel. 0222 31700). *Last week.*

28c St Clear's: Annual Pilgrimage and Service in the churchyard. *Last Sunday.*

33i Cwmbran/Newport: Welsh Folk Dancing Society Summer Festival, with all-day displays of traditional dancing in both town centres; also evening events at various venues (details tel. Cardiff 0222 568221 or Newport 0633 52962). *3rd weekend.*

36h St David's Cathedral Choral concerts. See 37e Fishguard.

37e Fishguard Music Festival (tel. 0348 873612). International professionals perform orchestral and choral music; also films, lectures, art exhibitions; choral concerts in St David's Cathedral (36h). *Last week.*

40b Llanybydder: Horse Fair. *Last Thursday.*

50b Llandrindod Wells: Carnival Day. *Last Saturday.*

50e Builth Wells: Royal Welsh Show, Llanelwedd Showground. Wales' annual agricultural show, with livestock, crafts, sideshows, etc. (details: tel. 098 22 3683). *Mid-week during last full week: 0900-1900.*

All Wales Sheepdog Trial, at Llanelwedd Showground. *1st day of Royal Welsh Show from 0900.*

58c Llanfyllin: Annual Festival. *1st two weekends.*

Eisteddfod Powys, with all the traditional events. *3rd weekend.*

62a Porthmadog: Yacht Racing. Dinghies and cruisers on alternate weekends.

62c Llyn Trawsfynydd: Yacht Racing. Dinghies and cruisers on alternate weekends.

65b Llangollen: International Musical Eisteddfod (tel.0978 860236). World famous event, with over 12,000 singers from 30 nations taking part in solo, choral, folk and instrumental music. *2nd week: competitions 0900-1700, concerts 1930-2200.*

67b Caernarfon: Festival. *3rd week.*

71a Ruthin: Mediaeval Days. See April.

75i Menai Straits: Regatta fortnight (details from Royal Anglesey Yacht Club tel. Beaumaris 0248 810295 or 810883). *Last week.*

77a Llandudno: Ladies Open Bowling Competition, Craig-y-Don Bowling Club (details: tel. Colwyn Bay 0492 49309). *1st Tuesday and Wednesday from 1000.*

August

21e Swansea: Patti Pavilion. See July.

21f Mumbles: Swimming Race to Aberavon.

23g Llantwit Major: Horticultural Show at the Town Hall (tel. 044 65 3707).

24e Cardiff: Royal Salute in Bute Park, Cardiff Castle to celebrate the birthday of the Queen Mother. *4th at noon.*

Searchlight Tattoo. *2nd/3rd week.*

Lord Mayor's Parade. *3rd Sunday.*

28d Saundersfoot: Round the Island Race and two regattas. *Last weekend.*

28g Tenby: Bowling Week, Carnival and Regatta.

35a Monmouth: Annual Bed Race through the main streets. *Last Tuesday from 1900.*

36h St David's: Arts Festival (tel. 021 472 1735). *All month.*

37c Newport: Annual Regatta.

38c Cilgerran: Annual Coracle Regatta. Contestants row up and down the River Teifi in 5½ft oval craft built to the traditional design.

39i Carmarthen: United Counties Agricultural Show. *2nd week.*

40h Llanybydder: Horse Fair. *Last Thursday.*

40i Llandeilo: Annual Agricultural Show.

50b Llandrindod Wells: Welsh National Bowling Championships.

56b Barmouth: Art Exhibition.

56i Machynlleth: Royal National Eisteddfod (details tel. 0654 2801). *1st week.*

71a Ruthin: Mediaeval Days. See April.

75i Menai Straits: Regatta Fortnight. *1st week.* See July.

September

35a Monmouth: Raft Race. Contestants travel 5 miles down the River Wye to Whitebrook. *1st Sunday.*

40b Llanybydder: Horse Fair. *Last Thursday.*

48f Tregaron: Eisteddfod. *2nd Saturday.*

67b Port Dinorwic: Angling Festival on the Menai Straits. *3rd Sunday.*

70a Llyn Brenig: Yacht Racing. GP14 Team Race. *Last Sunday.*

71f Plas Madoc: Annual Basketball Tournament, Leisure Centre. *3rd Sunday.*

78e St Asaph: North Wales Music Festival (tel. 0745 583429). Many international artistes perform in the cathedral. *Last full week.*

October

21e Swansea: Swansea Festival. The largest professional arts festival in Wales; events take place in Brangwyn Hall, Grand Theatre and the Glynn Vivian Art Gallery. Tickets and details from the Guildhall (tel. 0792 50821). *1st two full weeks.*

27a Haverfordwest: Portfield Fair. Traditional 'hiring' fair which has been held for centuries. *5th.*

27h Pembroke: Autumn Fair. Another long established, traditional event.

40b Llanybydder: Horse Fair. *Last Thursday.*

50b Llandrindod Wells: Eisteddfodd in the Albert Hall.

75g Llangefni: Welsh National Drama Festival. Plays performed in Welsh.

November

24e Cardiff: Festival of 20th Century Music, University College (tel. 0222 44211). Artistes are both established and new, the music is both popular and esoteric; also concerts by the college choir and orchestra. *Last week.*

December

24e Cardiff: Festival of 20th Century Music. *1st 2 weeks.* See November.

Wales - Key to map pages

Motorways	**M5**	National Parks		Battlefields	✗
M'ways under const. & proposed		Forest Parks		Lighthouses	
Motorway Junction Numbers	23 24 Restricted Access	Woods & Forests		Lightships	
Motorway Service Areas	EXETER	Car Ferries		Summits	△ 672m
Dual Carriageways		Passenger Ferries		Spot Heights	. 223m
Dual C'ways under construction		Railways	STA L.C. (Level Crossing) Tunnel	Waterfalls	
Main Roads		Mineral Railways		Marshes	
Secondary Roads		Disused Railways		Caves	⌒
Other Good Roads		Canals		Churches	+
Minor Roads & Tracks		Long Distance Footpaths		Coast Guard Stations	CG
Route Classification Numbers	A69 B631	Footpaths & Bridle Paths		Lifeboat Stations	LB
National Boundaries		Youth Hostels	▲YH	Sandy Beaches	
County Boundaries		Airfields	⊕	Rocky Foreshore	
Military Danger Zones		Windmills	⚥	Low Water Line	
National Trust Property ·	NT ●	Antiquities	∴	Cliffs	

HEIGHT OF LAND IN METRES AND FEET

	0	165	330	490	655	985	1310	1640	1970	2295	2625	2950	3280	3610	Feet
Land below sea level	0	50	100	150	200	300	400	500	600	700	800	900	1000	1100	Metres

Activities covered in the gazetteer (with page numbers)
Where appropriate, these may be overprinted on the relevant black symbol above

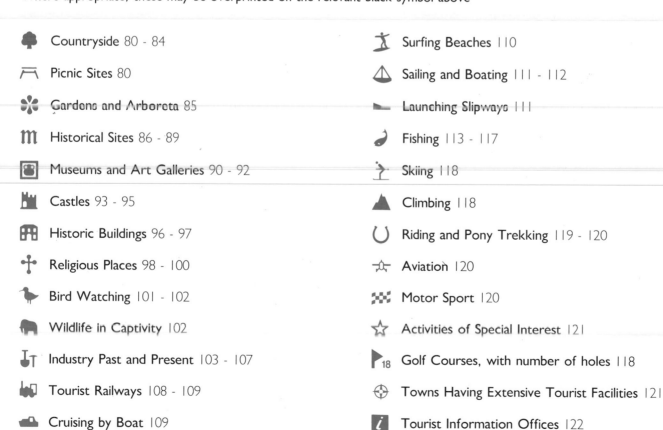

- Countryside 80 - 84
- Picnic Sites 80
- Gardens and Arboreta 85
- Historical Sites 86 - 89
- Museums and Art Galleries 90 - 92
- Castles 93 - 95
- Historic Buildings 96 - 97
- Religious Places 98 - 100
- Bird Watching 101 - 102
- Wildlife in Captivity 102
- Industry Past and Present 103 - 107
- Tourist Railways 108 - 109
- Cruising by Boat 109
- Water Sports 110
- Surfing Beaches 110
- Sailing and Boating 111 - 112
- Launching Slipways 111
- Fishing 113 - 117
- Skiing 118
- Climbing 118
- Riding and Pony Trekking 119 - 120
- Aviation 120
- Motor Sport 120
- Activities of Special Interest 121
- Golf Courses, with number of holes 118
- Towns Having Extensive Tourist Facilities 121
- Tourist Information Offices 122

20

a	b	c
d	e	f
g	h	i

29	30
20	21

0   1   2   3   4   5 Miles

0   1   2   3   4   5   6   7   8 Kilometres

DANGER ZONE

20'

DANGER
ZONE

DANGER ZONE

Pembrey

Forest

Pembrey Burrows

B 4311

Country Park

Low Water Mark

0'

A 484

B 4317

Pen-y-bedd

Pembrey

Burry
Port

Achddu

Dafatty

PEMBREY &
BURRY PORT STA
Power Sta

Cen-rhos

Craig capel

Plas
newydd

Morfa

Pwll

Cefn Patrick

Sandy

Rhiw-las

Bigin

Ty gwyn

Mynydd Pen-bre

190m

165m

141m

Dythel

Rhos

Pant
Barclay

Cil-y-maen
llwydd

Pen y fui

Cwm bach

Cil-y-maen
llwydd

Stradey

Mudlescwm

Pen-y-bont

Syddyn-melyn

Cil-feri-
isaf

Ty canol

Horeb

Five Roads

Troshill

Myrtlehill
Gelli-galed

Cil-wnwg

Clochyrie

Blaen
hiraeth

Cil-Dewi-fay

185m

119m

Troserch

Cefn-y-bryn

Gelli fawr

Pant y Dydu

Cilau-gwyn

Upper
Lliedi Resr

Soho

Bylch y
Fedwen

Pisaf

A 476

Ystrad fai

Allt-y-fran

Morlais R.

A 4138

B 4309

Lower
Lliedi Resr

Felin-foel

Llangennech

Corn-hwrdd

Clyn-gwernen

Allt

Plas-isaf

Pen llwyn-gwyn

Bryn

Pen-coe

Felinfoel

Dafen

A 476

A 484

LLANELLI

Hosp.

LC

Halfway

A 4138

Blwyn-hendy

Bynea

BYNEA
STA

Berwic

Ysp

5m

Pen-y-bryn

Morfa Bacas

Machynys

River Loughor

BURRY RIVER

20c LLANELLI

Burry Pill

Whiteford Pt

BURRY   INLET

Llanrhidian   Sands

Dalton's Pt

Berth

Pen-cla

Salthouse Pt

Salthouse

Crofty

Llanrhidian Chap

Pound

Cefn

Llan-morlais

Pen-llwyn
Robert

Wern-ffrwd

Mynyd
Bachy-ca

Gelli-groes

Cil-oner

Whiteford Sands

Whiteford Burrows

NT

Landimore
Marsh

North Hill

Cwm Ivy

Hills Tor

Prissen's Tor

Broughton
Bay

Foxhole Pt

Bluepool Corner

Minor Pt

62m

Broughton
Burrows

Burry Holms

CHAPEL

Llangennith
Burrows

Cockstreet

Llanmadog

SETTLEMENT

Cheriton

Llanmadog
Hill

186m

CAIRNS

THE BULWARK

Tankeylake
Moor

Kennexstone

NT

Ryer's
Down

Burrygreen

Landimor

CAS

Llanrhidian
Marsh

5m

Leason

WEOBLEY CAS

FORT

Mansel
Fold

Stembridge

Oldwalls

Stouyford

Newton

Cae Morgan

Freedown

Wern-halog

NT

Bryn

NT

Welsh
Moor

NT

Cillibion

Llethrid

Pengwern Common

Bryn gwas

Carter-ford

Pengwern

Swa

Furzehill

W

Willoxton

Bryn-afel

Luxom

Park
Wood

Park le Bruce

Park Pt

Parkmill

A 4

CAS CH

San

Rhosili
Bay

NT

Rhosili Beach

Low Water Mark

Rhosili
Downs

93m

The Beacon

Rhosili

WELL

Middleton B 4247

NT

BURIAL
CHAMBERS

Sluxton

Coety
Green

Hillend

SETTLEMENT

Llangennith

Hardingsdown

Hardings
Down

Druids Lo.

Cathan

Hen-llys

CAS

G   O

W   E

R

Bryn

186m

Burry

Reynoldston

Stout Hall

Ty-bryn
CROSS

Fairyhill

Llwyn y bwch

BURIAL
CHAMBER

HOLY WELL

Walterston

Longoaks

Holy Well

Llanddewi

Knelston

EARTHWORK

Scurlage

A 4118

Berry

Penrice
Cas

MOTTE

Penrice

Ch

Nicholaston

NT

Penmaen

CAS CH

Penard

Penard
Burrows

18

WORMS HEAD
(Pen Pyrod)

Devil's Bridge

Blow Hole

Low Neck

Inner Head

Crabart

Sears Pt

Mew's lade Bay

Red Chamber

Kitchen
Corner

NT

SETTLEMENT

Pitton

Pilton Green

Monksland

Margam

Hangman's Cross

Moorcorner

Norton

Sanctuary

Pitt

Oxwich

Oxwich
Burrows

Low Water Mark

Great Tor

Threecliff Bay

Shire Combe

Mitchin
Hole

Oxwich   Bay

Bac

Paviland

Paviland Cave

Blackhole Gut

NT

Littlehills

Horton

Overton

Port
Eynon

The Cove

Slade

Oxwichgreen

CAS Ch

Oxwich Pt

76m

Congnon
Cliff

Culver
Hole

Harry's Watch

Port Eynon Bay

Overton Cliff

Port Eynon Pt

4°20′W

10'

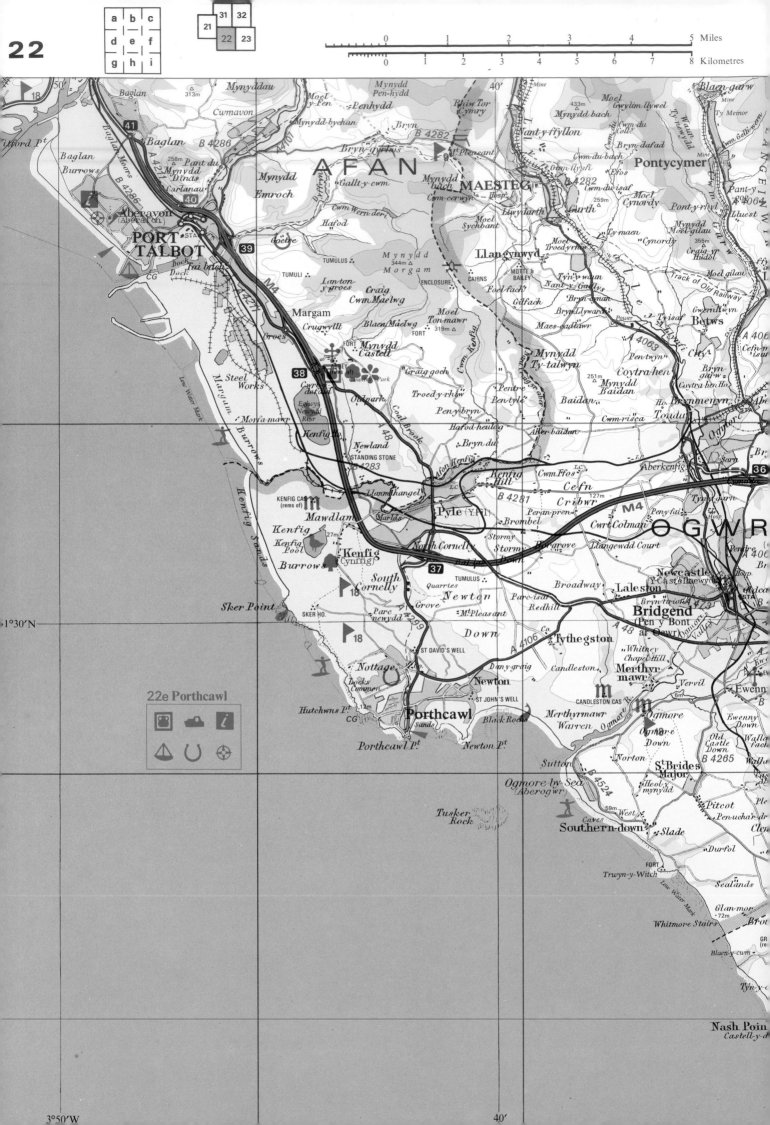

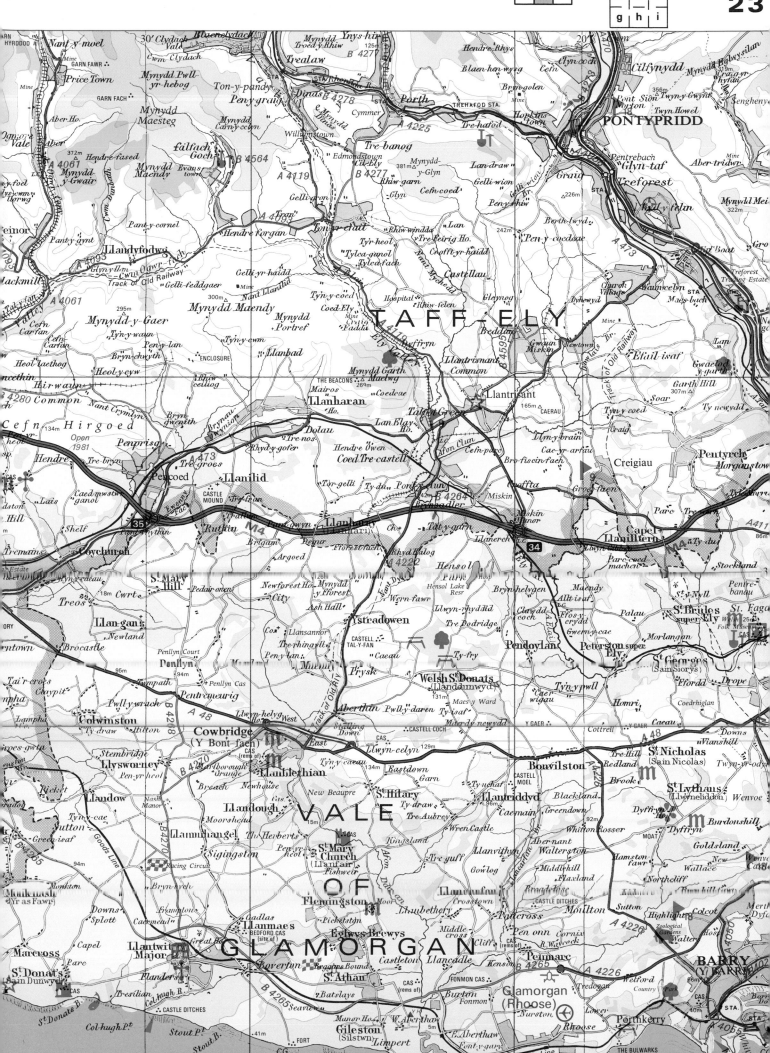

37 38
26 27 28

a b c
d e f
g h i

27

27h Pembroke

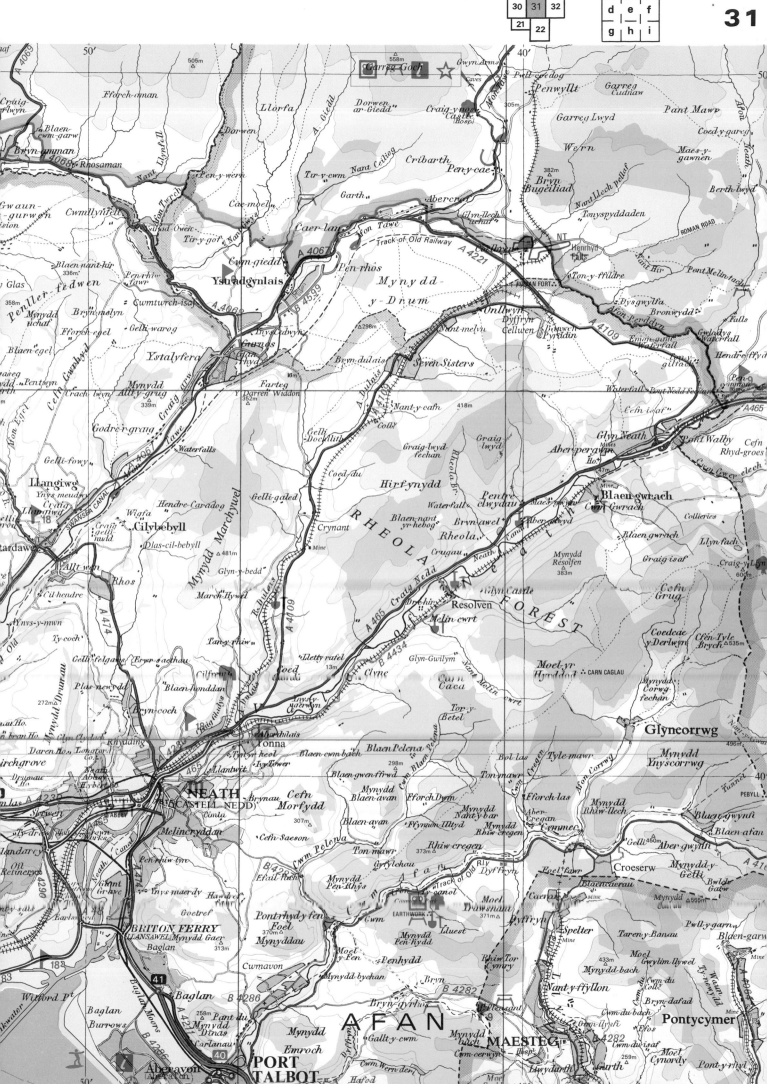

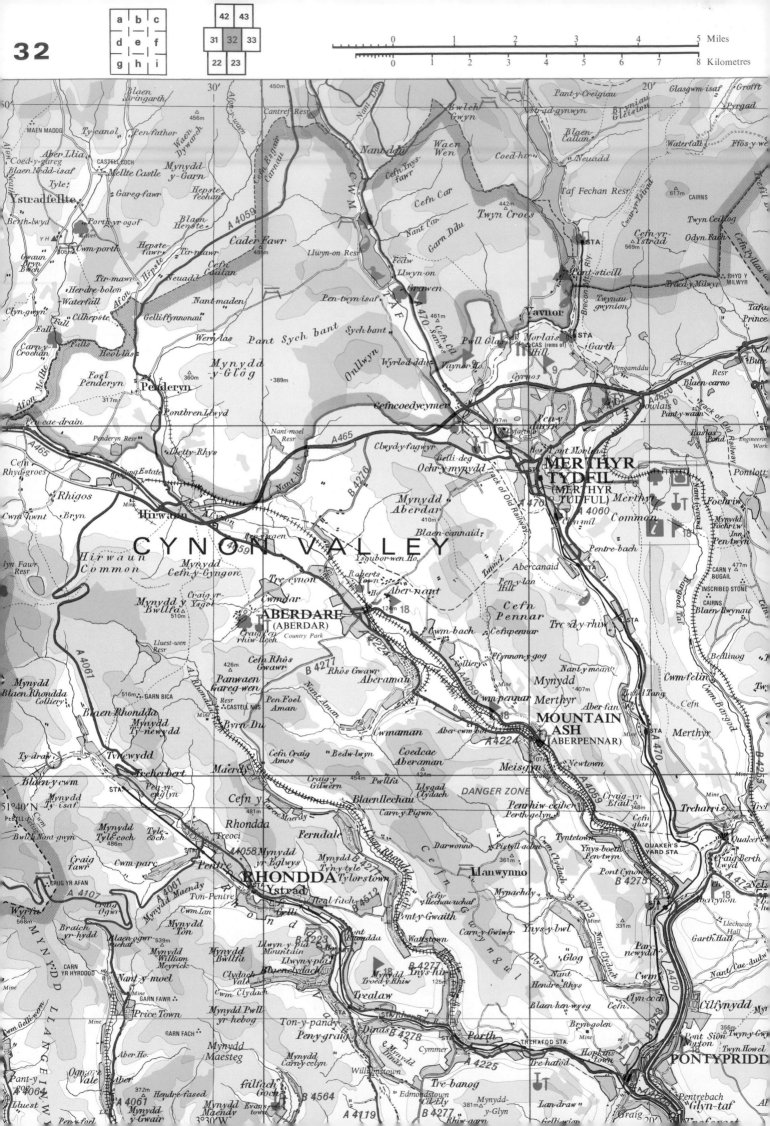

43	44
32	33	34
23	24

a	b	c
d	e	f
g	h	i

33

NEWPORT

M4

35a Chepstow

MICHAELWOOD

AUST

| 48 | 49 |

| 40 | 41 | 42 |

| 30 | 31 |

a	b	c
d	e	f
g	h	i

41

Bryn-teg
NT
Cefn y Bryn 434m
Craig Rhosan
Llanerch-fındıla
Fwng uchaf
358m
Sugar loaf

Glan-meddyg
Esgair Dderchon
Afon Gwenlais
Gwern-pwll
Coed-Ifan
Nant Hiraum
Bryn-ffoi

Alandre
Cefn y Bryn
Rhyd-lydan
Neuadd-fawr
Dolau-ddu
Dugoedydd
Cefn hir tryn
Allethr hir

Brummt
Banc yr Esgair
Afon Merchon
Glan Gwenlar
Cefn Ilan
CYNGHORDY STA
Cynghordy
Cefn-coch

Cothi
Banc Blaen-dyffryn
Dinas-bach
Cyngloty
Cefn Ho
Crychan
Banc Cefn garreg

Caio
Blaen dyffryn
CILYCWM
Aber Gwenlas
Ochr y fforest
Moelfre
A 483
Glan Bran
Llanfair-ar-y-bryn
Tre fawr

Llwyn Owen
Nant-iwrch
Pen y banc 365m
Byflyn
Cilycwm fforest
Afon Bran
Little Hall
Cefn Ho
Afon
Cefn garreg

Glan-yr-Annell
Albert Mount
Aber Bowlan
Gilwen
Pant glas
Glan Crychan
Cin coed
Clawdd Brit

Maes-glas
Pen-y-banc
Cefn-trenfa
Llwyn y Berllan
Tyn y coed
Aber crychan
Ystrad Walter
Pen y waun
M07

Goleugoed
Bwlch cefn sarth
Porth-y-rhyd
Wern-ddu
Emlyd
Maes y gwanllw
Pen y bont
Dolau gwynion
305m
Gelli felen
Babel

A 482
Banc Bwlch-cefn-sarth 335m
Esgair-afel
HenIlys
Dolau hiron
Maes Nedan Hall
Pentre-ty-gwyn
Cha

Nant-yr-Hogfaen
Troed y rhıw
Plas newydd
Llwyn cynhyrys
LLANDOVERY
EARTHWORK
Pen twyn
Gwernddon
Cefn-pwll hen

Hafod Bridge
Wern
Tal-yr-yn
Cwm Mynys
Garth
Velindre
Afon Bran
Gefn Arthur
Nant-y-Tresglen

Mynydd Llansadwrn 345m
Froed y rlaw
Gilfach
Cwm Mynys-uchaf
Blaenos
Pen-lan-telych
Pentre bach
Halfway
A 40
Gwyddgrug
Gellifain

Carmel Cha
Ty Tywyd
Garth
CAS
Fron Rock Fm
Dagfa
Pigwn ROMAN CAMPS
383m

Coed-hirion
Cwm-cilath
Mount Pleasant
Llwyn y brain
Pen y bont
Cwm Rhuddan
Cefn ceryg
Llanerch-goch
Gareg-lwyd
Belia

Plas newydd
Waen-clynda
Cha
Ystrad H
A4069
Glan Fenw Wood
Llwyn-wermwd Ho
Ffin fach
Hafod-fawr
Mynydd Trecastell

Fan
Llanwrda
Dol y garreg
Pant y gaseg
Nen twyn
Waun Ddu
Llwyn-cely

Banc-y-lan Aberdaunant
Llansadwrn
LLANWRDA STA
Cwm Cowdl
Cae gwyn
R Ydw
Tomen y Rhos 440m
Gelli-gam

Bryn
Fetindre
Pont Goleugoed
MYDDFAI
Esgair llaethdy
Daun

Aberntarlas Parks
Tyddyn
Cilgwyn
Gorllwyn-fach
Cefn gwrych
STANDING STONES
STANDING STONE
Pwll-uchaf
Ynys-fawr

Parc glas
Cefn gornoet
44069
Afon Bran
Cwm bran 101m
Rhyblid
Usk Resr
Pont ar Hydfer
Aber Hydfer

Llwyn-y-piod Cha
LLANGADOG
Glan Serw
Tyr-paen
Gwydre
Fedw Fawr
Rhyd-y-fallen

NETWR
Felindre
CASTLE MOUND & BAILEY
Man-ddinam
Olchfa
Gilfach
Pen y rhiw
Rhosfa Gareg Lwyd
Mynydd Wysg

Llwyn-yr-yn
Dan-yr-allt
Ta-mawr
Bryn glas
Rhiwiau Hill
359m
Cha
Tirclun
Ilechach
Moel Darw 424m
Blaenau-isaf
STONE CIRCLES
Meity

Tyle
Pen-y-banc
Casait-bychan-mawr
Panthowell
Cilmaen
Mynydd Llan 423m
River Usk
Troed-rhiw-fer
Ford
Meity-fawr

Manordeilo
A 4069
Twyn Mann
LLANDDEUSANT
Bryn Mawr
Carn Las

Bethlehem
Pen-Arthur-isaf
Pont ar-llechan
Pen-crug
Sawdde
Ford
Fords
Pen-careg
Source of Usk
Twyn yr Esgair

Carn Goch
GAER FAWR
Pen-Arthur
Hen-Bont
Pont Newydd
Gelli-gron
Blaen-Sawdde
Moel Feudwy 591m

Capel-ty-dyst
Crug-las
Cwm coy Melwch
Beiti
Pont Aber
Pant-y-turnor
Carn y Gigfran
802m
Source of Tawe
Belia

Bryngwyn 336m
Dafadfa 287m
Gwynfe Ho Capel Gwynfe Sch
Llan
Garreg yr ogof 586m
Llyn y Fan Fach 750m
BANNAU SIR GAR MOUNTAIN
Llyn y Fan Fawr
STANDING STONE

Neuadd
Ford
Hirllwyn-isaf
Truman
Bwlch y Giedd
Naw y Llan
CERRIG DUON

Cefn-bedw
Ferdre
Glan-brwynant
Breast Rhiw-ddu
Pont Clydach
Cefn-y-Cylchau
Garreg-las 633m
Brest Twrch
Carnau Gwys
Cefn Rhudd
721m
Blaen-Ca

The Forge
CARREG CENNEN CAS
Blaen-Gemen
Rhiw Wen
Cefn-y-Truman
MYNYDD DDU
Blaen Llynfell
Bwlch y Garreg-lem
Llwyn-yr-yn
Dderi

CWRT BRYN-Y-BEIRDD
Banc Wern Wgan
Clogau Mawr
Foel Fawr 493m
Foel Fraith 604m
616m
Blaen Tywrch
Garreg-Kem
Gwyn Arms

Tair Carn Uchaf 482m
Carn Pen-y-Clogau 521m
Garreg-lwyd
Bytchau Rhos Facn
Carn Fadog
505m
Dysgwylfa
Afon Haffes
A 406

BLACK MOUNTAIN
Tair Carn Isaf 459m
Ffarch-aman
Garreg-Goch 558m
Gwyn-Coch
Afon Tawe

42f **Brecon**

Hay

Crickhowell

53
48 49 50
41 42

a b c
d e f
g h i

49

Tan-y-rhydiau
Disgwylfa
Lleth-Lwyd
Bryn-yr Hyddod
Llyn-Cerig Uwydion uchaf
Nant Caletwr
Pen Cwm-yr-hafod
Esgair-pen-y-garreg
Rhydoldoy

50'
Esgair Mwn Mines
Bryn Eithinog
Esgair-Gris
Dam
Esgair Gris
Pen-y-garreg Resr.

Ffuir-rhes
Esgair Hengae
Bryn Hir
Pen-y-garreg Resr.
Peny Bwlch
Nant-yr-haid

Esgair y Garn
Llyn Teifi
Claerwen
Claerddu
T R U M A U
Gwaelod-y-Rhos
Nant Madog

Pen-y-Banau
Llyn Hir
Afon Claerwen
Esgair Nant y beddau
Moel Fryn 486m
Nant Methan
Crug Dutdaeneg
B4518

SETTLEMENT
Gargoed
Llyn Egnant
459m △
Claerddu
Llethr Hir
Nant-y-Beddau
Esgair-y-Gader
538m△
Craig Dyffaint
Cefn Cwm-Coel
Ty ny Llidiart
Y Foel
Filter Beds
Craig Foel

rhydfendigaid
Troed-y-rhiw
Esgair Wen
Esgair-y-Gader
Craig Fawr
Cefn Blaen Coel
Waterfalls
Elan Village
466m

Strata Florida
Berthgoed
Craigen Ddu
Dibyn Du
Banc y Llyn
Esgair Garthen
Claerwen
483m
Rest.
Cefn Blaen Coel
Craig Fawr
Waterfalls
Allt Goc

Glasffrwd
Pen-y-Magn Berthgoed
Llyn Gynon
Afon Arban
Craig y Bwlch
Gors Goch
Cil-oerwynt Waterfall
Rhosygelynen
Caben Coch Gro Hill
Talwrn

calwrn
Peny Bwlch
Crug Gynon
Crug yr Wyn
Cureg Wen Fawr
Pen Maen-wern
Rhiwnant
Craig y Bwlch
Caben Coch Resr.

Bryn-y-Crofftiau
Blaen Glasffrwd
Llyn Gorast
Bryn Garw
Rhiwnant
Llanerch-y-Cawr
Waun Llwyd
Waterfalls
Crugiau Ferlen

Carn Fflur
Llethr Brith
Esgair Llyn-du
Moel-prysgau
Cnol Wen
Cerig Llwyd y rhestr
Llyn Carw
Esgair Ganol
Dalrhiw
Waterfalls

Llyn Crugnant
Llyn Ddu
Esgair Saeson
Cors-yr-Hwch
Pant Glas
Creigiau Hirion
Waun
Gorllwyn

Carn Gron
548△
Drum Nant-yr helyg
Drum Nant-y gorlan
Drugarn yr-Eira
645m
Blaen Rhiwnant
Drygarn Fawr
Bwlch y Ddau-faen
Carnau
Lan Wen
Gyrnos

Esgair Hirnant
Hirnant
Bryn Crwn
Esgair yr Adar
Drygarn Fach
Bryn Glas
Nant Melyn
Nant Cerwyn
Esgair Fraith
Daren
Cwm Dulas

Cefn Crwe △527m
Esgair Gerwyn
528m
Cureg yr Adar
Bryn Du
Nant y Fedw
Bryn Mawr
Esgair Gul
Blaen Gwnfel
Y Gart

Nant-y-maen
487m
Esgair Gelli
Bwlch Esgair-gelli 471m
Nant-ystalwyn
Esgair Gloddiad
Creigiau Duon
Pen-cae
Moelydd

Bryn glas
Esgair Cerig
Gamallt
Cefn Isaf
Nant Crm du
Pen y Cnwe
Nant-yr hwch
Llanerch yrfa
Afon Gwesyn
Pen Careg dan
Blaen-cwm
Bryn
Cefn Drum

Bryn Du
Maes glas
Nant Crm du
Creigiau Duon
Camddwr
Esgair Irfon
Llednant
Argoed
Tyn-y-Uwyn Erw dlo

Doethie Fach R.
Nant y graig
Esgair Gors
Llanddewi Abergwesyn
Craig Nant y Fleiddast Cnuach
Nant Hir
501m
Cefn Coch
Bryn Clun
Glan Gwesyn
Bryn Mawr
Croffriad
Chapel
Troedy rhiw
Gilwern

Llethr-Llwyd
Goyallt
Tyn-y-corryd
Chapel
Rhyd Goch
Cefn Tyn-y graig
Nant y brain
Ty mawr
Llethr Melyn
Loft y bach
Garn Wen
Cefn-hafdref

Maes-y
Pen rhiw clochdy
Nant-llwyd
Cefn Fanog
Llwyn derw
Nant Rhydwen
Pwll y bo
Crug
Cefn Crug
Cefn Pen-y-bont
Bryn
Llwyn Madog

RHIW-LLWYDOG
65m
Cnuach
Cefn Gurnos
Cae gwyn
Abergwesyn
BANC PONFFROI
Coed-mawr
Bryn-mwelo

Bryn ambor
Esgair Gwair
Llyn Brianne Rest.
Pen-y garn
Cefn Cwmlles
Craig Dinas-fach
Nant y cerdau
Cefn Blaen-Einon
Nant Einon
Coed caeper corn
Beulah
Llwyn-eu

Pwr Las
Nant Cwm-lles
Cefn Uchaf
Carcwm Pen-y-bont uchaf
488m
Pen Y Garn
Carcwm goch
Pen-y-fed
Brenith coed
Pant teg
Llwyn-Cadogan
Llanlleonfel

Bird Reserve
Cefn Cwm-Irfon
Cefn Alltwineu
Ffos-yr-hyddod
Nant-yr-odyn
Bwlch-tua-tbre
Lluwes-heli
Prysiau-fach
Trefiys

Craig Bysgotwr
Craig Ddu Pen-Rhiw-bie
391m
Mynydd Trawsnant
Nant Henog
Cwm Henog
Pen-y-banc
Garn Dwad
Nant Cerlan
Y Foel
Tyn-y-pind
Prysiau fawr
Llangammarch Wells

Cefn Gwenffrwd
Bird Reserve
Craig Clyn-gwyn
Croes Llwyd-fach
Allt-wineu
Glen View
Dol-y-coed Hotel
A483
Pen-hewyn-fach
Cefn-gast
Ford

STANDING STONE
Ch.
Twm Shon Catti's
Ystrad Ann
CERRIG CEUN
Hafod Llewelyn
Waun Coli
Llanwrtyd
Llanwrtyd Wells
Aber-nant Lake
Esgair Fnoel
Pen-rhiw

DING STONE
Craig Beynon
Bron-y-rwrt
Nant y Bai
Cynnant
Esgair Berfedd
Pen-maen-llwyd
STANDING STONE
Waun Rhydd
Llwyn-y-finwent

Mallaen
GARN WEN
Rhandir-nwyn
Bryn Nichol
Fwng uchaf
Ffos-gou
Sugar Loaf
Nant Hirawm
Afon Dulas
Aber-geliau
Llwyn-y-finwent
TRI CHRUGIAU
Maes-xt-on

Craig Rhosan
Dolau-ddu
Gwern-pwll
Llanerch-findda
Coed-Ifan
358m
Cefn Llwydlo
Craig Rhosan
Pen-lan-wen
at Bray

50'
40'

55
50 51
43 44

a b c
d e f
g h i

51

a b c
d e f
g h i

56
52 53
48

0 1 2 3 4 5 Miles
0 1 2 3 4 5 6 7 8 Kilometres

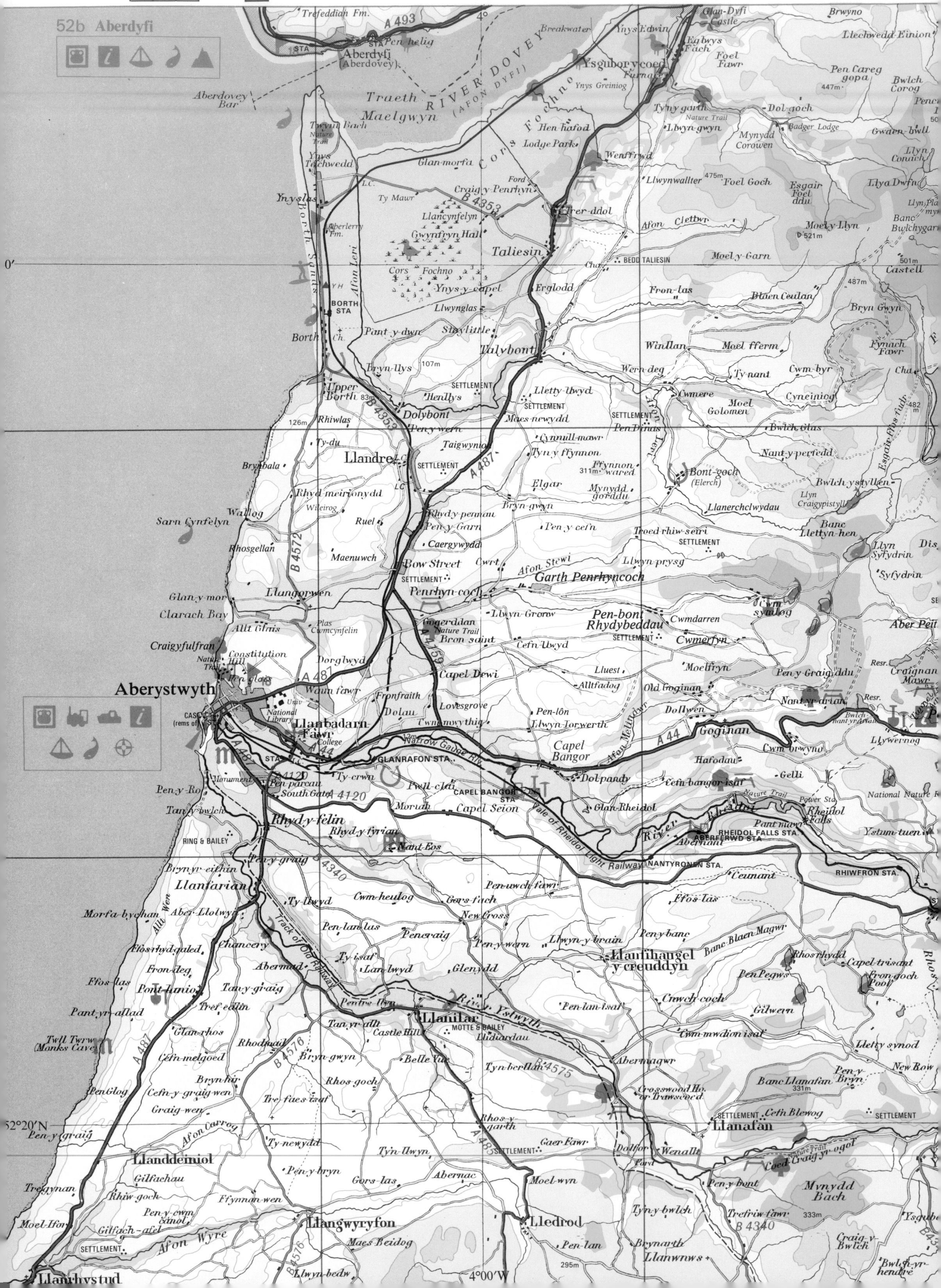

52b Aberdyfi

Trefeddian Fm.
A 493
Breakwater
Glan-Dyfi Castle
Brwyno
Llechwedd Einion
STA Penhelig
STA
Aberdyfi (Aberdovey)
Ynys Edwin
Fabys Fach
Foel Fawr
Ysguborycoed
Furnace
Pen Careg gopa
447m
Bwlch Corog
Pencl
Aberdovey Bar
RIVER DOVEY (AFON DYFI)
Fochno
Ynys Greiniog
Ty'n y garth
Nature Trail
Dol-goch
Badger Lodge
Gwaen-bwll
Llyn Conach
Twyni Bach
Nature Trail
Ynys Tachwedd
Traeth Maelgwyn
Hen-hafod
Lodge Park
Wenffrwd
Llwyn-gwyn
Mynydd Corowen
Llechwedd Einion
Glan-morfa
Craig y Penrhyn
Ford
Trer-ddol
Llwynwallter
475m
Foel Goch
Esgair Foel ddu
Llyn Dwfn
Llyn Plas mys
Ynyslas
Aberleri Fm.
Ty Mawr
B 4353
Afon Cletwr
Moel-y-Llyn
521m
Banc Bwlchygarn
Borth Sands
Afon Leri
L.C.
Llancynfelyn
Gwynfryn Hall
Taliesin
BEDD TALIESIN
Moel-y-Garn
Castell
487m
501m
0'
Cors Fochno
Ynys-y-capel
Erglodd
Fron-las
Blaen Ceulan
Bryn Gwyn
BORTH STA
Llwynglas
Stoylittle
Windlan
Moel ffrm
Ty nant
Cwm-byr
Cyneiniog
Cha.
Borth Ch.
Pant-y-dwr
Talybont
SETTLEMENT
Wern-deg
482m
Bryn-llys
107m
Lletty-Uwyd
Moel Golomen
Upper Borth
83m
Henllys
SETTLEMENT
Maes-newydd
Cwmere
Pen Dinas Leri
Bwlch olas
Rhiwlas
126m
Dolybont
B 4353
Pen-y-wern
Taigwynion
Cynnull-mawr
Ffynnon-wared
311m
Bont-goch (Elerch)
Bwlch ystyllen
Brynbala
Llandre
Ty-du
LC
A 487
Elgar
Mynydd gorddu
Llanerchcelwydau
Rhyd meirionydd
Wileirog
Rhyd-y-pennau
Bryn-gwyn
Llyn Craigypistyll
Wallog
Ruel
Pen-y-Garn
Pen-y-cefn
Troed rhiw seiri
Banc Llettyn-hen
Sarn Cynfelyn
Rhosgellan
Maenuwch
Caergywydd
Cwrt
Afon Stewi
Llwyn-prysg
SETTLEMENT
Llyn Syfydrin
Syfydrin
Dis
Bow Street
SETTLEMENT
Garth Penrhyncoch
Craigyfulfran
Glan-y-mor
Llangorwen
Penrhyn-coch
Llwyn-Gronw
Cefn Uwyd
Pen-bont Rhydybeddau
SETTLEMENT
Cwmdarren
Cwmerfyn
Cwm sy-alog
Aber Peit
Clarach Bay
Allt Ddu
Plas Cwmcynfelin
Gogerddan Nature Trail
Bron saint
Moelfryn
Lluest
Alltfadog
Old Goginan
Dollwen
Pen-y-graig ddu
Craignant Mawr
Resr.
Craigyfulfran
Nature Trail
Constitution Hill
Dorglwyd
Capel Dewi
Fronfraith
Lovesgrove
Pen-lôn
Llwyn-Iorwerth
A 44
Goginan
Cwm brwyno
Llywernog
Resr.
SE
Aberystwyth
Penglais
Waun fawr
Univ.
National Library
Dolau
Cwm mwythig
Capel Bangor
Hafodau
Cefn-bangor-isaf
Gelli
National Nature R
CASTLE (rems of)
Llanbadarn-Fawr
College
Narrow Gauge Rly
GLANRAFON STA.
Capel Bangor
Dolpandy
Nature Trail
Power Sta.
Pen parcau
STA
A 44
Ty-crwn
CAPEL BANGOR STA.
Glan-Rheidol
Rheidol Falls
RHEIDOL FALLS STA
Rheidol
Ystum-tuen
Monument
South Gate
A 4120
Fwll-clai
Morum
Capel Seion
Vale of Rheidol Light Railway
River Rheidol
Aberffrwd
ABERFFRWD STA.
Pant mawr
RING & BAILEY
Rhyd-y-felin
Rhyd-y-fyrian
Nant-Eos
Capel Seion
NANTYRONEN STA.
Pen-y-Ro
Tan-y-bwlch
A 4120
Bryn-yr-eithin
Pen-y-graig
A 4340
Peruwch fawr
Ceunant
RHIWFRON STA.
Llanfarian
Track of Old Railway
Cwm-heulog
Gors-fach
New Cross
Ffos-las
Morfa-bychan
Aber-Llolwyn
Pen-lan-las
Pencraig
Pen-y-wern
Llwyn-y-brain
Pen-y-banc
Banc Blaen Magwr
Ffosrhydgaled
Chancery
Ty isaf
Lan-lwyd
Glenydd
Llanfihangel-y-creuddyn
Rhosrhydd
Capel trisant
Fron-deg
Abermad
Pen-lan-isaf
PenPegws
Fron-goch Pool
Rhos
Ffos-las
Pont-llanio
Tan-y-graig
Pentre-dwr
Tan-yr-allt
Cnwch-coch
Gilwern
Pant-yr-allad
Glan-rhos
Cefn-melgoed
Rhodfai
Bryn-gwyn
River Ystwyth
Cwm-mwdion isaf
Lletty synod
Twll Twrw (Monks Cave)
A 487
Bryn-hir
Cefn-y-graig wen
Graig-wen
Tre faes isaf
Belle Vue
Llanilar
MOTTE & BAILEY
Lldiardau
Castle Hill
B 4575
Abermagwr
Banc Llanafan
331m
Pen-y-bryn
New Row
Pen Glog
B 4576
Rhos-goch
Tyn-bellun
Crosswood Ho. or Trawsgoed
SETTLEMENT
Cefn Blewog
SETTLEMENT
Moel-Ifor
52°20'N
Pen-y-graig
Afon Carrog
Ty-newydd
Rhos-y-garth
Gaer Fawr
SETTLEMENT
Dolfor
Wenallt
Llanafan
Nature Trail
Coed Craig-yn-ogor
Llanddeiniol
Gilfachau
Pen-y-bryn
Abernac
Moel-wyn
A 485
Pen-y-bont
Mynydd Bach
Rhiw-goch
Pen-y-cwm canol
Gilfach-afel
Afon Wyre
Maes Beidog
Pen-lan
Brynarth
Llanwnws
333m
Craig-y-Bwlch
Ysgube
Tregynon
Llangwryfon
Lledrod
B 4340
Bwlch-yr-hendre
B 43
Llanrhystud
Llwyn-bedw
4°00'W
295m
Trefriw fawr
4°

57
52 53 54
49

a b c
d e f
g h i

53

| 59 |
| 54 | **55** |
| 51 |

a	b	c
d	e	f
g	h	i

55

Bryn-derwen · Llandyssil · Llwynoliw · Lr. Gwarthlow · Up! · Rhiston · Alport · Brynyn · Brithdir · Woodgate

Pentre · Fron · Weston-Madoc · Penbry · Rockley · ChurchStoke · Hurdley · Old Church Stoke · Llanerch · The Hollies · Pultheley

White Hall · Drain Llwyn Ellen · Penyllan · Brompton Hall · Meadow · Covey · Broadway · Ivy Ho. · Up! Snead · Pitchods · Hall

Abermule · Cwm Bromley · Pentrehyling · Bacheldre · L! Mellington · Camlad · Aston Hall · Plas Madoc · Snead · FORTS · Lind Partroe

Maenllwyd · Hodley · Goetre · Caeliber Isaf · NewHo. · Gwerney-go · Mellington Hall · Pentre B · Aston · Owlbury · Upper Broughton · Lower · More

Pen-y-gelli · Goetre Hill · Caeliber Uchaf · Cwm-berllan · Lake · FORT · Aston · Plas Madoc · Lydham · Newton

Cloddiau · Llwyn Cowrid · Cwm-earl · Bachaethlon · Pentrenant · G! Argoed · Tan Ho. · Pentre cwm · Lower Heblands · Lydham Manor · 179m

R. Mule · Sarn · Pant Hill · Cwm Llädron · Castlewright Boarded Ho. · Aston Hill · Bankshead · B 4383

Glan mihely · Upper Trefeen · Hopton Uchaf · Caer Din · Bishopsmoat · Cabin · CAS.

Borfa-wen · Highlands SETTLEMENT · Hopton Bank · Pantglas · L! Edenhope · Woodbatch · **Bishop's Castle**

Drefor SETTLEMENT · Round Bank · L! Dolfowr · Edenhope Hill · Reilth Top · Oakeley

Bedran · Cefn-gwyn · 470m · Mainstone · Colebatch Hill · Colebatch · Conery

Cefny Coed · Churchtown Hill · Reilth · Bryn Hill · Lydbury North

Cantlin Stone · Long Pike Hollow · Two Crosses · EARTHWORK · New Ho. · Cefn Einion · Brockton B 4385

Clun Forest · Three Birches · Pant-y-Llidan · Shadwell Hall · Llysty · Lower Garde · Walco

Nanty-rhuan · Rose Grove · Crossways · Brook Ho. · CAER-DIN RING · Burlow · Argoed · Acton · Lower Down · The Da Walcot Park

Anchor · CASTLE BRYNAMLWG · Bryn Mawr · Gogin · Mardu · Llanhedrick · Colstey · Stepple · New H.

Rhadnor Br. · Black Mountain · 448m · Hall of the Forest · Folly Br. · Graig Hill · Whitcott Keysett · STONE · Bicton · Guilden Down · Steppleknoll · Kempton

Hendre · Poundgate · Cha. · CAMP · Bryndrinog · Little Hall · EARTHWORK · Ford · Radnor FORT Wood · Clunton Hill

Feindre · Craig-y-byddar · R. Clun · EARTHWORK · Newcastle · Lower Spoad · EARTHWORK · Teagsawew · CAS · Hospital · Chinton B 4368

Rhydy-cwm · Bettws y cerwyn · Hongnans · Spoad Hill · Springhill · Llwyn · **Clun** · Hurst

The Moat · Dowke Hill · 429m · Llanfair Hill · Churchbank · Woodside Lords Rock of Woolbury

Beguildy · Quabbs · Upper Wain · Turgun · Green · Cwm Collo · Rockhill · 344m · Clun Hill · Pen-y-wern · Black Hill · Llan Howell

Bryn-draenog · Pantycaragle · Lower Wain · ENCLOSURE · STONE CIRCLE · 442m · Llanadevey

Datlas · Feaburlwyd · Tregodfa · Treverward · Hobarris · New Ho. · Cha. · Obley

Fair Well · Beacon Hill · 548m · Mellin-y-Grogie · Black Hall · Garbett Hall · Darloque · Bwlch · Menutton · Hopton Titterhill

Fron Rocks · Werny-geufron B 4355 · Llanfair Waterdine · Selley Hall · New Invention · Pentre Hodre · G! Hagley · Meeroak · CASTLE DITCHES

Pool Hill · Beacon Lo. · Guytro · Graig · Bwlch · Chapel Lawn · Bryncalled · Bucknell Hill · Mynd

Source of R! Lugg · Cnwch Bank · Bwlch-y-Plain · Monaughty Poeth · Five Turnings · CAER CARADOC · Garn Bank · R! Redlak · Fron

Llanlwest · Dol-y-telin · Hryop · Skyborry Green · Lurkenhope · Stow Hill · 434m Holloway Rocks · Bucknel

Ffos-llabiriau · Cefn-coch · Knucklas · R. Teme · Nether Skyborry · Stowe · Weston · STA

Rhos-grug · Cha. · Llan-coch · STA · Panpunton · STA · Stanage · A 4113

Cefn-yr-eryri · Crug · LLANGUNLLO · ENCLOSURE · Creignant · Bailey Hill · **Knighton** (Trefyclo) · BRYN CASTELL · Milebrook · Heartsease · Stanage Park

LLANBISTER ROAD STA · Cringoed Bank · Llangunllo · Coed-harbour · Cwm gilla · Hosp · 9 · Llanshay · Mynd

Cwm-y-geist · Cefn-suran · Upper Weston · Griffin Lloyd · Rhôs-y-meirch · Mount Flirt · EARTHWORK · Hill Ho.

MOTTE & BAILEYS · Treboeth · L! Weston · 359m · Treburfaugh · 391m · Gwernaffel · Llanwen Hill · Farrington · Boresford

Tyn-y-wann · Llysin Hill SETTLEMENT · 366m · Glôg Hill · Dolassey · **Bleddfa** · Pilleth · Black Hill · CAMP · Hawthorn Hill · B 4357 · B 4356 · Rheyes Hill · Willey Lo · Harleys · Stonewall Hill · Cha. · Boresford Mountain

63
56 57 58
53

a b c
d e f
g h i

5

66 67
60 61 62

a b c
d e f
g h i

61

Mount easant
Llithfaen
203m
251m Mynydd Carnguwch 359m
Carnguwch-bach
nnus
Ysgubor-plas
Penfras-uchaf
Tyddyn-cestyll
Llwyn-dyrys
Trallwyn Hall
oedilan
Gors-goch
Cefn-pentre
Mynydd-mawr
Pen-rhos
Tyddyn
Ty-corniog
Mela
Pentre uchaf
Bryn-yr odyn
Ty Du Isaf
llannor
el Hall
Llannerch
Cefncoch
Rhosydd
Bryngoleu Fm
Bryn-llaeth
Bryn-coch
Pont y Gribin
Pen-llwyn
Bryn hynog
Yoke Ho
Gorphwysfa
Glanllon
47m
Efail-newydd
Denio
43m
Bodegroes
Afon fly
Pennaen
Hosp.
Pwllheli
STA
li-dara
A 499
18
West End
Harbour titan y don
LB
Carreg yr Imbill
Traeth Crugan
Y Gamlas
arreg y Defaid

Caer-Gribin
Tŷ y gors
138m
Bryn-bychan
Caer-ferch
Mynachdy-bach
20'
Ynys-wen
Pont y Gydrhos
Glasfryn
Coed cae-bach
Cefn-caer-ferch
Llyn Glasfryn
Glasfryn-fawr
Pentyrch
Tyn-lon
Castell-Gwgan
Orsedd-fawr
Penchenewydd
CARN PENTYRCH
Llangybi WELL
Penbryn
Plas-du
Caer-fron
Ynys-Lapri
Penarth-uchaf
Bryn-llefrith
Llanarmon
Plas Chwilog
B 354
Rhedynog
Chwilog
Penarfynydd
Penybryn
Pen y bryn
m
PENARTH FAWR
Ysgubor hen
Afon-wen
BURIAL CHAMBER
Brook Hall
A 497
Hendre
Holiday Camp
STA
Pen-y-chain
Glogwyn
Penrhyn
Cerig y Barody
Pen-y-chain

Llechriddler
Glan Dwyfach
Pont-Felin
Dolbenmaen
Tower
STANDING STONE
10'
Bryn Hynion
Forfi
Ysguber Gerrig
Cefn-pen-coed
Gaerwen
Ty-cerrig
Muriau
Ystum Cegid
179m
Ystum-Cegid
Clenenney
Cefn coch
Golan
Cefmperaidd
Gesail-gyfarch
Gareg-frech
114m
Penmorfa
Braich-y-Saint
Bettws-bach
Rhos-gyll
Dwyfor
TALHENBONT
Gwynfryn
Llystumdwy
Pen y bryn
Cricieth
(Cridieth)
YSTUMLLYN
Bron Eifion
Muriau
NT
Ynysgain
Low Water Mark
6m
Pont Fechan
STA
18
Dyfnant
Trefan
Mynydd Ednyfed
Gell
B 4411
Pentrefelin
A 497
Wern
Bron-y-foel
Coed-llyn
Tyddyn-ad
Cabes
Morfa-bychan
Morfa Bychan

D W Y F O R

Criccieth

T R E M A D O C
B A Y

20'

L'S
50'

Tudwal's Island
East
Careg y Trai
wal's Island
Llanbedrog

A 499
A 487
A 417
A 354

71 72
64 65
59

a b c
d e f
g h i

65

WYN
Foel
Ceiriog Forest
△522m
△560m
Tynnewydd
Tan-y-graig
TOMEN Y MEIRW
Plas-Nantyr
Bonc
Old Cambrian Slate Quarries
Glyn Ceiriog
Fron Bache
Llangollen
Plas Newydd
Pengwern Hall
Tyndwr Hall
VALE OF LLANGOLLEN
Plas yn y Pentre
Newbridge
Pentre
Cwmalis
A 5
353m
Froncysyllte
Plas Offa
Fron Isaf
Halton
River Dee
Sodylt Bank
Plas-Warre
Rock Fm.
Pen-lan
875m
Nant y Bache
Rhos-Pengwern
Finger Fm.
371m
Pontfadog
River Ceiriog
Pennant
Wern Tower
Pen-y-bryn
Duffws Dyke
New Hall
Chirk Green
Brynkinalt Hall
Glynmorlas
Street Dinas
Ifton Hall
Bryn Gole
Pentre
131m
△405m
Dolywern
Llangwryd Issa
Penisar Glyn
Bronygarth
Pont faen
Fron Isaf
Tyn-y-Rhos
Gledrid
Chirk (y Waun)
CHIRK CAS.
STA.
Ifton Heath
Crosslanes Fm.
St. Martins
B 5070
Pentre Cilgwyn
Bryniau
Llwynmawr
Plas-crogen
Plas Onn
Creignant
Fron
Rhos
Preesgweene
Weston Rhyn
Moreton Hall
Henlle Hall
Etnal Hall
Wiggington
New Marto
LLANGOLLEN CANAL
B 5069
Rhos-y-gadfa
Y Fawnen
△561m
Pandy
Cam-helyg
Pont-y-meibion
Cwmclwyd
Spring Hill
444m
Llech-rhydau
Tyn-y-rhyd
Nant
Selattyn Hill
△372m
Selattyn
Morlas Brook
Upper Hengoed
Mardy
Daywall
Hengoed
Tre-wern
Gobowen
Rhewl
Little Fernhill
Henlle
Whitner Fm.
Hindford
Coed-y-go
Tregeiriog
Ael-y-coryn
Tower
A Ceiriog
Plas Tregeiriog
Tyn-y-fedw
Cefn-y-braich
Siambr-gerrig
Foel Rhiwlas
Rhiwlas
Ty-draw
Pen-y-gwely Resr.
Cefn-y-maes
Tyn-y-drain
Caregy big
Pant-glas
310m
Hafod
Cefnbyrallt
Old Race Co.
CASTLE MOUND
Brogyntyn
Old Oswestry
Pentre-clawdd
Pentre-pant
Oakhurst
Park Hall Camp
Halston Ha
Llanarmon
Dyffryn Ceiriog
Blaen Rhiwlas Uchaf
434m
Cefn Hir-fynydd
Cyrchynan-isaf
Cae-hir
Mynydd Lledrod
△404m
Cefn Canol
Rhydleos
Lledrod
Llwynt
Rhydycroesau
311m
B 4580
Parc Uchaf
The Hayes
Oerley Hall
Broom Hall
Oswestry
A 495
Middleton
Aston Sq.
A 4083
Whitehall
Wootton
Whittington
Babbinswood
Pantglas Ucha
Lawnt
Llangadwaladr
Ty-gwyn
Hafodty
Lledrod
Bryncoch
Cynynion
Pen-y-llan
Llwynymaen
Mile Ho.
Mile Oak
His land
Queen's Head
Fox Hall
Locks
Ashfield
Bromwich Park
Cymdu
Gilfach
Glas-hirfryn
△523m
Gyrn Moelfre
Bodlith
Berwen-deg
Nant-y-gollen
Rhandir
R. Morda
Trefarclawdd
Weston
Morda
Sweeney Hall
Sweeney Mountain
Rhydairy
Maesbury Marsh
Maesbury
Llyn Moelfre
Moeliwrch
Moelfre
Ty-du
Glan-yr-afon
Llansilin
Glascoed
Llyn Rhaeadr-wyn
Pentregaer
Croesau Bach
Craig-llwyn
Mynydd Myfyr
340m
299m
Trefonen
Woodhill
Trefonen Hall
Ty-canol
Treflach Hall
Treflach
Sweeney
Treflach Fm.
88m
Nuttree Fm.
Morton
Well
Woolston
Oddi-ar-y-llyn
Lloran Isaf
Talwrn
Tynewydd
Pentre-cwm
Wern ddu
MOTTE & BAILEY
Glyn
Rhydygaled
Lloran Uchaf
Cefnhir fawr
Cefnhirfach
Tre-brys
Craig Orllwyn
314m
Tyn-y-graig
Wenallt
Pen-y-bryn
Golfa
Ty-gwyn
Glanyr-afon
Cefn y blodwel
Ty-isaf
Nant-mawr
Quarry
Old Canal
A 483
Morton Hall
Trewern
Glanwrch
Pentrefelin
B 4396
Banhadla
Plas-uchaf
Bryn-gwalia
Llangedwyn
A Tanat
Scrwgan
Pen-y-bont
Cefn Aber-Tanat
Llanyblodwel
Blodwell Hall
Quarries
Waen Wen
Crickheath
Osbaston
MOTTE & BAILEY
Glantanat Isaf
Allt Tair Ffynnon
Pen-yr-allt
Llanerch
Lluner John mrys
Plas-gwyn
Cefn Ucha
Brynfedwyn
Fownwy
Aber-Tanat
OFFA'S DYKE
Caregtwfa Hall
Pant
Trepenal
Maesbrook Ho.
Pentre-uchaf Hall
The Wood
B 4398
Waen
Knockin
Kinnerley
389m
Glyn
Pen-y-nant
Bwlchyddar
Aithnen
Ffinnart
Glasgoed
Llanymynech
Llwyn-y-go
Pen-y-parc
Llwyn-y-groes
Argoed
Tyfryd
Pentre-heylin Hall
Llwyntidmon Hall
Ty-n'-twll
Ty-canol
Llanfechain
Bodynfoel
Llansantffraid-ym-Mechain
B 4393
Bryn-coch
Clawdd coch
Wern
Pentref
Pentre-heylin Hall
R. Vyrnwy
Llandysilio
Calcott Hall
Pentre-heylin Hall
Pentre-heylin
Hall
Tir-y-coed
Pentre-heylin Hall
Melverley Hall
Crosslane
Llanfyllin
Green Hall
Bryn derwen
Pentre
Tyn-y-rhos
Waun
Domgay
Four Crosses
Rhos Common
Gwernowddy
Haughton
Sychpwll
Melverle Green
Ponther
Rhysgog
Bryndwyn Hall
Godor
Bwlch-y-cibau
Fferm
Rhosddu Fm.
149m
FLAG VIN DINAS
Trewylan Ho.
Court Ho.
Cefn Briw
Trewylan Hall
Rhysnant Hall
Llandrinio
Pentre-fechan
R. Severn
Gwern-y-go
Twern
Hainwood
Melverle Ha
Allt-y-Gadair
A 490
A 495
Ystym Colwyn
Moel-y-Main
Pant-y-sgawhryd
Tan-y-fron
Gil-mawr
Peniarth
Pen-y-foel
Ford
Trefnanny Fm.
Sarnau
Tan Ho.
Fawnog
Dyke Pool
FORT
Gaelford
Rhos Hall
△356m
Ardd-lin
Trederwen
B 4392
B 4393
Rhyd-esgyn
Red Hall
Rodney's Pillar
△365m
FORT
Breidden
Criggion
The Hall
Bausley Hill
Crew Green
Kempster's Ho.
SETTLEMENT
△130m
3°
Peny lin
Graig

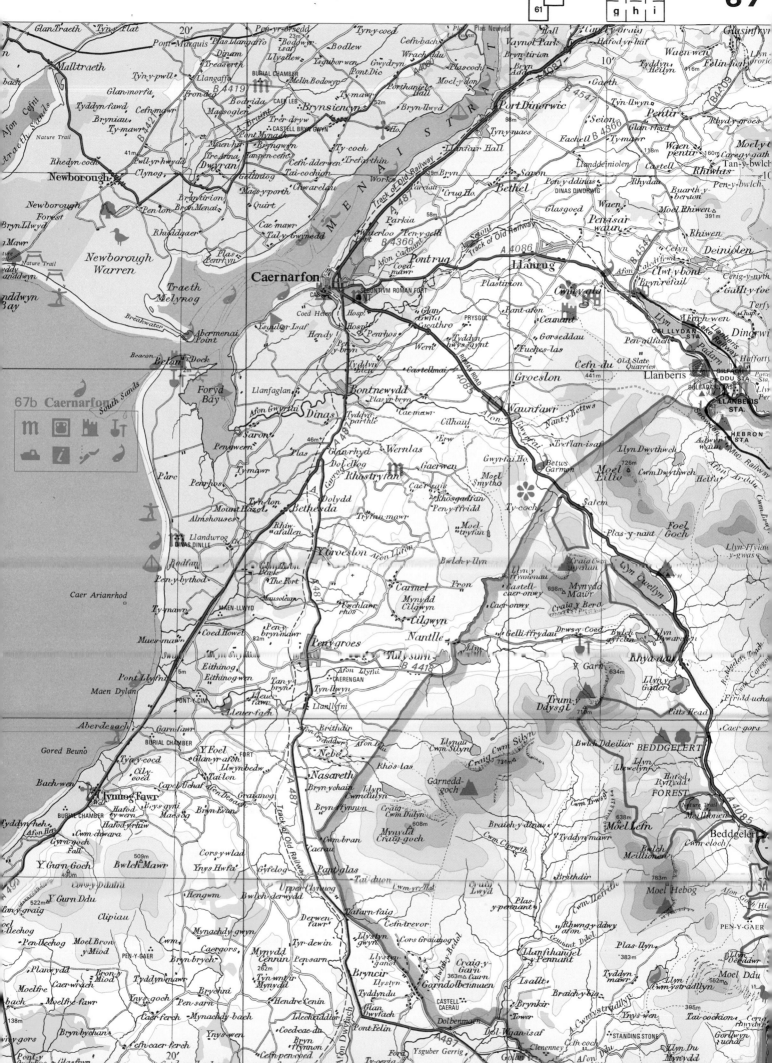

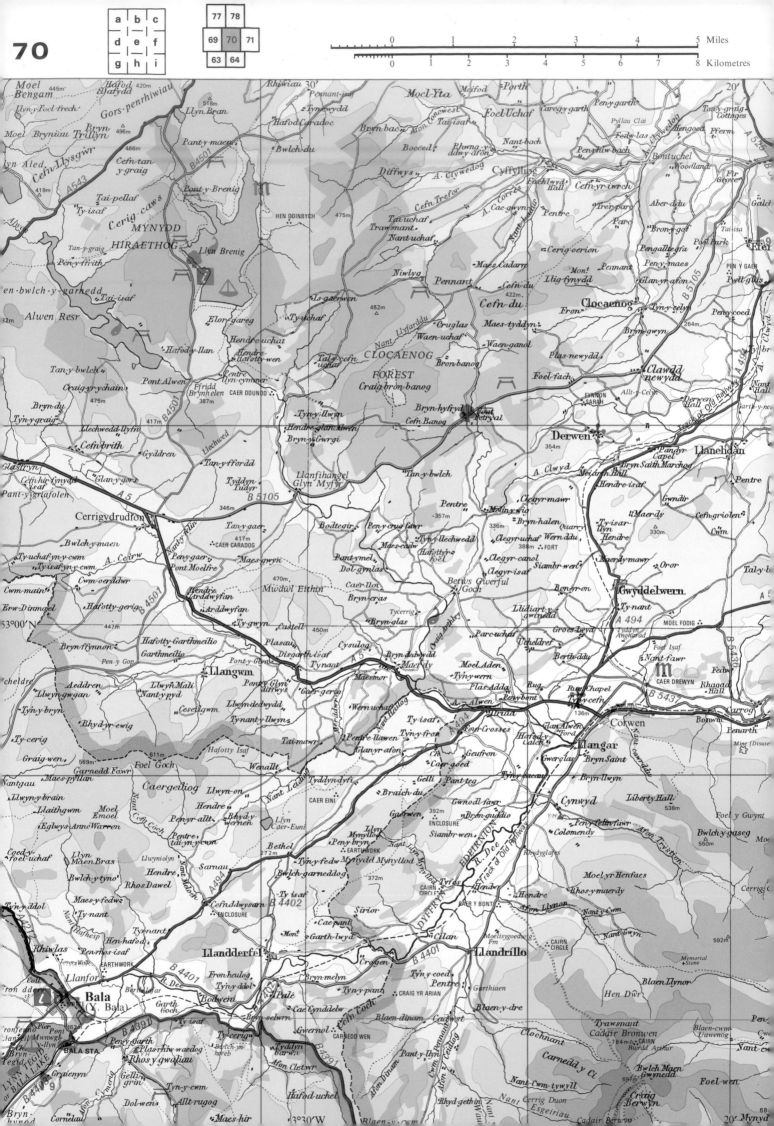

a	b	c
d	e	f
g	h	i

79
71 72 73
65

Miles 0 1 2 3 4 5
Kilometres 0 1 2 3 4 5 6 7 8

Hope
Caergwrle
CAERGWRLE STA.
Abermorddu
CEFN-Y-BEDD STA.
Llay
Windy Hill
Gwersyllt
Rhosrobin
New Broughton
Rhostyllen
Johnstown
Ruabon
Brynfields
St. Martins
Gobowen

Pulford
Poulton
Lavister
Rossett
Marford
Trevalyn
Gresford
Borras Head
Plas Bostock
Hugmore
Ridleywood
WREXHAM (WRECSAM)
Acton
Rhosnesni
Bryn Estyn School
Wrexham Industrial Estate
Bowling Bank
Sutton Green
Marchwiel
Erddig
Cock Bank
Eyton
Bangor-on-Dee
Overton
Erbistock
Knolton
Pentre-coed
Dudleston
Dudleston Heath
Ellesmere
Penley
Hanmer
Bronington
Bettisfield
Welshampton

Aldford
Churton
Handley
Tattenhall
Coddington
Farndon
Holt (BOVIVM)
Stretton
Tilston
Shocklach
Malpas
Threapwood
Higher Wych
Worthenbury
Bettisfield
Whixall Moss
Fenn's Moss
Colemere
Lyneal

River Dee
LLANGOLLEN CANAL
SHROPSHIRE UNION CANAL

72 | 73

a	b	c
d	e	f
g	h	i

73

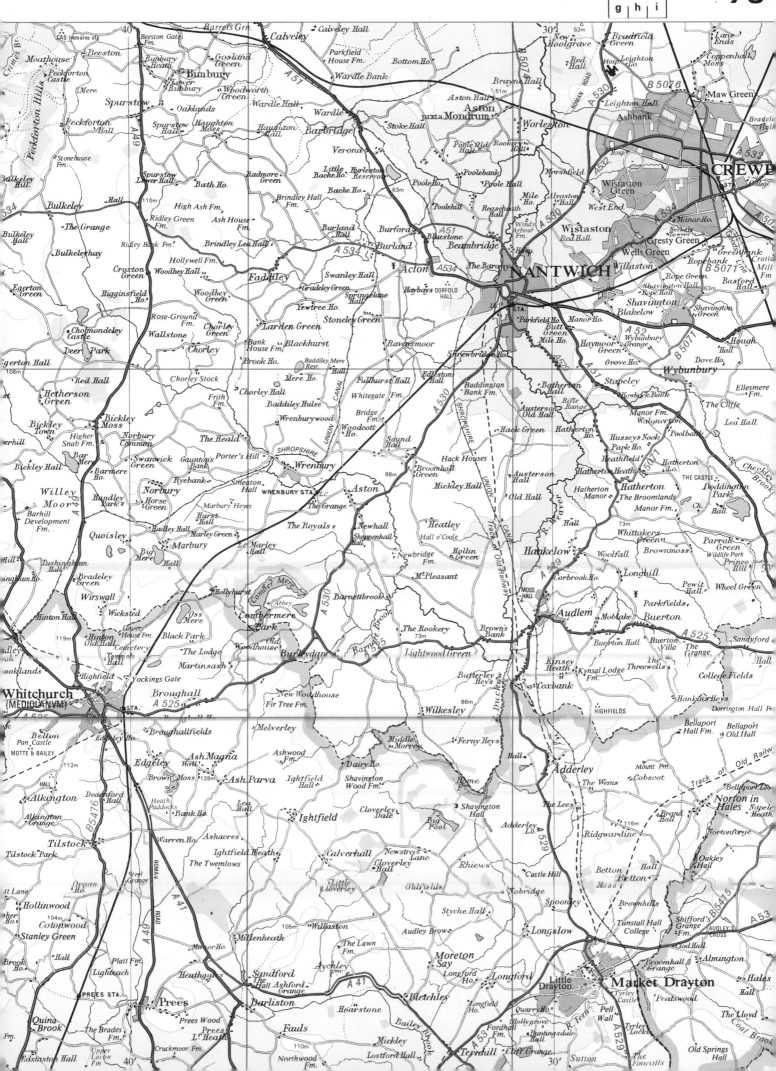

a	b	c
d	e	f
g	h	i

74 75
66

0 1 2 3 4 5 Miles
0 1 2 3 4 5 6 7 8 Kilometres

40' 30'

Middle Mouse
(Ynys Badrig)
NT Hells

The Skerries
Ynys Arw
Porth Llanlliana
Dinas Gynfor
NT
Br
Llanbadrig
Llewe

West Mouse or
Maen-y-Bugail
Harry Furlongs Rks
Porth-y-castell
Cemaes
Bay
Llanfair-yng-Nghornwy
Wylfa
Nuclear Power Sta
Cemaes
CG
Neuadd
Bettws
Cemaes

Carmel Head
Hen Borth
NT Cemlyn
Cemlyn Bay
Penrhyn
Simdde-wen
Nant-y

Porth-y-Dyfn
Plas
Cafnan
38m
Tre-gele

Mynachdy
Penyr-orsedd
Caer-degog-uchaf
Gors
Rhosbeirio
Tai heh

Nanner
Ty-Wion
Foel-fach

Ynys-y-fydlyn
Caerau
Hen-dy
11m
Cefn-coch
Llanfechell
Bodew

Porthybrihys
Llanfair-yng-Nghornwy
119m
Llanddyfnael hir
Pentre

Craig-y-gwynt
Bothedd
Rallt-goch
Bodegri
Llyn Llygeirian
Coeden

Porth Swtan
Ch.
Bodwin
Gamog
Creigiau-fawr
Carreg-lefn

Church Bay
Rhydwyn
A5025
Clwch-dernog
Llanfflewyn
Llannol
Llyn Hafodol

Crugmor
Llanr-hyddlad
Meiriogan
Ynys-yr-hw

Porth Trwyn
Carreglwyd
Bron-heulog
Ucheldref-goed
Tyn-y-rhos
90m
Pen-Padrig

Careg-y-fran
Brynmaethlu
Cerig-camog
Ucheldref-uchaf
Penbol
Uchaf

Creigiau
Borthwen
83m
Llanfaethlu
Fadog-frech
Brwynog
Llanbabo
Glan-y-gors

Porth Trefadog
Tre-fadog
Plas uchaf
Pant-Ednyfed
Clwch-dernog
Bodfordden-ddu
Caer-gwrle
Alaw

Craig Dafydd
Ty-croes
Bodfardden ddu
Gronant
Tan-llan
Llanddeusant
Bod Deiniol
Glan-Alaw

Creigiau Clipera
Tre-lywarch
Bodfardden wen
Llidiart-y-Facsen
Nantanog

Porth Tywyn-mawr
Plas-y-glyn
Bryn-Eglwys
Graigdryn
42m
Llantrisant
Chwaen-hen
I L S

Llanfwrog
Peniel
Strydy-Facsen
Penllyn
Tre-Gwehelydd
Chwaen-wen
Ty-croes
Carn

Porth-Penrhyn-mawr
Tyn-llan
Ty-croes
Pen-yr-orsedd
112m

Ty-croes
Bodlasan fawr
Llanfigel
Llyn Llawr-y-tyddyn
Clwch
B 51

Holyhead
To Dun Laoghaire
HOLYHEAD BAY
Bodlasan groes
Llanfachraeth
Llanynghenedl
Erw-goch
Llywenan
Bodsuran
Llechcynfarwy

3°20'N
Porth Namarch
Breakwater
Salt I.
Yr-allt
Mrydd-y-gof
Prysaeddfed
Treforwerth
Trefor

North Stack
LB
CG
Nimrod Rocks
Fadog
11m
Bodedern
B 5109

Gogarth Bay
SAER Y TWR
Porth-y-Felin
Traeth y Gribin
Cleifiog fawr
Tyhen
Tyn-y-graig
Rhyd-y-defaid

Holyhead
Mountain
(Mynydd Twr)
219m
Llanfawr
Mon
Beddmanarch Bay
Cleifiog isaf
Bodowyr
Tre Angharad
Manaw
Parc

South
Stack
Holyhead
(CAERGYBI)
Stanley
Hosp
A 5025
Ysbyllir
Pen-rhiw

Pen-las
Rock
Ty-mawr
Pen-y-banc
Kingsland
Cerig-y-Gwyr
Penrhos
Embankment
Valley
Caergeiliog
A 5
24m
Bryngwran
Party Trebay
Clear-mawr

Gors-goch
Penrhos-Feilw
Tre-Figneth
Is-allt-bach
18
Four Mil
Bridge
Penny-bont
Ty-mawr
Gwmael
Pen-rhw
Treban
Bryn-Aldd

Llwyn-y-berth
CYTIAU'R GWYDDELOD
Valley
Llanfihangel
-yn-nhowyn
Plas Llechylched
Fach
Caerglaw

Penrhyn Mawr
Treiddu Bay
Glan-traeth
B 4545
Rhyd-bont
Llyn Dinam
Bryn-gors
Traffwll
Gwaenfynydd
Treddolphin

HOLY ISLAND
(YNYS GYBI)
4m
Cair-Scais
Fadog
Trefle
Llanfair-yn-neubwll
Plas
Llyn Penrhyn
12m
Tyn-coed
Cemais

Porth-y-Garan
Pwll-pillo
Bodior
Pwll-preban
Plas Iago
Carnau
Cymmeran
Tywyn
Tyn-twyn
Tai-croesion
Ty-mawr

Bwa-Du
Bronddel
Valley
Cefn-ysgwydd
Bryn Hyfryd
Bodfeddan
Tyn Coed
Cemais

Rhoscolyn Hd
Rhoscolyn
Hirfron
Pentre-gwyddel
Brynmeran
Tywyn Trewan
Glan-tywyn
A 4080
INSCRIBED STONE
Dryrill
A N C

Maen-y-fran
Borthwen
Cymmeran Bay
Pentre-traeth
Llainwen
Cefn Du

Rhoscolyn Beacon
Ynysoedd Gwylanod
Ynysfenrig
Traeth Crugyll
RHOSNEIGR STA
Plas Marlog
Neuadd
Ty-Newydd
Cerig-cafael
Tynrhos

Porth Nobla
CHAMBERED CAIRN
Barclodiad y Gawres
Porth Tre-castell
Rhosneigr
Cerig-y-brain
A 4080
Llyn Maelog
Llanfaelog
Bryn Ciay
Bryn Du
STA
Rhos Badric
Tai-moelion
So
Bod

Porth Tre-castell
Tre-castell
Bodelwa
Meddyn
Y Bryn
Plas
Llangwyfan
Tyn-y-pandy
Clae-mawr

DANGER ZONE
Caethle
30'
Cerig-y-brain
Pensarn
10m
Pen-lon
Rhosmor
Gorgl-gam
Tynrhos
Bwlan
Llyn Coron

Ynysoedd Duon
Llangwyfan isaf
Bod
Feirig
Aberffraw (Abberffro)
Llangadwaladr
Tyn
A 4080

4°40'W

74 75 76
67

a b c
d e f
g h i

75

76 77 78
69 70

a b c
d e f
g h i

77

50'

40'

Llandudno

GREAT ORMES HEAD
(PENYGOGARTH)

Great Orme
Tramway
207m
BISHOP'S PALACE
(rems of)
Maes-
y-Facrell

CG Pen Trwyn
Ormes Bay
or
Llandudno Bay
Toll

Llandudno

A 546
Rhiwledyn Cliffs
141m
hydro

Little Ormes Head
(Trwyn y Fuwch)

Penrhyn-side

Conway
Sands

Vessel Banks

on Conway

Mark

Conway
Marsh

Deganwy

STA
18

Bodlondeb
246m
NT

Conway

Crows Nest

Hendre
chwaith
Gwestfordd

Castell
Llanbedr-y-cennin

B 5106
Fach
leidiog

Baglaw

Henryd

Glan
Isaf

Glyn-
uchaf
B 5106

Tal-y-cafn

Tyny-groes
STA

B 5279

Pont Waen

Caerhun
Ch.
CANOVIUM
ROMAN FORT

Tal-y-
Bont

Careg-y-
fraldd

Dolgarrog
Fall

Dolgarrog

DOLGARROG
STA
7m

Pont Dolgarrog

Aqueduct

Chalybeate
Wells & Baths

Tyddyn Wilym

B 5106

Coed
Creiciau

Trefriw
STA

Gelli-Tydan

Clundan
288m

Tyn-Twll

400m

Llyn
Crafnant

Llyn
Geirionnydd
50'

Nature Trail

Penrhyn

Gloddaeth
Isaf'
Bryn
Mael-gwyn
Hafod-y-coed

TOWER

B 5115
CAS
(rems of)
108m

Llandrillo
Rhos Neigr

Glan
Wydden

BODYSGALLEN

Pydew

Esgyryn

Llandudno
Junction

Graianllyn

Pen-y-bryn-uchaf

Llandudno
JUNC STA

Pabo

Mochdre

Mynydd

Glyn

Pant-y-gloch

YH
St. Kross

COLWYN BAY

Colwyn Bay

Rhos-on-Sea

Rhos
Hotel

Dinarth

LLYS EURYN

133m

BRYN EURYN

Llangystennin
Hall

B 5104

A 55

Zoo

Old
Colwyn

COLWYN BAY
(BAE COLWYN)

Pennarth
Rhos

quarry

Penmaen
4m

Llanddulas

A 547

STA

Pensarn

Abergele

A 55

Ty-mawr

Llysfaen

Cefn yr Ogof
204m

Rhyd-y-foel

Pencorddu
mawr

CASTELL
CAWR
FORT

18

Conway
Elsteddfod
CAS

Bryn
23m

Coed teg

Cadlwyn-mawr

Meifod

Chapel

Llanelian-yn-Rhos

Plas newydd

Bryngwenallt

Llansantffraid
Glan Conwy

STA
B 5381

Geuffion

Bryn-y-maen

Ty-newydd

288m

Teirdan

Cefnen

Plas Uchaf

Cefn Isaf

Bryn ffanigl

Gwreiddyn

Top-y-glol

B 5381

Plas-uchaf

Penrhiwuchaf

Ffridd y
Mynydd

B 5383

Dôl-wen

Bryndansi

L Fawnog

Coed-coch

Gwydy isaf

Bron-y-pistyll

Gwern-uchaf

Peny-bryn

Strior-bach

Pwlly-cibau

Moelfre
isaf
317m

Pentre-
felin
91m

Mynydd
Llanelian

Tyddyn-uchaf'

Nant-y-cywarch

Deunant

Cefn

Tyn-ddôl
A Dulas

Betws-yn-Rhos

B 5381

Peniarth-bach

Tycelyn

A 548

Rodnoehwyn

Mynydd
Bodrychwyn

Fron
faw

Glyn
Isaf

Tan-y-
bryn

Erw-goch

Tyn Twll

Topan-bach

Bodrod-uchaf

Gofer

Dawn

Bryn
Hill

Deheufryn

Mynydd
Branar

Cil-Uidiart

Pant-y-clyd

Cynnant uchaf

Moelfre-uchaf
308m
Mynydd-dir

Bron-heulog

Mynydd Bodran
229m

Wern

Medrifynt
Bodnant
Gardens

Cae Forys

Graig

Ty-uchaf

Brymbo

Moel
Gyffylog

Bodlondeb

Hafotty

Trofarth

Glyn-bâch

311m

Dafarn-
bara-ceirch

Peny-
Ciddin

Plas-isaf

Tynyffrith

Gwaenynog

Ysgubor-newydd

A 548

Llanfair
Talhaearn

Eglwys-bach

Tan-yr
allt

Cefn-gwyn

Dolgoch

Ty-isaf

Pen-
mynydd

Gelli

Henbryn

Tui

Pen-twich

Wenallt

Llwyn-du

Dyffryn

Peny-
ffrith

Nantmawr

Hendys

Glan Aled

Pentre-r-felin

Croes onen

Hafod-y-bennau

Cefn goch

Ynys Rhys

Pentre Isaf

Tyn-y-cyll

Tau-duon

Cefn
trefiech

Pentre du

Trefloch

Dylu

Mwdwl-eithin
389m

Ty-mawr

Camaes

Tre-pys-llygod

Cynycaeau

Plas bychan

Mynydd
Unben

Moel
Emwnt

Mostyn Isaf

Plas-isaf

Merllyn

Bodyfryd

Cadair Ifan Goch
NT

Foel
Cleftairiau

Dolau

Hafodunos

Llangernyw

Hafod-lom

Melai

Bedwen

Ffrith
bedwen

Pen-y-mwdwl

Foel

Plas-yn-cornel

Pennant

Tyny-celyn

Pennant-ganol

Maesol

Pont-syllau

Hendre-ddu

B 5382

Llansannan

Plas-newydd

Penglogo

Copy

Plas-draw

Rhos-y-mawr

Wenlli

Bryn-barcut

Plas-on

encleden

The Abbey

Bryn-glas

Ffrith
isaf

Ffrith-uchaf

Tyny-fford

Wern

Tyn-y-ddol

Plas Mattw

Rhyd eidion

Pwllffordd

Cae-fatran

Trwyn-sych

Caer fadan

Plas yn blaenau

Tyn-y-caeau

B 5384

Bont-garreg

Tan-y-fron

Bryn-rhwd

Belmont

Pen-y-garth

Maes Madog

A 548

Afon Gledwy

Pandy-tudur

Tyr-felin
isaf

Hafod

Beidiog uchaf

Cae Goronwy
Eithin-fferwd

Llanddoged

Plas-uchaf

Plas Madoc

Henffrith

Swch-yr-hafod

Ty-isaf

Bodwrach

Cefn-y-cefn
Peny-cefn

Hendre

Cornewal

Cae du

Bryn

Pen-caer-com

Fforest

Trefriw

Pentre
Tafarn-y-fedw

Llwyn Rhisiard

Maelogen

Graig-bach

Bryn-tan

Nant Merddyn

Rhos Pen
Uwyd

Pant-y-carw
STA

Brynsyllty

Gwytherin

Bryn-y-clochydd

Glany-gors

Rhiwiau

Llanrwst

Moel Maelogen
424m

Meliny Coed

Bertifoddau

Bryniog-uchaf

Tyddyn-uchaf

Afon Euryn

Llwyn-Saint

Moel
Bengam
445m

Beaver
Grove

Aled Isaf
Resr

Gors-penrhiwiau

Hafod
420m

Penyparc

Cytryd

Merddyn

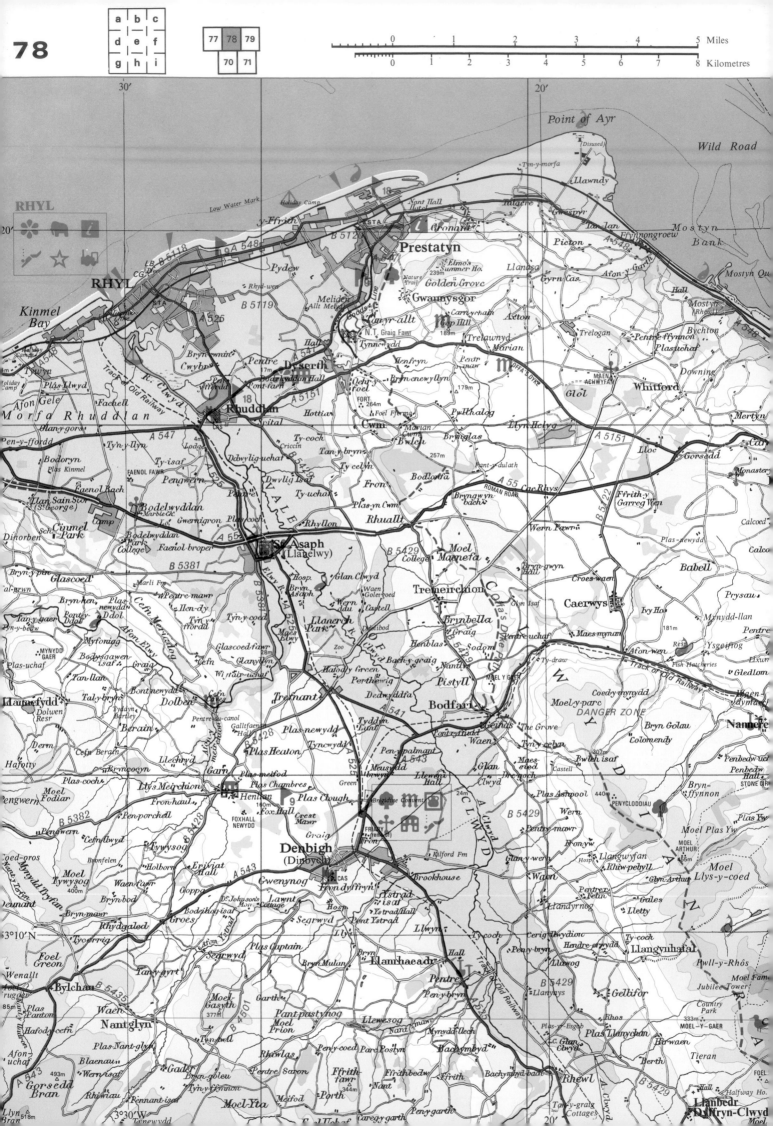

78 79
71 72

a b c
d e f
g h i

79

Countryside

Nature trails, scenic walks, country parks, field and nature study centres and areas of outstanding natural beauty, including woods, waterfalls, moors, coastline and interesting natural features. See page 82 for details of long distance walks and page 83 for National Parks.

20a Pembrey Forest. Six miles of sand dunes with remains of wartime defences. Now a country park.

20e Llanddewi: Gower Farm Trails. One walk with three distances that explores West Gower farming methods and animals.

20g Kitchen Corner. Rocky causeway to Worms Head. Access from Rhosili. *Safe crossing times from nearby CG station.* ✦

20h Port Eynon: National Trust Reserve. Combines magnificent coastal views with interesting bird and plant life in seashore and cliff habitat.

20i Oxwich Burrows. 8 stage trail tracing the movement and influence of sand. ✦

20i Mitchin Hole: prehistoric caves; splendid cliff walk between Caswell Bay and Three Cliffs Bay.

21d Mumbles: Oystermouth Castle. Small beautifully laid out park. *June to August: daily 1100-1730. September to May: weekdays 1100-1530.* ♜

21e Brynmill: Singleton Park. Wide green vista of tree-sheltered meadowland. ▣

21g The Knap: Bishopston Valley. Narrow, steep-sided ravine leading to remote Pwll-du Bay; notable limestone flora.

21g Mumbles Head. Stunning cliff top walk to Langland and Caswell Bays.

22b Margam Park (tel. Port Talbot 063 96 87626). An 823 acre country estate with way-marked walks through woods and pastureland. *April to end October: Tuesday to Sunday and Bank Holiday Mondays 1030-1800. November to end March: Wednesday to Sunday 1330 to 1 hour before dusk. Free.* ◗ ❊ ▣ ✝ ⋒

22e Kenfig Burrows: 3 mile nature trail, recognised by the Nature Conservancy Council. ✦

23b Mynydd Garth Maelwg. Series of forest paths overlooking the Vale of Glamorgan. ⋒

23c Gwaelod-y-garth. Steep footpath to heather-covered moorland with impressive views over the lower vale of the Taff.

23e Welsh St Donats: Tair Onen Forest. Two walks of 1-2 miles.

23i Porthkerry Country Park. 250 acres mainly of wooded slopes with a large grass area in the valley down to the sea. Bull cliff has rock with fossil strata. ⋒

24a Nature Trail: Caerphilly Common. 7 stage trail with heathland, limestone plants, exposed rock formations and good views.

24a Cefn Onn Country Park. Walk through glades of most types of rhododendron and azalea—unforgettable in early summer.

24a Gwaelod-y-garth. See 23c.

24c Tredegar Country Park (Newport 0633 62275). Extensive grounds including woodland. *Free.* ◗ ⋒ ♞ ♪

24d Forest Farm: Glamorganshire Canal Nature Reserve. 1½ mile walk along banks; rich bird and plant life. ↧T

24e Cardiff. City Council organised walks in Bute Park, Nant Fawr Park, Rumney Hill Gardens and many more in the City's 2,700 acres of land.

24h Penarth. Cliff walks south to Lavernock Point and Sully Island; north to 100 ft high Penarth Head.

25c Caldicot Castle Country Park. (tel. 0291 420241). 50 acres of grounds provide a beautiful setting for leisurely walks. *Daily. Free.* ▣ ♜ ⋒

25c Blackrock. Waymarked coastal walk along the Severn Estuary to Gold Cliff (25d). ✦ ⋒

26d Skomer Island: Nature Reserve. 16 viewing points for bird and seal life. Island reached by boat from Martin's Haven, near Marloes. *Summer only.*

26e Marloes Sands. Nature trail exploring sandstone cliffs, Iron Age fort, Marloes Mere with its reeds and cotton grass, and giving spectacular coastal views.

26e Dale. A walk around the peninsula and St Anne's Head. Booklet available locally gives notes on the geology, scenery and history.

26e Dale Fort Field Centre (tel. Dale 064 65 205). Courses and information on all aspects of the surrounding countryside.

26e Kete. 168 acres and a mile of beautiful coastline with views to the islands of Skomer and Skokholm; National Trust Village.

27b Picton Castle (tel. Rhos 043 786 296). The extensive grounds and gardens provide delightful walks. Only grounds and garden open. *April to end September: Tuesday to Thursday and weekends 1030-1730.* ◗ ❊ ▣

27c Blackpool: Minwear Wood. 2 mile walk from Canaston Bridge through Forestry Commission property overlooking the Eastern Cleddau River. *Easter to end September. Free.*

27e West Williamston: Nature Reserve. 21 acre mediaeval deer park of Carew Castle maintained by West Wales Naturalist's Trust. *No car park; access by footpath only.*

27e Upton Castle. The grounds provide a beautiful setting for many varied walks. An all-weather footpath leads round the more formal gardens. *February to October: daily 1000-1630. Free.* ❊ ⋒

27f Manor House Wildlife and Leisure Park, St Florence (tel. Carew 064 67 201). 12 acres of wooded grounds which include 43 different species of tree (name tags attached for identification). There is also a large variety of wild flowers in the park and gardens. *Easter to October: daily 1000-1800.* ◗ ♞

27g Orielton Field Centre (tel. Castlemartin 064 681 225 or 204). Courses and information on the natural history, flora and fauna of the surrounding area.

27h Pembroke. Walk around the ancient town, taking in the mighty castle. Leaflet showing route available locally.

27h Stackpole. 8 miles of National Trust coast, including Barafundle Bay and Broad Haven, with paths that give access to the cliffs, bays, woods and lakes. Area supports a wide variety of flora and fauna.

27i Lydstep Caves (tel. Tenby 0834 2402). The caverns can only be entered at low tide; a nature trail (1½ miles) which runs along the headland signposts the way.

28b Pentre Howell: Redgate Forest. Short, easy walk of 1 mile that explores this wooded valley up the Afon Taf. ⋒

28e Amroth. Eastern end of the Pembrokeshire Coast Path (see page 82). On the shore at low tide, the blackened stumps of a prehistoric drowned forest can be seen.

28g Tenby. A selection of cliff, coastal and country walks in and near the Pembrokeshire Coast National Park is available in a local publication, "Rambles around Tenby".

28g Penally. 3½ mile nature trail which uses the roads and paths in and around the ancient Ridgeway route to Pembroke. 13 viewing stations.

28g Caldey Island. Footpath to the highest point of the island (the lighthouse), which gives good views of the coast and its seal and seabird colonies. Boats from Tenby (*summer only*).

29d Tregoning Hill. Good viewpoint for the Taf/Towy Eastuary. ✦

29e Pembrey Forest. See 20a.

30b Ty-Isaf Adventure Centre (tel. Warwick 0926 41961). Teenage holidays arranged, including hill walking and orienteering. All equipment provided, except for rucksacks and cagoules. *July and August.* ⛺ ▲ ∪

30h Brynmill. See 21e.

31b Craig-y-nos Country Park (tel. Abercrave 063 977 395). Series of walks in 40 acres of woodland. Also: conducted walks, demonstrations of skills like sheep shearing and horseshoeing and a country fair ▣ ⋒ 𝐢 ☆ at nearby Dan-yr-Ogof Caves.

31c Coelbren: Henrhyd Waterfall. A walk to the spectacular 90 ft high falls.

31f Craig-y-Llyn. Waymarked 2½ mile walk along a ridge giving panoramic views of the wild, wooded valleys of Rhondda, Aberdare and Neath.

31h Afan Argoed Country Park (tel. Cymmer 063 983 564). Series of walks in the surrounding forest (1-5 miles) starting from the Countryside Centre. *Park: daily. Centre: Easter to end September daily; also winter weekends; dawn to dusk.* ◗ ▣ ⋒ ↧T

32a Porth-yr-ogof. Signposted route south, down a remarkable wooded ravine with a series of waterfalls unequalled in Wales. ⋒

32a Falls: Scwd-yr-Eira Waterfall. 50 ft high fall with such a powerful flow that one can walk behind it.

32b Llwyn-on Reservoir. Walk explores the conifer forest of the Taf valley. ⋒

32b Llwyn-on: Garwnant Forest Centre (tel. Merthyr Tydfil 0685 3060). Circular forest walk starts

Picnic Sites

These are usually situated in areas of natural beauty, often with a nature trail or walk nearby. They generally consist of wooden tables, log seats, litter bins (please use) and, if near a road, parking spaces. Do not expect any conveniences or other facilities. Although mainly run by the Forestry Commission, others are maintained by local councils, National Parks, the National Trust and by private concerns.

Although the blue symbol above is used to indicate a picnic site on the maps, many locations are marked 'on the ground' with signs bearing the symbol shown here.

Above are three species of trees among the most widely planted by the Forestry Commission.

Norway Spruce *Sitka Spruce* *Contorta Pine*

from the centre where information, exhibitions and lectures are given on the Brecon Beacon forests. *Easter to end September: weekdays 1030-1600; weekends and Bank Holidays 1400-1700. Free.*

32d Llyn Fawr. See 31f Craig-y-Llyn.

32d Dare Valley Country Park. Series of mountain and forest walks, including 4 trails illustrating the natural history of the coalfield and local industrial archaeology.

32f Merthyr Tydfil: Glamorganshire Canal. Circular 4 mile walk along the canal from car park at the Technical College. Guide book available locally.

33a Trefil. Marvellous walk north and east, following the circuitous route of the Trefil Tramroad around Llangynidr Mountain and down to the Abergavenny Canal at Cwm-crawnon (43h).

33c Garn-ddyrys. Tramroad from Pwll Du Quarry now makes a good footpath with views of the Black Mountain.

33c Abergavenny. This area of the Brecon Beacons National Park has much to offer the walker: mixed farmland, high rolling hills, attractive villages, historic buildings and the only canal within a National Park. A guide called "Thirty walks in the Abergavenny area" shows all the waymarked footpaths in the district.

33e Pen-y-fan Pond Country Park. Small park with a wealth of recreational facilities.

33f Pontypool Park. 2½ mile waymarked walk around the park taking in points of interest like the Georgian stables.

33h Glan-Shon: Cwm Gwddon Trail. 1½ mile walk round the northern area of the Ebbw Forest.

33h Cwm-carn Scenic Forest Drive (tel. Newbridge 0495 244223). A 7 mile drive through mountain forest with spectacular views of the Bristol Channel and Brecon Beacons. Also: adventure play areas; forest and mountain walks up to 1370 ft. *Easter to August: daily 1100-2000; September to October: daily 1100-1800.*

34a Abergavenny. See 33c.

34a Clytha Hill: Coed-y-Bwynydd. 25 acre hilltop with magnificent views of the Usk valley.

34d Llandegfedd Reservoir. Six walks, totalling 19 miles, through varied countryside, with hills, woods and steep valleys.

34h Wentwood Forest. 6 waymarked walks in ancient 3000 acre forest with historic royal hunting associations. Guide available locally.

34h Wentwood Reservoir: Gray Hill Countryside Trail. Varied walk of forest, hill-commons, a quarry and plantations.

34i Caldicot Castle. See 25c.

35d Tintern Parva: Forest Trails. Two demanding walks with views of the beautiful Wye valley.
Nurton's Field Centre (tel. 029 18 253). Residential courses available for the study of surrounding natural habitats.

35d Wynd Cliff. A forest trail through a nature reserve to a 700 ft high viewpoint over the Wye; views to the sea.

35g Chepstow: Offa's Dyke. Start of the footpath which finishes at Prestatyn (78b). See panel on page 82.

35g Blackrock. See 25c.

37c Dinas Island. Circuit walk of 3 miles along the spectacular cliff path of this 400 acre promontry; includes 500 ft high Dinas Head.

37h Treffgarne: Nant-y-coy. Nature walk in private grounds noted for Great Treffgarne Rocks, prominent for miles around.

37h Scolton Country Park (tel. Haverfordwest 0437 3708). An estate of 40 acres, especially rich in

trees and ornamental shrubs; nature trail. Leaflet available. *Tuesday to Sunday.*

37i Llys-y-fran Reservoir Country Park. 7½ mile footpath circling the reservoir; nature trail.

38c Cardigan Wildlife Park, near Cilgerran (tel. Llechryd 023 987 662). 250 acre park with an interesting nature trail. *Daily 1000-1800.*

38e Crymych: Presely Mountains. Walk west on Bronze Age road (6 miles all at over 1000 ft). Numerous relics from Bronze and Stone Ages visible on route.

39a Cenarth. Magnificent waterfalls and pools where coracles can still be seen.

39c Llandyssul: Maesllyn Woollen Mill (tel. Rhydlewis 023 975 251). Nature trail in beautiful 20 acre valley. *Monday to Saturday 1100-1800; Sundays 1400-1800.*

39i Carmarthen: Town Walk. Exploring Carmarthen on foot can reveal anything from a Roman amphitheatre to coracles on the river. Leaflet available locally.

39i Abergwili: Carmarthen Museum, Old Bishop's Palace (tel. 0267 31691). Nature trail in the grounds illustrates local natural history; also an interpretative centre with exhibition. *Monday to Saturday 1000-1630. Free.*

40f Abergorlech: Brechfa Forest. 1½-2 mile walk north west into extensive forest which covers the northern slopes of the beautiful Vale of Cothi.

40i Ty-Isaf. See 30b.

41a Dolau Cothi Estate. A walk through 2577 acres of grounds designed to show some aspects of managing a large country estate containing woodland, lowland and hill farms. Also 2 nature trails showing areas of Roman mining activity from 1st century AD.

41c Sugar Loaf. This conspicuous landmark, rising to 1950 ft, is an extinct volcano. Walk to summit signposted from the car park.

42e Mynydd Illtyd: Brecon Beacons National Park Mountain Centre (tel. Brecon 0874 3366). Small centre providing toilet and rest areas and an interpretative display for better understanding of the area. *Daily.*

42f Brecon. Walks in and around this ancient town are described in two leaflets: "A look at Brecon" and "Some short walks around Brecon", both available locally.

42f Modrydd: Cwm Llwch. Start of one of 10 walks over the 2950 high red sandstone mountain range that dominates the National Park; each walk selected by the Brecon Beacons National Park Committee and featured in the booklet "Walking in the Brecons", available locally.

42f Cwm Gwdi. One of 10 selected walks over the Beacons (see 42f Modrydd).

42i Bryn Du: Storey Arms. One of 10 walks to Pen-y-Fan summit (see 42f Modrydd).

42i Neuadd Reservoir. Pont Cwm-y-Fedwen Forest. A 2 mile walk high in the beautiful and isolated Taf Fechan Valley. Footpath to Pen-y-Fan peak also starts from here (see 42f Modrydd).

43b Talgarth. Leisurely walk around 30 points of interest in this old market town, described in locally available guide.

43d Llanfrynach: Cefn Cyff. One of 10 walks to Pen-y-Fan and the Brecon Beacons (see 42f Modrydd).

43f Ffawydden: Mynydd Du Forest. An 11 stage trail through 150 acres of forest rich in plant and animal life.

43g Nant Menascin. One of 10 walks to Pen-y-Fan and the Brecon Beacons (see 42f Modrydd).

43g Bryn. One of 10 walks to the Pen-y-Fan peak in the heart of Brecon Beacons (see 42f Modrydd).

43g Aber Cynafon: Talybont Forest. 4 trails exploring the afforested headwaters of the Caerfanell river.

43i Crickhowell. 1½ mile walk showing 21 interesting features of the town, including castle, church and the site of the ancient 'Great Gate'.

44d Ffawydden. See 43f.

44g Twyn-yr-Allt: St Mary's Vale. A 7 stage nature trail winds through this fascinating valley up to the moorland around Sugar Loaf hill.

44g Abergavenny. See 33c.

46f Ynys Lochdyn. National Trust 'island' reached by a cliff path from Llangranog. An abundance of seals and seabirds add to the sense of isolation this bold coastline gives.

46g Penrhyn. Start of the Pembrokeshire Coast Path (see panel on page 00).

48c Bwlch-yr-hendre: Tynbedw Forest. 2 mile walk illustrating the life and growth of the forest and gorge scenery.

48c Cors Goch: National Nature Reserve. One of the largest bogs in Wales (4 miles long). Contains many rare plants: sundews, bladderworts, sedges and bog rosemary.

49g Dinas Nature Reserve (tel. Rhandirmwyn 055 06 228). 10 stage trail through oakwood gorge on the beautiful upper section of the Towy.

49h Llyn Brianne Reservoir. Series of walks around recently constructed reservoir and the vast Towy forest. (See also 39i Carmarthen).

49h Cwm-Irfon Forest. Number of short walks in the hills behind Llanwrtyd Wells.

49h Sugar Loaf. See 41c.

50a Rhayader: Waun Capel Park. Situated on the banks of the Wye, this park is one of the most beautiful in Wales.

50i Aberedw Rocks. Impressive rocks which tower over the Wye in a steep-sided gorge covered in thick foliage.

51a "Water-breaks-its-neck". Above the A44 is a delightful waterfall with this curious name.

This symbol is used to designate the route of many long-distance footpaths

This symbol is often used 'on the ground' to mark the route of nature trails

Long Distance Walks

Offa's Dyke Path *(Llwybr Clawdd Offa).* Stretching from Chepstow (35g) on the Severn Estuary to Prestatyn (78g) on Liverpool Bay, a distance of 168 miles, this path is unique among designated long-distance footpaths in that it follows an archaeological feature rather than a geographical one, like a coastline. It was built by Offa, King of Mercia between 750 and 800 AD, as a series of defensive earthworks along his frontier to keep marauding Welsh hillmen out of the Kingdom of Mercia. Throughout the walk, history is brought to life with ancient hill forts, mediaeval castles and small market towns and villages. While Offa's Dyke is its theme, the path does detour from its course, using old drover's roads and prehistoric trackways, to give a more attractive walk. The landscape varies from the pastoral lowlands of Monmouthshire and the level floodplain of the River Severn, through the rolling cultivated country of the foothills of the Black Mountains and the thickly wooded Wye Valley, up to the Clun Hills and the high open walking country of the Clwydian Range.

The route is readily accessible even by car and many sections are suitable for walking in short distances. The entire length is marked with wooden signposts. Clothing should be suitable for overgrown, muddy ways and for tough hill-walking, but there is no rock work. An invaluable guide is "Offa's Dyke Path" (published by Her Majesty's Stationery Office) which gives detailed maps and essential information for the serious trekker, but the casual visitor or holidaymaker will find the path clearly marked with a red hatched line on the maps in this atlas.

Pembrokeshire Coast Path. The first long-distance footpath in Wales, this path hugs the coast from Amroth in the south (28e), around the Pembroke and Milford Peninsulas (maps 26 and 27) to St Dogmaels (46g) on the Cardiganshire border, a total distance of 167 miles. Running almost entirely within the Pembrokeshire Coast National Park, it reveals a coastline of immense variety: magnificent, remote cliffs with wide views; busy industrial harbours and peaceful fishing and sailing ports; secluded bays and sandy coves; bustling, popular holiday resorts and beaches. There is an abundance of wild flowers and wildlife all around the coast and the offshore islands hold some of the largest and most diverse seabird populations in Great Britain.

Walkers should wear tough clothing and stout shoes because of the predominance of gorse and heather and because the path is often very close to the edge and can be slippery with mud. An invaluable guide for anyone attempting a serious trek along all or part of the walk is "The Pembrokeshire Coast Path" (published by Her Majesty's Stationery Office) which provides detailed maps and explanations of all that is seen about you on the walk. For the casual visitor or holidaymaker, however, the maps in this atlas are more than adequate and the path is clearly marked with a red hatched line. The only restricted access is in the area around Castlemartin Firing Range (27g) when those ranges are in use (indicated by red flags and/or lights).

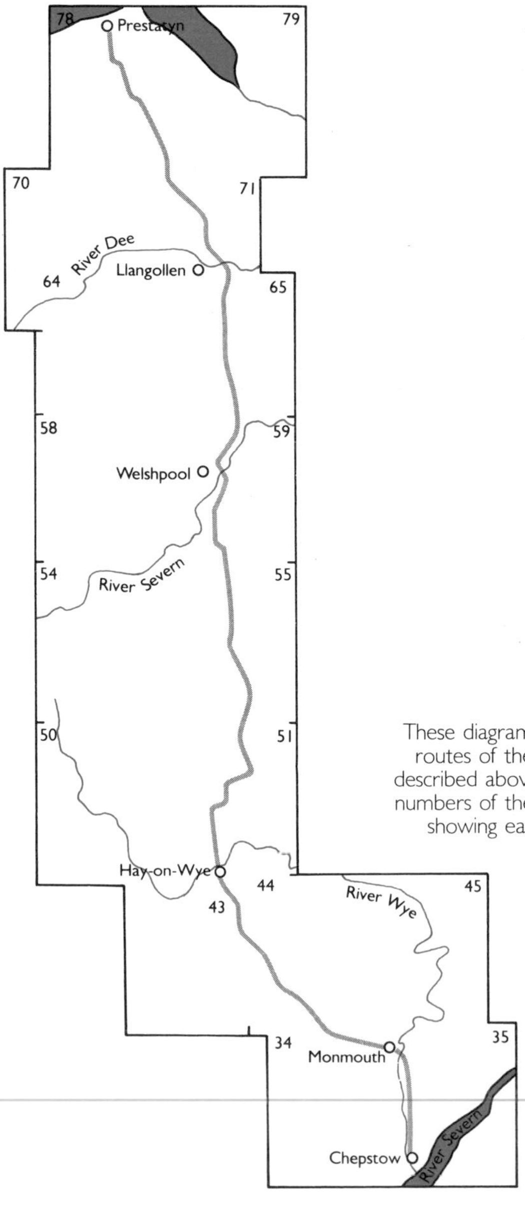

These diagrams show the complete routes of the long distance walks described above, along with the page numbers of the 1:100,000 scale maps showing each section in detail.

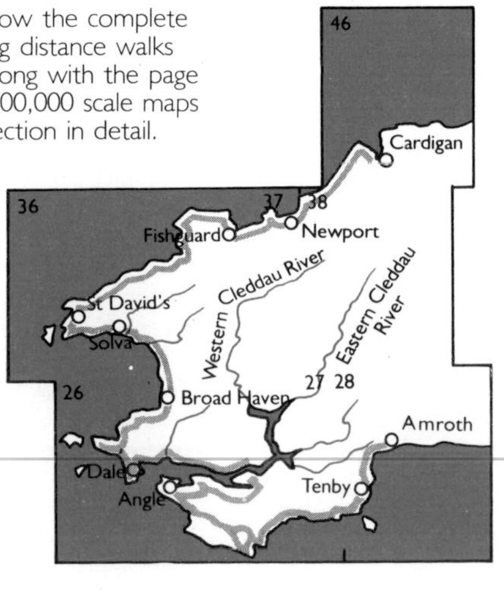

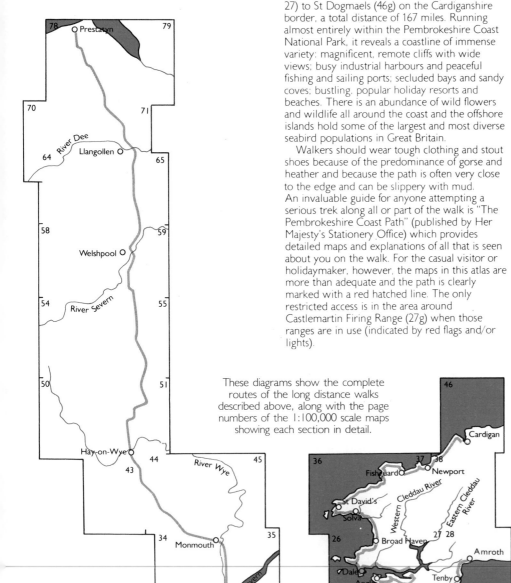

52b Twyn Bach. 3,525 acre reserve of sandbanks and saltings, noted for its birdlife.

52b Cors Fochno: Ynyslas Nature Reserve. A duneland trail of great interest revealing much unique flora and fauna.

52b Wenffrwd: Plant Glas Forest. Set of 3 way-marked walks in beautiful forest setting.

52c Ty'ny garth: Taliesin Forest. 1 mile walk up Artist's Valley; explanation boards en route.

52d Aberystwyth: Constitution Hill. 2 nature trails on the hills and cliffs with fine views of the Plynlimon Mountains and Cardigan Bay.

52e Plas Gogerddan: Rheidol Forest. Easy and interesting walk through woodlands.

52f Nant-yr-arian Forest Centre. Operated by Forestry Commission, the centre has spectacular views over the foothills of the Plynlimon Mountains (53d). Contains an exhibition on the history of and man's influence on the forest. Two superb walks—the Jubilee Walk and the Forest Trail—explore the wooded mountains of the area. *Easter to October: daily 1000-1700; July and August: daily 1000-1900. Walks open all year.*

52f Cwmrheidol Reservoir. Nature trail encircling the reservoir (part of a hydroelectric scheme completed in 1963) with 11 viewing points. Information and leaflets available from CEGB reception centre at power station.

52h Trawscoed: Black Covert Forest provides a walk in pleasantly hilly, forested landscape.

52i Mynydd Bach: Tynbedw Forest. 2 mile way-marked walk giving spectacular views of the gorge and forest.

52i Bwlch-yr-hendre. See 48c.

53c Llyn Clywedog. Pleasant 2½ mile trail, with 13 stages, through wooded dingle on the hills surrounding the reservoir. An informative leaflet is available locally.

53e Hafren Forest. Cascades Trail, Blaenhafren Falls Walk and Source of the Severn Walk. A series of walks in 17 square miles of forest, all of which start from the car park on Old Hall road. See leaflets: "Hafren Forest Walks" and "Cascades Forest Trail", available in Llanidloes.

53g Devil's Bridge. A set of 9 walks through the wooded gorge, with wonderful views of the many waterfalls below the bridge. Beware—some of the paths are very steep.☆

53g Bryn Llwyd: The Arch Forest Trail. 1½ mile walk through plantations with many interesting views.

54c Newtown: Dolerw Park. A beautiful 32 acre park across the Severn river from the town centre.

54g Rhayader. See 50a.

56b Barmouth: Dinas Oleg. 4 mile panoramic walk offering superb views of the Mawddach Estuary, the Cader range to the south and Diffwys to the north. Reached by steep road from Porkington Terrace.

56b Cregennen. Walk to Llyniau Creggennen past impressive waterfalls. Another footpath continues into the mountains to open moorland and an old Roman road.

56c Foel Ispri: New Precipice Walk. High level footpath with magnificent views of the Mawddach Estuary and Cader Idris.

56c Penmaenpool. Walk south from former signal box along the path of the disused railway overlooking the Mawddach Estuary. 🐦

56c Craig y Castell: Talywaen Farm Trail. Privately-owned walk on the flanks of Cader Idris high above the Mawddach Estuary. No dogs; play area. *Easter to October.* 🏠

56e Dolgoch Falls. Magnificent series of waterfalls which drop a total of 125 ft.

56h Twyn Bach. See 52b.

56h Cors Fochno. See 52b.

56i Ty'ny garth. See 52c.

57a Braich-y-ceunant: Torrent Walk. Scenic walk of 1 mile along the banks of Clywedog river. Many beautiful waterfalls.

57d Aberllefenni: Foel Friog Forest. 7 stage trail in area of outstanding beauty. See local guide for interpretation of the scene. 🏠

57d Esgair geiliog. 2 mile walk through Dovey Forest. Waymarked in red (short walk) and yellow (long walk). 🏠

58i Gregynog Hall. Small but interesting woodland nature trail in the grounds of the hall, now part of the University of Wales. ✿

58i Newtown. See 54c.

60e Porth Ysgo. Delightful, isolated bay reached by a path from a small car park at the head of the valley (15 minutes walk). Superb coastal scenery and sandy, shingle backed beach (completely covered at high tide).

60e Mynydd-y-Graig. Footpath to a wild bracken-covered rock surrounded by a heather moor. Magnificent views to the curving shore of Porth Neigwl; on the moor the remains of an Iron Age defensive camp can still be seen.

61b Llanystumdwy: Cabin Wood Walk. Easy to follow for 1 mile through mixed woodland.

Afon Dwyfor. Waymarked walk through the wooded valley (north-east of village); large number of interesting tree species.

62a Tremadog. A trail that demonstrates local levels of nature conservancy; starts by the church.

62b Llyn Mair. Nature trail through oak woodlands and meadows overlooking this small lake. 🐦

62b Maentwrog: Plas Tan-y-bwlch National Park Study Centre (tel. 076 685 324). Residential courses given on various aspects of the countryside. ✦T

62c Cynfal-mawr Falls. Noted beauty spot with Hugh Lloyd's Pulpit—a column of rock rising from the stream. 🏠

62c Llyn Trawsfynydd. 3 mile walk along the shore of the lake from CEGB Power Station car park; also extensive walk to Llyn Celyn (63b) along the route of an old railway line.

62e Pentre: Cefn Isaf Farm Trail. 2 mile walk from near Salem Chapel, which explains the workings of a typical Welsh hill farm.

62e Cwm Nantcol. A nature trail along the riverside with explanation boards en route. 🏠

62e Llyn Du Nature Reserve. Beauty spot with fine views and a lake formed and maintained by rain and dew.

62f Maesgwm Forest Visitor Centre, Coed y Brenin Forest (tel. Ganllwyd 034 140 210). Run by the Forestry Commission to interpret the forest as part of the landscape, as a habitat for wildlife, as an industry and as a place for recreation. *Easter to October: daily 1000-1700 (1900 in July and August).*

62f Pont Dolgefeiliau: Coed y Brenin Forest Walks. 50 miles of waymarked walks clearly identified on a map available at the Maesgwm Forest Visitor Centre (see above). 🐦 🏠

62g Morfa Dyffryn: Nature Conservancy Reserve. Creeping willow and many other plants grow in the 'slacks' or hollows between the dunes. Permit needed for central/northern parts, from Nature Conservancy, Plas Gogerddan, Aberystwyth. 🐦 🏠

62i Rhaedr Ddu Falls. Series of waterfalls reached through carefully maintained oak woodland on path from village hall. Moist conditions favour rare ferns and mosses.

62i Foel Ispri. See 56c.

62i Penmaenpool. See 56c.

62i Craig y Castell. See 56c.

National Parks

The national parks of Britain are large areas of country, usually wild and sparsely populated, where special care is taken to conserve the natural landscape. However, most of the land is not nationally owned and even the open moorland usually belongs to someone, so that rights of access may be limited. National parks are run by local planning committees and the Countryside Commission. They receive government aid for a range of activities: control of design and development of buildings; conservation measures such as the removal of eyesores, tree planting and laying out footpaths; and the provision of facilities like car parks, camp sites, information centres and country parks. The boundaries of all national parks are clearly marked on our maps with heavy green lines.

Pembrokeshire Coast (Parc Cenedlaethol Arfoidir Penfro). This is the smallest national park in Wales and is the only one which is primarily coastal-no land in the park is more than 10 miles from the sea. The coastline is exceptionally beautiful, with the ancient geology which includes old red sandstone and carboniferous limestone, and can be best viewed from the Pembrokeshire Coast Long Distance Footpath (see opposite) which bounds the park. Other features of the area include the fine deep-water harbour at Milford Haven; the rolling uplands of the Presely Mountains with their abundance of prehistoric relics; and the chain of castles which mark the extent of the Norman colonistaion and which divides the area into two distinct cultural districts — English-speaking in the south and Welsh-speaking in the north.

SNOWDONIA NATIONAL PARK

PEMBROKESHIRE COAST NATIONAL PARK

Snowdonia (Parc Cenedlaethol Eryri) is a national park made up mainly of mountain ranges-14 peaks are over 2900 ft high — and glacier-scoured valleys. It covers an area of 838 square miles and is set in the heart of the ancient kingdom of Gwynedd which is and always has been the stronghold of Welsh language and culture. The many prehistoric burial chambers and hut-circles, Iron Age and Roman forts and castles of both English and Welsh origin are testaments to man's occupation of the area. The high passes that connect the valleys, in which small lakes and spectacular cascades can be seen, enable the motorist to view the area at close quarters. The area is probably best known to the climber, however — the section on climbing (page 118) gives details of the best climbing areas.

Brecon Beacons (Parc Cenedlaethol Bannau Brycheiniog). 519 square miles in area, the park takes its name from the mountain range at its centre which is part of a ridge of old red sandstone that forms a 'backbone across the entire length of the park. The only gap in this high ridge is the broad and fertile valley of the River Usk. Elsewhere, vast stretches of open moors clad with bracken are flanked by softer pastoral country, where farming predominates. Other features of the park include the only canal in any national park and a limestone area which contains Britain's longest known cave system.

The best way to see all three parks is on foot or on horse back. The section on the Countryside

(page 74, describes some of the best footpaths, nature trails and country parks. Remember when walking on open moorland or through mountainous country that it is essential to wear good shoes and weatherproof clothing, as you can often walk all day without seeing any signs of human habitation. For those who prefer travelling on horseback, pages 116-118 give a detailed list of the riding establishments in all three areas.

This map shows the area covered by the three national parks of Wales, all of which are described above. They are: A Snowdonia, B Pembrokeshire Coast, C Brecon Beacons.

63a Rhaiadr Cwm Waterfall: spectacular 200 ft high fall. ⌂

63d Rhaeadr Mawddach: two remarkable waterfalls merge into the one river. ↓T

63g Ganllwyd. 2 mile forest walk from the Ty'n-y-Groes Hotel; illustrates the wildlife, plants and trees in the forest. ⌂

63g Llyn Cynwch: Precipice Walk. Steep walk encircling high ridge offering magnificent views of the Mawddach Estuary, Cader Idris and Snowdonia.

63g Braich-y-ceunant. See 57a.

64f Pistyll Rhaeadr Waterfall. 150 ft fall which is one of the most spectacular in Wales.

65c Froncysyllte: Tan-y-cut Wood. Nature trail which starts by a canal tunnel. *Easter to September.* Also 10 miles of canal bank to north and south.

66i Craig Ddu: Ty Canol Walk. Remarkable wooded mountain giving good views of Caernarfon Bay. Exciting walking country.

67a Newborough: Hendai Forest. 7 stage trail through forest planted to hold dunes. Mediaeval houses of Rhosyr village exposed by blown sand.

67a Newborough Warren: Ynys Llanddwyn National Nature Reserve. 6 routes through 1565 acres of sandhills, salt marshes and dune grassland. ↘ ⌂

67c Llyn Padarn Country Park. 3 trails through lakeside park formed from Dinorwic Slate Quarry and Allt Wen woodlands of the Vaynol Estate. Visitor centre in former quarry hospital. ↓T 🐾

67i Beddgelert Forest. Series of waymarked walks exploring the forest and providing superb views towards Snowdon. ⌂ ▲

67i Nature Trail. ¾ mile trail through Beddgelert Forest and its spectacular scenery. ▲

68a Llyn Padarn Country Park. See 67c.

68b Cwm Idwal National Nature Reserve. Nature trail of 11 stations illustrates past glaciation in 984 acre nature reserve.

68b Pen-y-pass Youth Hostel: The Miner's Track. Easiest route (2 miles) to Snowdon summit via Llyn Llydaw See ▲ for details.

68d Beddgelert Forest. See 67i.

68d Nature Trail. See 67i.

68e Glandber. Short walk, steep in places, giving fine views of the Snowdon Massif and beautiful Llyn Gwynant. ⌂

68e Nature Trail. Follows part of Watkin trail to Snowdon summit. See ▲ for details.

68e Nantmor Valley: Cae Ddafydd Forest. Peaceful 2 mile walk through coniferous forest. ⌂

68g Tremadog. See 62a.

68h Llyn Mair. See 62b.

68i Maentwrog. See 62b.

68i Cynfal-mawr Falls. See 62c.

68i Llyn Trawsfynydd. See 62c.

69a Llyn Geirionnydd. ¾ mile forest trail showing various aspects of forestry work and the once flourishing local lead mines. ⌂

69a Nature Trail: Lady Mary's Walk. An undemanding, 7 stage 1 mile walk introducing the work of the Forestry Commission. See locally-available information.

69a Glyn: Cae'n-y-coed Arboretum. Two walks, the longer being very steep in places, through an Arboretum providing fine views of Snowdon and the Llugwy Valley. ✿ ⌂

69a Tyhyll: Gwydyr Forest Trail and Swallow Falls. 3 mile, 13 stage walk illustrating the work of re-afforestation in the area. Also notable beauty spot with superb waterfalls. ✿ ⌂

69a Pentre-du: Garth Falls (tel. Llanrwst 0492 640578). Route, past tall spruce trees, a stream and a waterfall, on paved surface suitable for handicapped and elderly; guide rail for blind.

69a Clogwyn Cyrau: Gwydyr Forest. 10 walks explore the forest and provide some breathtaking views. Guide available locally.

69b Betws-y-Coed. 9 short walks in the area—through woods, over hills and along public footpaths—which are described in a leaflet available from 🛈 at Betws-y-Coed.

69b Plas-rhyd-y creuau: Drapers' Field Centre (tel. Betws-y-Coed 069 02 494). Short residential courses available on a wide variety of subjects related to the countryside.

69b Conway Falls. Magnificent twin waterfall in a steep-sided rocky gorge. 🐾

69g Rhaiadr Cwm Waterfall: spectacular 200 ft high fall, just off B4391.

70a Brenig Reservoir. A series of trails surround the 919 acre reservoir. A field study and interpretive centre, with a library and laboratory, are available to visitors. 🅼 ⌂ ⛵ ⚓

70b Pont Petryal Visitor Centre. Exhibition presenting the forest in its ecological and historical setting is displayed in an old keepers cottage. Waymarked walks, up to 2¾ miles, through varied woodland. *Centre: Easter to October daily.*

71a Ruthin. Starting in Cae Ddol car park a walk is routed round this ancient and historic town, with its mediaeval, Georgian and Regency buildings. 🏛

71c Waun-y-Llyn Country Park. Situated on a moorland ridge of Hope Mountain beside a small lake, this park offers good views and walks.

71c Hope Mountain Walk. Footpath waymarked in yellow. Free map/leaflet available.

71c Bwlch-gwyn. Geological trail (1½ miles) around disused quarry illustrating the geology of sedimentary rocks, fossil plants and marine shells, plus evidence of glaciation. ☕ 🖼 ↓T

71e Worlds End. Nature trail of 1 mile over Ruabon Mountain; spectacular views. *June to August.*

71f Talwrn: Legacy Nature Trail. Study plant and animal life established on landscaped ground around an electricity substation. *By arrangement with CEGB, Deeside* (tel. 0244 817607).

71f Wynnstay Park. A large and beautiful park with many pleasant walks. 🏛

71i Froncysyllte. See 65c.

72d Wynnstay Park. A large and beautiful park with many pleasant walks. 🏛

72e Bangor-on-Dee. Town trail taking in many fine old houses. Booklet available from Clwyd County Council.

72e Overton. Walk through the town featuring an interesting church and many other fine buildings. Booklet available from Clwyd County Council. ✝

74c Wylfa. 1 mile, 8 stage trail around the headland at Wylfa Head Nuclear Power Station (tel. Cemaes Bay 040 789 471). Noted for coastal flowers and seabird colonies. ⌂ ↓T

74d South Stack. 9 viewing points on a guided walk down 350 steps and 150 ft to South Stack Lighthouse. *May to mid July. Free.* ↘ ▲ ☆

74e Penrhos Nature Reserve (tel. Holyhead 0407 2522). 5 mile trail with 13 viewing stages. Varied habitat: rocky and sandy coast, woodlands, lakes and archaeological remains. 🐾 ⌂

76e Pont Newydd: Coed Aber Nature Trail. Scenic walk (3 miles) through woods to the spectacular 150 ft Aber Falls on Rhaiadr-fawr.

76g Llyn Padarn Country Park. See 67c.

77a Great Orme's Head. Three short nature trails start from Happy Valley. Points of interest include rock gardens, superb views, old mine shafts, abbey remains and St Tudno's Church. Leaflet "Discovering the Great Orme" available locally. ✿ 🐾

77a Llandudno. Short walk around the town's main points of interest, starting at Cenotaph on promenade. Booklet available.

77b Bryn Euryn Nature Trail. Scenic 1½ mile walk in an area of natural beauty. Excellent views of the coast and Snowdonia; notable flora and fauna.

77b Colwyn Bay. Walk around Victorian seaside resort overlooked by wooded heights. Brochure available from Civic Society.

77d Conwy. Walk round interesting sites in ancient walled and castled city. Descriptive leaflet 'Conwy Town Trail' available at 🛈

77d Bodnant Garden. Many pleasant walks in one of Britain's finest gardens. *Mid March to end October daily 1000-1700.* 🐾 ✿

77g Llyn Crafnant. Tiny mountain-ringed reservoir with idyllic woodland walk and viewpoint.

77g Gwydir Forest Information Centre (tel. Llanrwst 0492 64057). Forestry Commission exhibition illustrating various aspects of the forest: planting, harvesting, the timber crop, re-afforestation and wildlife. 12 forest trails in the area. *Easter to end September: daily 1000-1630.* 🏛 ✝

77g Llanrwst. Tour round ancient buildings of this historic town, "Llanrwst and District Trail" available locally. 🅼 🏛

77g Llyn Geirionnydd. See 69a.

78b Gwaunysgor: Bishopswood Nature Trail. 2 mile walk with 12 viewing stations and panoramic views over North Wales.

78h Denbigh. Town trail, established in 1965, takes you through an area with many historic buildings. Guide book available. 🏛

78i Moel Arthur Country Park. Moorland park which has within its boundaries a hill fort, Offa's Dyke (see page 82) and fine views of the Vale of Clwyd. Two trails and various walks.

79d Holywell Nature Trail. 3 mile walk covers wooded valley, Basingwerk Abbey and a holy well. Booklet available locally.

79g Rhyd-y-mwyn: Leete Nature Trail. Walk from village to Trail Hill, Pontnewydd and return via Pen-y-fron (3¾ miles). Limestone gorge with fossils in quarry.

79g Loggerheads Country Park. Woodland park with views and 12 stage nature trail along the River Alyn and the leete (water channel) of an old mill.

79g Moel Famau Country Park. Moorland park with fine views, a reservoir, the Jubilee Tower, a hill fort and Offa's Dyke (see page 82). Various walks, including a 2-4 mile Forest Trail with 12 viewing points en route to Moel Famau summit (78i). ↘ ⌂

79h Ewloe Green: Castle Nature Trail. 1½ mile walk with 6 stages exploring farmland, wooded valley and remains of Ewloe Castle. 🅼

Wepre Park. Footpath from Ewloe Castle north to Wepre along 7 miles of wooded defile.

79i Higher Kinnerton. Walk explores the Brad Brook area for 1 mile (waymarked in yellow). Free map/leaflet available locally.

Gardens and Arboreta

21d Clyne Gardens: late-spring displays of azaleas and rhododendrons; also fine collection of primulas, herbaceous plants, conifers and other trees. *Daily 0800 to dusk. Free.*

21e Brynmill: Singleton Park, off A4067 south of Swansea. Education Gardens feature a large collection of shrubs, including many sub-tropical species; also trees, herbaceous and alpine plants. *Daily: 0900-1630 (1900 in summer). Free.* ♣ ▣

22b Margam Park (tel. Port Talbot 063 96 87626). 18th century Orangery, the longest in Britain (327 ft), surrounded by 8 acres of gardens with unusual trees and shrubs. The rhododendron garden is especially attractive in May. Adventure playground, boating and pony rides. *April to end October: Tuesday to Sunday and Bank Holiday Mondays 1030-2000. November to end March: Wednesday to Sunday 1030 to 1 hour before dusk.* ☕ ♣ ▣ ✝ 🅿

23i Dyffryn Gardens (tel. Cardiff 0222 593328). 72 acres of gardens with many rare shrubs and trees; also palm house with citrus, orchid, banana, cocoa, pineapple and coffee plants. Arboretum covers 25 acres. *End March to September daily; October weekends; 1000-1800 (1900 May to August).*

27b Picton Castle (tel. Rhos 043 786 296). Extensive grounds with shrub gardens and woodland (at their best in spring). Only grounds and garden open. *April to end September: Tuesday to Thursday and weekends 1030-1730.* ☕ ♣ ▣

27d Milford Haven: Hamilton Terrace. Fine walks and gardens with a pleasant view to St Annes Head.

27e Upton Castle. The grounds contain over 250 species of trees and shrubs and are at their best in spring, although the flowering season starts in December and continues until early summer. *February to October 1000-1630. Free.* ♣ 🅿

30h Clyne Gardens. See 21d.

34c Lydart: The Yew Tree (tel. Monmouth 0600 2293). Garden of 3 acres with superb views. Large and unusual range of plants, rare trees and shrubs and a stream garden. *By appointment only (not Tuesdays or Fridays): January to November 1000-1600; May to October 1100-1800.*

43h Gliffaes Country House Hotel (tel. Bwlch 0874 730371). Excellently placed high above the River Usk, this large garden has shrubs, ornamental trees, fine maples and rhododendrons. *March to December.* ☕

52c Cymerau (tel. Glandyfi 065 474 230). Superbly positioned garden with panoramic views over the Dovey Estuary. Contains flowering shrubs and unusual bushes. New owners; telephone first.

56b Ty'n-y-Coed. A large house set in peaceful woodland grounds, with waterfalls and peacocks. The woodland shrubs are at their best from mid-May to mid-June. Only grounds open. *Mid April to mid October weekdays 1030-1700; Sundays 1230-1700.* ☕

56i Ynyshir Hall Hotel, on A487 (tel. Glandyfi 065 474 209). Large garden with shrubs, fine trees, rhododendrons, azaleas and hydrangeas. *March to October daily 1400-1700.* ☕

56i Plas Machynlleth. Public park with rose garden, tennis courts and childrens playground. *Any reasonable time.* ▣

56i Cymerau. See 52c.

57d Corris: Brynhyfryd (tel. 065 473 278). 4-acre garden on a rocky mountainside containing

Bodnant Garden (77d)

rhododendrons, roses, flowering shrubs, alpine and water plants. *Daily by appointment only.*

58i Gregynog Hall. Early 19th century house with large garden. Includes rhododendrons and azaleas, a dell with specimen shrubs and a formal garden. A short nature trail starts from the car park.

59d Powis Castle (tel. Welshpool 0938 2554). The gardens were laid out in 1720 and have world famous hanging terraces. Other features are enormous yew hedges, lead statuary, an Orangery and a large wild garden. *Easter Weekend; then May to late September, Wednesday to Sunday 1300-1730; also Bank Holiday Mondays 1130-1730.* ☕ 🏚 🅿

60e Plas-yn-Rhiw (tel. Rhiw 075 888 219). 16th century house with large grounds and woodlands stretching to the west shore of Porth Neigwl. Ornamental gardens contain flowering trees and shrubs, including sub-tropical specimens, with streams and waterfall rising to a snowdrop wood. *By appointment only: April to end June Wednesdays and Thursdays 1300-1630.* 🏚

62a Portmeirion (tel. Penrhyndeudraeth 089 284 228). The Gwyllt Gardens are some 20 miles of coastal, cliff and woodland gardens surrounding the scenic village. They are famous for rhododendrons, azaleas and sub-tropical flora. *Easter to end October daily 0930-1730.* ☕ 🏚

67c Bryn Bras Castle (tel. Llanberis 028 682 210). Extensive gardens including stream, waterfalls, pools, hydrangeas, rhododendrons and woodland and mountain walks with panoramic views. *Spring Bank Holiday Monday to mid-July 1350-1700 mid-July to end August 1030-1700; September 1330-1700; but closed Saturdays throughout.* ☕ 🏚 🅿

67f Betws Garmon: Hafodty House. Delightful walks in rock and water gardens with azaleas, hydrangeas, flowering shrubs and trees standing beside the Nant Mill waterfalls. *Daily 1030 to dusk.*

68a Betws Garmon: Hafodty House. See 67f.

68h Portmeirion. See 62a.

69a Tyhyll: Cae'n-y-Coed Arboretum. Many species of trees, numbered for identification in guide available from Gwydyr Uchaf Forestry Commission, Llanrwst (Map ref 77g; tel. 0492 640574). *Daily.* ♣ 🅿

71f Erddig. Garden restored to its 18th century formal design and containing fruit known to have

grown there during that period. *Easter to late October: Tuesday to Sunday and Bank Holiday Mondays 1200-1730.* ☕ 🏚 ⬆ ∪

72d Erddig. See 71f.

75h Plas Newydd (tel. Llanfairpwll 0248 714795). Gardens with massed shrubs, fine trees and lawns sloping down to Menai Strait, with superb views to Snowdonia. *Easter to late October: Sunday to Friday and Bank Holiday weekend Saturdays 1230-1700.* ☕ ▣ 🏚

75i Bangor: Bible Garden. This unique garden places every tree, shrub and flower, capable of growing in the Welsh climate, in the order in which it appears in the Bible. *Any reasonable time.*

76d Bangor: Bible Garden. See 75i.

76d Penrhyn Castle (tel. Bangor 0248 53084). The garden and grounds command superb views of the mountains and Menai Strait. Fine and rare trees and shrubs; Victorian walled garden. *April, May and October daily 1400-1700; June to end September and all Bank Holiday weekends, daily 1100-1700.* ☕ 🏚 ⬆

76g Bryn Bras Castle. See 67c.

77a Llandudno: Rapallo House (tel. 0492 76517). Ornamental and secluded garden. *April to November weekdays 1000-1600. Free.* ▣

77b Colwyn Bay: Botanic Gardens (tel. 0492 2938). Range of flora of all types. *April to October 0930-1900; October to March 1000-1600.* ☕ 🐘

77d Ro-wen: Gilfach. Small but attractive garden specialising in shrubs. *April to September weekdays.*

77d Bodnant Garden. One of the finest gardens in the country. Planned and begun by Henry Pochin in 1875, the 87 acres contain a famous rhododendron and camellia display, a rock garden, terraces, a rose garden and pinetum. *Mid March to end October daily 1000-1700.* ☕ ♣

78a Rhyl: Royal Floral Hall, off East Parade (tel. 0745 31515). Contains many magnificent tropical plants. *Easter to early October: daily 1000-1900 (later in summer).* 🌿

78b Bodrhyddan Hall (tel. Rhuddlan 0745 590414). Beautiful grounds and gardens. *June to end September Tuesdays and Thursdays 1400-1730.* ☕ 🏚 🅿

79i Hawarden Old Castle. Ornamental gardens of note. *Easter to mid-September Saturdays, Sundays and Bank Holidays 1400-1730.* 🅪

ⅿ Historical Sites

Ruined fortifications from prehistoric to modern times, including the remains of many castles (those preserved in good order are listed on pages 93-95); also the sites of Roman camps, ancient tombs, battlefields, monuments, etc.

20d Burry Holms: limestone island with remains of an Iron Age earthwork fort. On the Rhosili Bay side are the remains of the *City of Bristol*, which ran aground in 1840. *Access to island when causeway is dry.* ✝

20f Burial Chamber: Megalithic tomb notable for its huge, 25 ton capstone. It was said to have been split open by King Arthur's sword, and it is therefore known as 'Arthur's Stone'.

20f Parc le Breos: well preserved Neolithic burial chamber, 70 ft long with central passage and 4 side 'rooms'. *Free.*

20h Paviland Caves: Goat's Hole, where in 1823 was found the skeleton of a Stone Age hunter who died 19,000 years ago. The discoverer, Dean Buckland, was a firm believer in Biblical Creation, however, and never accepted the antiquity of his find. The skeleton is now in London's Natural History Museum. The cave was occupied at various times right up to the Roman occupation, evidenced by many subsequent finds.

20h Culver Hole. Famous Gower cave, unique in being largely man made. A 60 ft cleft in the cliffs has been enclosed by a limestone wall with 'windows' cut into it. Local folklore about a smugglers' den or pirates' hideaway is sadly inaccurate: it was simply a 15th century pigeon house. *Low tide only. Free.*

20i Oxwich Castle. A fortified manor house built in the 16th century and including parts of a Norman castle. Home of the Mansel family, who moved here from nearby Penrice Castle. Now used as a farmhouse.

21a Loughor Castle. Remains of a Norman fortification built on the site of a Roman camp overlooking the strategic ford which provided access to the Gower. In later years it was defended and rebuilt several times by the Welsh. *Any reasonable time. Free.*

21c Neath Castle. Remains of a Welsh fortification, with characteristic D-shape towers, built in the 14th century on the site of a destroyed Norman castle. *Exterior only at any time.*

21e Swansea: New Castle, Wind Street. Remains of fortifications and private rooms built in the 13th/14th centuries. The castle was defended in the Civil War, but saw no action, and it was later used for diverse purposes, including a glassworks. The Old Castle, incidentally, stood just to the north, but the last traces of it disappeared under buildings in 1913. *Any time. Free.*

22e Kenfig Castle. Slight remains of the castle of old Kenfig, a village which has now been completely buried by the surrounding sand dunes. Records of the lost town are in the National Museum, Cardiff.

22f Newcastle. Ruins of the New Castle, built in the 12th century and expanded in later years. Impressive Norman gateway. *Weekdays 1000-1900 (dusk in winter); Sundays 1400-1900 (dusk in winter). Free.*

22f Candleston Castle. Pleasantly situated remains of a fortified manor house built in the 15th century and abandoned in the 19th century. *Any time.*

22f Ogmore Castle. Built on a site fortified from very early times, because it overlooks the important crossing of the River Ewenny, whose stepping stones can still be seen. The existing defences include 12th century earth banks and 13th century stone walls, up to 40 ft high in places. *Daily. Free.*

Glossary of terms

Stone Age (or Paleolithic): characterised by the first use of tools, including stone axes, etc. Normally taken to date from about 650,000 to 8000 BC.

Neolithic: late Stone Age, characterised by the use of polished tools, usually flint; the first domestic animals and the beginning of agriculture. From about 8000 to 4000 BC.

Bronze Age: the first use of metal for tools and weapons (also to time of ancient Troy). From about 4000 to 800 BC.

Iron Age: officially the age in which we still live, it began about 800 BC.

Prehistoric: a general term covering all the above Ages; often used on these pages to describe sites whose precise origins are hard to date.

Mediaeval (or Middle Ages): an ill-defined historical period, usually taken to run from about 1000 AD (the fall of Rome; the Norman Conquest of England) to about 1500 (the start of the Tudor era in Britain).

23d Coity Castle. Typical Norman fortress built in the 12th century, although it was rebuilt in the 14th and extended in the 16th centuries, soon after which it was abandoned. It saw action during the Welsh uprisings, withstanding a long siege by Owain Glyndwr. *Daily.* ✝

23f St Fagan's. Curtain walls of 13th century castle containing Welsh Folk Museum (tel. Cardiff 0222 569441) and 16th century house. *Weekdays from 1000; Sundays from 1430.*

23h Cowbridge: Porte Mellin (Mill Gate), one of the 3 town gates built in the 14th century, is the only survivor. Nearby, at the southern side of the town centre, are two towers and some remains of the town walls, also 14th century.

23h Llanblethian: St Quentin's Castle. Started early in the 14th century, this castle was never completed, as the owner died at Bannockburn in 1314. There is an impressive 3 storey gatehouse and traces of 8 ft thick walls. It was used as a prison for many years. *Free.*

23h Flemingston. Burial place of Iolo Morgannwg (real name Edward Williams), a literary forger who invented the Gorsedd of Bards which is now part of the National Eisteddfod.

23i St Nicholas: Tinkinswood Burial Chamber. Neolithic tomb in fine condition despite 5000 year age: the main chamber is 16½ by 13 ft, with a 40 ton stone lid. When excavated in 1914, the bones of 50 people were found. *Any time. Free.*

23i St Lythan's Burial Chamber. 3 upright stones supporting capstone. Dates from about 2000BC. *Any time. Free.*

24d St. Fagans. See 23f.

25a Caerleon: Roman Fortress and Amphitheatre. One of the major Roman sites of Britain, this was Isca, headquarters from 80AD of the 2nd Augustan Legion, whose 6000 men were one of 3 legions permanently based in Britain. Isca covered more than 50 acres, its HQ block standing on the site of the present parish church. Much of the modern town is based on the Roman street plan: Broadway was once Via Principalis, for example. The most visible remains are those of the magnificent oval amphitheatre, where up to 6000 spectators watched men and beasts fight to the death: this site has

been cleared. In a nearby field, the foundations of neat rows of barracks can be seen, and some of the cooking facilities have been reconstructed. *Daily from 0930 (winter Sundays from 1400).*

25c Caerwent: Roman Town. Unlike Caerleon (25a), this was a civil settlement, built in 75AD to house the warlike Silures tribe, who were forced to move here from their hill fort north of Llanmelin, 1 mile to the north west. In Venta Silurum, they were expected to adopt Roman ways, including such new habits as bathing. The limestone walls are 17 ft high in places, but little else remains, the city having been laid waste by Irish raiders after the Romans left. *Free.*

27a Haverfordwest Castle. (tel. 0437 3708) Ruins of a 12th century Norman stronghold, impressively sited on an 80 ft mound overlooking the town centre. The steep natural defences are backed up with 12 ft thick walls. The defenders withstood a long siege by Owain Glyndwr and a force of 3000 Frenchmen, but the castle was slighted during the Civil War, since when it has served as prison, police headquarters and, now, a museum. *Daylight hours. Free.*

27c Llawhaden: Bishop of St David's Castle. The site was fortified in the 12th century, but was captured by the Welsh in 1192. The Normans recaptured it and levelled the defences, and the existing buildings date from the 13th/14th centuries, when they were erected to protect the Bishop's estates—his soldiering was done by mercenaries. *Daily.*

27f Carew Cross. Monument of historical importance, being the most advanced slab cross of its type. It was erected in 1035, with an inscription that translates as "The Cross of Maredudd, son of Edwin", Maredudd having ruled south-west Wales until he was killed in that year. It stands at the entrance to Carew Castle.

27h Lamphey Bishop's Palace. Impressive remains of an extensive 13th century residence from the days when Bishops held much secular as well as religious power. *Daily.*

27i Burial Chamber: King's Quoit. A group of prehistoric standing stones, topped by one measuring 15 ft by 9 ft.

28c Llansadurnen: Coygan Cave. Limestone cavern in which the bones of mammoths, woolly rhinos and other prehistoric animals have been found.

28c Roche Castle. Slight remains; now part of a 'castle' let by Hoseasons for holidays (and always booked well in advance). *Exterior can be viewed from the road.*

28c Laugharne Castle. Two towers and other remains of a 13th century castle, together with the ruins of residential buildings added in Tudor times. Made famous in a painting by Turner. *Exterior at any time.*

28e Marros Beacon. Unusual war memorial designed like an ancient cromlech.

28g Tenby: Castle. Built in the 13th century on an easily-defended headland, its main action was during the Civil War. It fell to Cromwell's forces after a heavy bombardment in 1644, but later became a Royalist stronghold again. *Any time. Free.*

Town Walls. Built over 50 years of the 14th century in an attempt to make the town impregnable. There were 4 gates, of which one—the West Gate (known as Five Arches)—survives, along with a good portion of the West Wall. *Any time. Free,*

29e Kidwelly: 14th century bridge over the River Gwendraeth.

29h Burry Holms: limestone island with remains of an Iron Age earthwork fort. *When causeway is dry.* ✝

30f Carn-Ilecharth. Prehistoric circle of 24 standing stones, with a burial chamber in the centre.

30g Loughor Castle. See 21a.

30i Swansea. See 21e.

31g Neath Castle. See 21c.

32c Morlais Castle. Remains of a 13th century fortification. *Any time. Free.*

33a Sirhywi: 4 large stones stand beside A4047 as a memorial to Aneurin Bévan, the famous Labour politician who was born in nearby Tredegar.

33c Abergavenny Castle. Fragmentary remains dating from the 11th to 14th centuries, first built by William de Braöse, a Norman lord famed for his cruelty. *Daily 1100 to dusk. Free.* 🔲

33i Newport Castle. See 25a.

34a Abergavenny Castle. See 33c.

34b Llantilio Crosseny: Hen Gwrt. Outline of a mediaeval house surrounded by a water filled moat. *Any time. Free.*

34c Monmouth: Castle. Dating from the 12th century, it was the birthplace in 1387 of Henry V. *Exterior only, any time.*

Shire Hall, Agincourt Square, has a 7 ft statue of Henry V in a niche.

Monnow Bridge has the only fortified bridge gateway in Britain.

34e Usk: Castle. Scant remains, including the main gateway, tower and keep of a 12th century Norman castle built for one of the Marcher Lords. Although extended during the 13th and 14th centuries, it was beseiged by Owain Glyndwr in 1404 and badly damaged. Repaired and defended by Royalists in the Civil War, it was taken by Parliament and slighted. The gatehouse is now part of Castle House. *By written appointment only: Mr R Humphreys, Castle House, Usk.*

Bridge. 5 arches built to span the River Usk in the 18th century.

Priory Gatehouse, dating from the 13th century.

34g Caerlon. See 25a.

34g Newport Castle. See 25a.

34i Caerwent. See 25c.

35a The Kymin. A 1794 bowling green and pavilion built for "the gentlemen of Monmouth" together with a Naval Temple added in 1800 to commemorate the Battle of the Nile.

35g Chepstow: Town Walls. Dating from mediaeval times and including the main gateway at which visiting traders paid their tolls. The gatehouse has served over the years as prison, tailor's shop and museum.

Prehistoric Earthworks can be seen at Bulwark village and in Piercefield Park, on the southern outskirts.

36h St David's Head Fort: a small promontory stronghold with a stone rampart and earth banks. Within are several rock shelters and stone huts. Spectacular views.

36h Whitesand Bay. Remains of the wreck of the paddle tug *Guiding Star*, which foundered here in 1882. *Low tide only.*

Pentre Ifan Cromlech (38a)

36h St David's Bishop's Palace. Extensive remains of an elegant residence built during the late 13th and 14th centuries and which accurately reflects the immense wealth of contemporary prelates. *Daily from 0930 (winter Sundays from 1400).* ✝

37a Garn-fawr. Remains of an Iron Age hill fort, hut circles and other fortifications.

37b Fishguard: the town was the site of the last armed invasion of Britain, on 22 February 1797, when 1400 French troops and ex-convicts under American command landed at Carreg Wastad (37a). They had planned to take Bristol in the hope of starting a peasants' revolt, but unfavourable winds forced them into Fishguard, where they were promptly rounded up by locals, including a woman, Jemima Nicholson, who captured several with a pitchfork. This fiasco is commemorated in the Royal Oak Inn, the Square; also in the churchyard, where a stone recalls Ms Nicholson's achievements.

37c Cerrig-y-gof: unusual Bronze Age burial mound with 5 oblong chambers arranged in a circle.

37c Newport Castle. Built on a circular mound in the 13th century, this stronghold dominates the town's southern approaches. The gate tower and little else remains. *Interior not open.*

37c Carningli Common: remains of early Christian hut circles.

37d Mathry Burial Chamber: long tomb with 7 upright slabs supporting a stone lid. Once covered by an earth mound.

37f Tre-newydd: Parc-y-meirw. Row of prehistoric standing stones. Nearby is a typical stone burial chamber known as Coetan Arthur.

38a Newport Castle. See 37c.

38a Carningli Common: remains of early Christian hut circles.

38a Burial Chamber: Pentre Ifan Cromlech. Neolithic tomb, with the 17 ton, 16½ ft long capstone held 7½ ft off the ground by three standing stones. It was originally covered with an earth mound, but was excavated in 1936/37. *Any time. Free.*

38e Foeldrygarn Fort: an 11 acre hill fort dating from the Iron Age, when it controlled the eastern Presellys.

38h Meini Gwyr: Neolithic chambered tomb, with outer ring of stones set into an unusual raised ring.

39a Newcastle Emlyn Castle. Originally built in the 13th century, it was much altered in the 15th century by Rhys ap Thomas, who made it his country seat. It saw action during the Civil War, when Royalist troops resisted so staunchly that the Roundheads demolished the castle after their victory. Some walls and part of the gate are all that remain. *Any time. Free.*

39i Carmarthen: Castle, Bridge Street. Built by the Normans in 1109, it fell to Llywelyn the Great in 1215, being much extended thereafter. Edward I made it the centre of his administration of south-west Wales and the castle was improved constantly. In 1403 it again fell to the Welsh, this time under Owain Glyndwr, who held it for 6 years. Only the gateway and some towers remain, all built in the reign of Henry IV. *Any time. Free.*

Roman Fort. Recently excavated remains of Moridunum can be seen, along with the excavated site of the Roman amphitheatre.

40h Dryslwyn Castle. Once impressive stronghold built by the Welsh princes in the 13th century. It was reapeatedly attacked during the Anglo-Welsh wars in 1287, having its defences literally undermined by English sappers, several of whom died when part of the castle fell into their tunnels. *View from road or nearby riverside picnic site.*

40h Wenallt: Paxton's Tower. Triangular, triple-towered monument to Lord Nelson built in 1811.

40i Dynevor Castle. Beside the river is the ruined keep of the original stronghold, built in the 11th century. During the 17th century it was replaced by the castle to the north, which is still the family seat of Lord Dynevor. *Not open.*

41a Dolaucothi Roman Gold Mines. Exploitation started almost as soon as the Romans had conquered Wales, in about 80AD, initially using opencast methods, but later driving many tunnels deep into the hillsides. Most of the bullion went to the Imperial Mint at Lyons, France. Traces of the extensive aqueducts and water supply system can be seen. There are two marked trails with red or white markers, and children should be kept to these. Displays of material found during excavation can be seen in the museum at Abergwili (39i). *Weekdays 1000-1630. Free.* ♠ ⌷

41b Llandovery Castle: 11th century ruins in the grounds of the Castle Hotel (tel. 0550 20343 or 20660). The defences were built by Welsh and English forces, as the castle changed hands frequently during the campaigns of Edward I. *By permission of the hotel. Free.*

41f Roman Camps: Y Pigwyn. Sites of two military bases.

41g Y Gaer Fawr. Once one of the largest hill forts in Wales, enclosing 25 acres in single earth walls which have long since collapsed.

42f Y Gaer Roman Fort. The largest and most important of the inland Roman strongholds, it was founded in about 75AD to guard the crossroads of the main north-south and east-west roads through Wales. Parts of the south and east gateways remain, up to 8 ft high in places, together with traces of the fort buildings. *Free.*

42f Brecon Castle, grounds of Castle Hotel (tel. 0874 2942). Built by a half brother of William the Conqueror, it was frequently fought over during the Anglo-Welsh wars and during Owain Glyndwr's uprising. It stood until the Civil War, when the townspeople demolished it to spare themselves any part in the fighting. *By permission of the hotel. Free.*

43b Bronllys Castle. Remains of a round tower and some walls of a Norman dry moated stronghold, captured by the Welsh in 1233.

43c Hay on Wye: Hay Castle, now part of Booth's Booksellers in the town centre. Scant remains of an originally Norman fort burnt—along with the rest of the town—by King John in 1216. It was rebuilt by the Lancastrians in 1380 to 1421, but was blown up during the Civil War. A Jacobean manor was built on the site and this houses part of the bookshop. *Free.* ☆

43h Tretower Castle. This was a typical Norman motte and bailey affair, of which the round keep with its polygonal outer wall is the main feature. It last saw action during the Owain Glyndwr rising of 1403. *Daily from 0930 (Sundays PM).* 🔲

43i Crickhowell Castle. A 50 ft mound in the town centre first fortified by the Welsh, but captured and much improved by the Normans. *Free.*

Bridge. Notable for its unusual design, with 12 arches on one side and 13 on the other, an inequality introduced for structural reasons.

44g Abergavenny Castle. See 33c.

44i Llantilio Crosseny. See 34b.

46f Carregifan: remains of an ancient hill fort called Pendinaslochdyn.

46h Cardigan: Castle. Two small towers are almost all that remain of this fortress, built in 1240. Most of the site is now a private residence. *Not open.*

Teifi Bridge. Very old structure, dating from before 1136, when it was the scene of a famous victory by the Welsh over a Norman army.

48f Llanddewibrefi: St Davids Church. Contains inscribed stones dating from the 6th to 9th centuries. ✝

48g Lampeter: castle mounds. The sites of two fortresses: in the grounds of St David's College was a Norman castle destroyed in 1136; the other stood to the north, beside the old railway line.

49g Twm Sion Catti's Cave. Refuge used by the local version of Robin Hood, recently made even more famous by a television series. *Reached via Dinas Nature Trail.* ♠

50b Castellcollen. Remains of a Roman fort of the 1st century AD, finds from which can be seen in the Museum at Llandrindod Wells. It guarded the important road from Caersws (54b) to Y Gaer (42f).

50d Cilmery: roadside monument to Prince Llywelyn 'the Last', whose death in the 13th century at the hands of an English soldier marked the end of the Welsh dynasty.

50e Builth Wells Castle, near the Lion Hotel. The site was first fortified in the 12th century, but that castle was destroyed by Llywelyn the Last in 1260. New defences were built by Edward I and in 1282, Llywelyn was ambushed and killed nearby. The castle last saw action during the Glyndwr uprising and only traces remain. *Free.*

50i Llywelyn's Cave. Hiding place of Llywelyn the Last, the only native born Prince of Wales, who in 1282 was caught and killed near Builth Castle (50e).

51e Old Radnor Castle. Built in the 11th century, it led an active life thereafter: King John destroyed it in the 13th century; it was rebuilt by his son, Henry III; and it was finally ruined by Owain Glyndwr, who captured it during his uprising early in the 15th century.

51g Painscastle Castle. Remains of a traditional Norman motte and bailey castle, with extensive keep surrounded by deep double earth banks. *Free.*

51g Clyro Castle. Slight remains of a Norman castle built by William de Braose.

51h Hay-on-Wye. See 43c.

52d Aberystwyth: Castle, New Promenade. Built in 1277-1279 as part of Edward I's subjugation of Wales, it has an unusual diamond shape intended to best defend the rocky headland on which it stands. It was captured by Owain Glyndwr during his 15th century rising, but was recaptured by English troops under Prince Hal, later Henry V. The Civil War 200 years later saw it used as mint for King Charles, until the garrison surrendered to Cromwell's forces in 1646, after which the castle was abandoned. *Any time. Free.*

Pen Dinas, south of town, is a double Iron Age hill fort, whose earth defences were once supplemented by stone walls and a timber pallisade.

52g Monk's Cave. Legendary entrance of a secret tunnel leading to the Abbey of Strata Florida (49a), although the latter is some 15 miles inland! It is now choked with seaborne rubble and reached only by a rather daunting footpath down the cliffs.

53g The Arch, B4574. Stone monument celebrating the Golden Jubilee of George III in 1810.

54b Caersws Roman Fort. Built in 74-77AD, this fort stood at the hub of the Roman network in central Wales, with main roads leading south to Castell collen (50b) and Y Gaer (42f), west to Pennal (56i) and north to Chester. It was garrisoned by a 500-man cohort of Spanish troops, and measured about 200 yards square, with 40 ft wide ditches and 35 ft thick earth banks. Traces can be seen where the main road cuts through the northern part of the camp.

54c Abermule: Castell Dolforwyn. An important border fortress of Llywelyn the Last during his wars with Edward I. The English built their own castle less than half a dozen miles away, at Montgomery (59h). Only a few traces remain here at Dolforwyn, which means Maiden's Meadow. *Free.*

54i Crugyn: Castlelltinboeth. Remains of a mediaeval castle and ancient earth hill fort.

55e→h Offa's Dyke. This immense fortification runs almost the full length of Wales and is followed for much of its route by a well marked long distance footpath. It was built in 784AD by King Offa of Mercia, to protect his country from marauding Welsh tribes. This area boasts some of the best preserved sections, with banks still 30 ft high and ditches 15 ft deep in places.

56a Pen-y-ddinas is the site of an Iron Age camp, of which traces can still be seen.

Carneddau Hengwm, to the south east, is a prehistoric site with the remains of two chambered tombs and traces of two circles, one of earth, one of standing stones.

56c Dolgellau: Afon Wnion Bridge, carrying the old A470, was built in 1638. Also, near the town's primary school is an old toll house.

56d Owain Glyndwr's Cave, off A493 at Cae-du Farm and walk south on beach. Said to have been used by this most famous of Welsh princes when he was on the run from the English. In 1401-1408, he led a successful revolt against the English, capturing much of the Principality, but Henry IV eventually regained the ascendancy and Glyndwr died in hiding in 1416. *Low tide.*

56e Castell y Bere. Dramatically situated on a high rock outcrop, this fortress was built by Llywelyn the Last to a typically Welsh design, with a D-shaped tower at each end and without any of the mechanical devices (drawbridge, portcullis, etc.) which were a feature of so many English castles. It was much fought over during the Anglo-Welsh wars, being sacked by Edward I in 1283, retaken by Llywelyn and finally falling to the English in 1283; ten years later it was abandoned. Magnificent views. *Daily. Free.*

56g Tywyn: St Cadfan's Stone. The inscription on this 8th century stone is the oldest known example of the Welsh language. It translates as "The body of Cyngen lies underneath". It can be seen in St Cadfan's Church. *Daily. Free.* ✝

56h Mynydd-y-Llyn: Carn March Arthur. A fallen cairn bearing a mark like that of a giant hoofprint, said to have been made by King Arthur's horse.

59c Breidden. Remains of a hill fort with multiple ramparts, occupied from the Iron Age until the first Roman invasion in 57AD.

59g Rhydwhyman Ford. River crossing which was the traditional site of negotiations between the English and Welsh during their years of conflict.

59g Abermule: Castell Dolforwyn. See 54c.

59h Montgomery Castle. Perched high above the town on the site of earlier Norman fortifications, the castle was built in 1223 by Henry III. It saw much action during the campaigns of his son, Edward I, whose stubborn Welsh opponents had their own castle only 6 miles away at Castell Dolforwyn (59g). Montgomery was again the scene of fierce fighting during the Civil War, when its owners, the Herbert family, announced for the King. It was taken by the Roundheads in 1649 and subsequently demolished, so that little now remains. *Free.*

Lymore Park, south east of the town, has preserved sections of Offa's Dyke (see 55e).

60c Garn Boduan. Remains of an Iron Age hill fort and stone huts. Rubble on the summit is thought to have been a defensive site during the English invasion in the 13th century.

60c Carn Fadrum: prehistoric hill fort site on the 1217 ft summit.

60e Mynydd Rhiw: on the northern slopes are traces of a Stone Age 'axe factory'.

61b Llangybi: St Cybi's Well. Pool covered by a domed structure of dry stone, the only one of its kind in Wales. *Any time. Free.*

61b Penarth Fawr. Remains of a mediaeval hall, once part of a larger house. *Any time. Free.*

62c Tomen-y-Mur. Site of a Roman Fort in the 2nd century, with signs of stone ramparts and of the accompanying bath house and amphitheatre. Inside the fort area is the mound of a much later mediaeval castle.

62d Muriau'r Gwyddelod (Irishmen's Walls). Ancient site, dating back about 2000 years, with remains of hut circles within an enclosure whose walls are still 18 ft thick and 4 ft high in places. The name derives from legends that Irishmen once lived in north-west Wales. *Free.*

62e Cwmbychan 'Roman Steps'. Some 2000 stone steps built into the mountainside; their purpose is unknown, although one theory (which led to the name) is that they enabled Roman sentries to guard the high pass.

62h Pen-y-ddinas. See 56a.
Carneddau Hengwm. See 56a.

62i Dolgellau. See 56c.

63c Bala: Tomen-y-Bala (Bala Tump) in Mount Street, is thought to have been the mound of a mediaeval fortress.

Bardic Circle, The Green, is a stone ring erected in 1967 for the Royal National Eisteddfod celebrations.

63f Caer Gai Roman Fort. Ditches and other traces are all that remain. A 17th century farmhouse stands in the centre of the site, which has legendary connections with Sir Kay, one of King Arthur's knights. *By permission of the farm owner.*

64a Bala. See 63c.

65b Offa's Dyke. Traces of the huge rampart can be seen in the grounds of Chirk Castle. For details of the Dyke, see 55e. *Open as for Chirk Castle—see page 95.* ☞ 🚋 🏘

65e Sycharth Motte & Bailey. Although only the mound and some earthworks remain, this is an important site in the history of Wales, for on it stood the castle of Prince Owain Glyndwr, prime mover of the Welsh rebellion against the English early in the 15th century. Most of the buildings were wooden and the surrounding slopes were said to have been covered in vineyards. The castle was burnt down in 1403 by forces under the command of Prince Henry, then only 16 years old; Glyndwr was away at the time. *Private land; visits by permission only. Apply at Cottage opposite.*

66i Yr Eifl: Tre'r Ceiri Fort. Standing at a height of 1500 ft, this is one of the most impressive Iron Age fort sites in Britain, with dry stone ramparts and hut circles which remained in regular use until Roman times. *Any time. Free.*

67b Bodowyr-isaf Burial Chamber. A communal tomb dating from about 4000 years ago, with standing stones topped by an 8 ft by 6 ft capstone. In Neolithic times, it was covered by an earth mound. *Free.*

67b Segontium Roman Fort, Caernarfon. Built to perform the same task as Edward I's castle 12 centuries later, Segontium was founded in 78AD to control the Menai Strait and the foothills of Snowdon and it remained in use for 300 years. The basically square site was extensively excavated in 1921–1923 by the famous archaeologist Mortimer Wheeler, whose work revealed much of the fort's extensive history. When local tribes rebelled during the 2nd century, it was rebuilt in stone, with further additions in the 3rd century, but the major rebuilding programme came in the face of Irish raiders in 383AD and most of the surviving remains date from this period. They include all four gateways, a chapel with underground strongroom, the commander's house and a room with underfloor heating. Many finds from the site can be seen in the adjacent museum. *Daily from 0930 (Sundays from 1400).* ▣

67d Dinas Dinlle. Grassy mound which was fortified by the local tribe before the Roman invasion in the late 1st century.

67e Rhostryfan. The shell of a cottage stands as a memorial to Kate Roberts, whose Welsh language novels are still popular.

67f Dolbadarn Castle. Welsh stronghold of the 12th/13th centuries, thought to have been the work of Llywelyn the Great. It dominates the entrance to the strategic Llanberis Pass. The substantial remains include 3 towers, one 40 ft high, and 4 ft thick curtain walls. *Daily from 0930 (Sundays PM).*

67i Beddgelert: Grave of Gelert. Supposed resting place of Llywelyn the Great's dog Gelert, which he killed in a fit of temper. Despite modern proof that the tale was invented by an 18th century innkeeper looking for trade, the site still attracts thousands of tourists.

68a Dolbadarn Castle. See 67f.

68e Beddgelert. See 67i.

68i Tomen-y-Mur. See 62c.

69b Chambered Long Cairn. Neolithic triple burial chamber with curved dry stone walls. It is 140 ft long and was originally covered by earth. *Any time. Free.*

69i Bala. See 63c.

70b Brenig Reservoir: Archaeological Trail covering 7500 years of history, including Hen Ddinbych (Old Denbigh), a fortified site containing mediaeval stone buildings. Other trails, starting from the information centre on the lake's western shore, pass many sites of interest, such as a 16th century shepherds' hamlet, several Bronze Age burial mounds and a Stone Age camp site. *Daily.* ♣ ⋈ ℹ ⛺ ♪

70f Caer Drewyn. Site of an Iron Age hill fortress.

70g Bala. See 63c.

71c Caergwrle Castle. Slight remains of a Welsh stone castle captured by Edward I in 1282. The surrounding earthworks date from the Iron Age. *Any time. Free.*

71d Owain Glyndwr's Mount. Grassy hill on which stood one of the Welshman's early 15th century forts.

71e Pillar of Eliseg. Erected in the 9th century, this 8 ft stone cross bears a lengthy Latin inscription recording how, in 603AD, Eliseg defeated the invading Saxons. The monument was erected by his grandson and may also mark the spot where Eliseg is buried. *Free.*

71e Castell Dinas Bran. The remains of a well sited Welsh fortress, standing on a 1000 ft summit and making full use of the site's natural defences. It dates from the 8th century, when the invaders were Saxons, but again saw action during the later campaigns against the English who captured it during the 13th century. *Free.*

71e Llangollen: Dee Bridge. One of the traditional Seven Wonders of Wales, this stone bridge was built in the 12th century and widened in the 14th century. It has 4 pointed arches.

71i Offa's Dyke. See 65b.

72a Caergwrle Castle. See 71c.

74c Dinas Gynfor. The northernmost point of Wales, where can be seen traces of a prehistoric fortress.

74d Caer-y-Twr. Remains of a 17 acre prehistoric earth fort on the 720 ft summit of Holyhead Mountain.

74d Holyhead: Caer Gybi Roman Fort, enclosing St Cybi's Church. This small, but important, stronghold was built to defend the harbour from Irish raiders over 1500 years ago. The remains are still impressive, with rubble ramparts 15 ft high and 5 ft thick, and a 27 ft high tower at the north east corner. *Free.*

74d Cytiau'r Gwyddelod (Irishmen's Huts—see also 62d). Remains of a village inhabited in the 2nd to 4th centuries. *Any time. Free.*

74i Barclodiad y Gawres Chambered Cairn. Restored Neolithic tomb which is the only one in Britain known to contain examples of megalithic art—there are five carved stones. The name, incidentally, means "Apronful of the Giantess", and the tomb is at least 4000 years old. *Daily. Free.*

75b Point Linas. Remains of a 19th century semaphore signalling station, part of a chain between Holyhead and Liverpool by means of which news of ships' arrivals was passed to their owners.

75b Moelfre. On the cliffs above the bay stands a monument to the *Royal Charter*, one of the 114 ships wrecked off the Welsh coast during the infamous night of 25/26 October 1859, when a north east hurricane blew. Despite being only a few yards from the shore, the wreck of the *Royal Charter* claimed 459 lives, many of them returning Australian gold miners, so that £500,000 of bullion also sank.

75e Din Lligwy: Fortified Village. Well preserved site of an ancient British settlement of 350 to 385AD, including the remains of 9 substantial stone buildings, whose walls still stand up to 6 ft high. Thought to have been the home of an Anglesey chieftain. *Any time. Free.* ✝

Lligwy Cromlech, on the opposite side of the lane, is an impressive Stone Age burial chamber, topped by a huge, 28 ton capstone. Excavations revealed the bodies of over 30 people. *Any time. Free.*

75h Chambered Cairn: Bryn-celli-ddu. The best preserved megalithic monument in Wales, it consists of a 160 ft diameter mound covering a narrow passage leading to an 8 ft burial chamber. It was built about 4000 years ago and the chamber includes a mysterious standing stone. *Daily from 0930 (Sundays PM); key from farmhouse. Free.*

Bryn yr Hen Bobl, between A4080 and the Menai Strait, is a kidney-shaped burial mound with an unusual 320 ft terrace added on, thought to be a phallic symbol. ✿ ▣ ⌂

75i Plas Llanfair: The Marquess of Anglesey's Column. This 112 ft monument was erected in 1816 by locals in honour of the 1st Marquess' military achievements during the Napoleonic Wars. It is crowned by a 12 ft statue of the man himself, in his uniform as Colonel of the 7th Hussars. A staircase leads to the gallery beneath his feet. Half a mile south stands a statue to Nelson.

75i Beaumaris Gaol, Steeple Lane. Bearing witness to the harshness of prison life in Victorian Britain, this 1829 jail includes a wooden treadmill, punishment cell and the passage along which a condemned man walked to his gallows. Documentary exhibits of 19th century prison life. *July to September daily 1100-1800.*

76b Penmon Dovecote. Square building dating from about 1600, with domed vault and a great many nests. *Any time. Free.* ✝

76b Motte & Bailey: Castell Aberllienawg. Remains of an 11th century Norman castle, destroyed by the Welsh in 1095; the surviving stonework dates from the 17th century.

76d Beaumaris Gaol. See 75i.

76f Craig Llwyd: start of the Penmaenmawr History Trail, which takes in Bronze Age, Iron Age and mediaeval sites. The 3½ mile walk, over 1500 ft moorland, takes about 2½ hours. Leaflet available locally. *Free.*

Stone Circle, south of Craig Llwyd, also has the remains of a Stone Age flint 'workshop' area.

76f Cam-y-neint: start of the Llanfairfechan History Trail, which takes in the Roman road, ancient stone circles and standing stones, some of which are shown on the map. 4½ mile walk takes about 3 hours. Leaflets available locally. *Free.* ⋈

77a Deganwy Castle. Remains of the keep, gatehouse and curtain walls of a once-mighty Norman fortress built in 1245, but destroyed by Welsh forces under Llywelyn ap Gruffydd in 1263.

77d Conwy: Town Walls. Magnificent example of mediaeval engineering, covering 1400 yards with 21 towers. *May to September daily from 0930 (Sundays from 1400).*

77f Penycorddyn-mawr Fort. Strongly fortified Iron Age hill fort used until the Roman invasion, during which it was abandoned.

77g Llanrwst: Pont Fawr (Stone Bridge). Until the suspension bridge at Conwy was completed in 1826, this was the major crossing point over the River Conwy. Built in 1636, it has 3 graceful arches totalling 169 ft.

78b Dyserth Castle. Built by the English in 1241, it was captured and totally destroyed by Llywelyn the Last in 1263, so that only traces remain.

78b Gop Hill: the largest prehistoric cairn in Wales is on the summit. It measures 350 ft across, stands 46 ft high, and is built entirely of dry stones.

78b Offa's Dyke: visible section south of A5151. See also 55e.

78d Cefn Caves. Relics of prehistoric man, together with the bones of now-extinct animals have been found here. They are thought to be over 50,000 years old.

78h Denbigh: Town Walls. Remains include one of the ancient gatehouses.

79e Flint Castle. The earliest of Edward I's chain of Welsh strongholds, it was completed late in the 13th century and is unique among Edward's castles in having a remote keep—a huge round tower intended as a last-ditch refuge built on what was then an island and linked to the main castle by drawbridge. Although probably best known as the scene of Act III of Shakespeare's Richard II, Flint Castle saw plenty of real action during the Civil War, changing hands several times before finally surrendering in 1646 to Roundhead forces, who then demolished it. *Daily from 0930 (Sundays PM).*

79h Ewloe Castle. This small Welsh castle, with its distinctive D-shape tower, was built in the early 13th century by Llywelyn the Great, being expanded soon afterwards by Llywelyn the Last, who included several Norman features. The site was significant for the Welsh, for it was in the surrounding woods in 1157 that they had defeated Henry II. *March to September daily from 0930 (Sundays PM). October to February any time. Free in winter.*

79i Hawarden Old Castle. Standing on the first high ground on the Welsh side of the border, the existing fortress was built by Edward I on a site fortified since prehistoric times. The castle was often attacked by the Welsh, forcing the English to replace its original wooden defences with stonework, and it was twice captured during the Civil War. A good portion of the keep survives. *Easter to mid September: weekends and Bank Holidays 1400-1730.*

Museums and Art Galleries

Collections of almost every size and kind are listed here, other than those of a purely industrial nature, which are described in the section on Industry Past & Present on pages 103-107. Many stately homes also contain fine collections of objets d'art and these are detailed under Historic Buildings (pages 96-97).

20c Llanelli: **Parc Howard Museum,** off A476 to Llandeilo (tel. 055 42 2029). Mansion house with paintings, porcelain and sculpture and items of local interest. *Daily 1000-1600 (1900 April to October).* ↓T

21e Swansea: **Royal Institution of South Wales Museum,** Victoria Road (tel. 0792 53763). The oldest public museum in Wales, it includes an extensive archeology collection in a modern gallery, with notable items from prehistoric and Roman times and an Egyptology section; also a valuable art collection, with many works depicting 18th and 19th century Swansea. Childrens' quizzes. *Monday to Saturday 1000-1630.*

Glynn Vivian Art Gallery and Museum, Alexandra Road (tel. 0792 55006). Drawings and painting by old masters, modern British art including paintings and sculpture, fine ceramics collection, plus programmes of dancing, poetry, lectures and concerts. *Monday to Saturday 1030-1730. Free.*

Attic Gallery, 61 Wind Street (tel. 0792 53387). Paintings, lithographs and etchings, including many by contemporary British artists. *Weekdays 1000-1700; Saturdays 1000-1300. Free.*

Maritime and Industrial Museum, South Dock (tel. 0792 50351). Converted warehouse housing displays depicting the history of Swansea. *Monday to Saturday 1030-1730. Free.* ↓T

Dylan Thomas Uplands Trail covers 2 miles in the Uplands district of Swansea, 1 mile north west of the city centre. Thomas was born at 5 Cwmdonkin Drive, Uplands. Takes about 2 hours. Leaflet available locally. *Free.*

21e University College of Swansea, Singleton Park, 2 miles west of city (tel. 0792 25678 ext 578). Regular visiting art exhibitions. *During term time: October to June weekdays 0900-1700; Saturdays 0900-1200. Free.*

The Wellcome Collection, University College. Over 2000 objects, mostly from Ancient Egypt, dating from prehistoric to Christian times. *By arrangement only during term times: October to June weekdays 0900-1700.*

22b Margam Park (tel. Port Talbot 063 96 87626). Small Abbey Museum houses collection of ancient stone crosses and memorials. *Weekends, Wednesdays and Bank Holidays 1400-1700 (1600 in winter).* 🍺♣✳︎✝

22e Porthcawl Museum, Old Police Station, John Street. (tel. 065 671 6639). Collection of local exhibits housed in the Information Office. *Weekdays 1430-1630; Saturdays 1000-1200, 1430-1630.*

23f St Fagan's: Welsh Folk Museum (tel. Cardiff 0222 569441). Part of the museum is in a restored Elizabethan manor, which includes displays of furniture and household equipment, but the grounds also contain an outstanding collection of reconstructed buildings containing a whole range of exhibits depicting life in Wales over several centuries. The main block includes an impressive Costume Gallery. *Monday to Saturday 1000-1700; Sundays 1430-1700.* 🍺🎪↓T

24d St Fagans: Welsh Folk Museum. See 23f (above).

24e Cardiff: National Museum of Wales, Cathay's Park (tel. 0222 397951). Extensive museum with collections and exhibitions in archaeology, art, botany, geology, industry, and zoology. The emphasis is on Welsh history and items, with bi-lingual labels backing up the bias, but there are important collections of European painting (including work by Augustus John, Cezanne, Rubens, Renoir, Monet, Poussin and others) and of modern glassware

(notably the unique collection of Maurice Marinot). Specialised library; bookshop; lectures and concerts. *Monday to Saturday 1000-1700; Sundays 1430-1700. Free.* ☕

Welch Regiment Museum, Cardiff Castle (tel. 0222 29367). Display of militaria, including the colour of the 4th US Infantry, captured by the regiment at Detroit in 1812. *Daily 1000-1800 (1600 in winter).* 🎪

Chapter Centre for the Arts, Market Road, off Cowbridge Road East (tel. 0222 396061). Touring exhibitions plus workshops where artists and art restorers can be seen at work. *Gallery: weekdays 1200-2200; Saturdays 1400-2100. Free.* 🍺 ↓T

The Albany Gallery, 74B Albany Road (tel. 0222 487158). Private gallery with monthly exhibitions, usually by Welsh artists. *Monday to Saturday 1030-1730 (but closed Wednesday PM). Free.*

Oriel Art Gallery, 53 Charles Street (tel. 0222 395548). Fortnightly exhibitions by Welsh artists; poetry reading; folk music; specialist bookshop. *Daily 0930-1730. Free.*

Sherman Theatre Gallery, University College, Senghennydd Road (tel. 0222 396844). Monthly touring exhibitions. *Monday to Saturday 1000-2200 (closed August). Free.* 🍺

24h Penarth: **Turner House Art Gallery,** Plymouth Road (tel. Cardiff 0222 708870). A branch gallery of the National Museum in Cardiff, it displays selections of paintings and other items from the main collection. *Tuesday to Saturday and Bank Holiday Mondays 1100-1245, 1400-1700; Sundays PM. Free.*

25a Newport: **Museum and Art Gallery,** John Frost Square (tel. 0633 840064). Displays of natural history, geology and art, including early English water colours, British oil paintings and Pontypool and Usk Japan ware. Also local history material, including items from the Roman town at Caerwent (25c) and relics of the Chartist Riots of 1839. *Weekdays 1000-1730; Saturdays 0930-1600. Free.*

Civic Centre, Godfrey Road (tel. 0633 65491). The Main Hall contains impressive murals. *Weekdays 0830-1630.*

25a Caerleon: **The Legionary Museum,** High Street (tel. 0633 421462). Contains items found on the site of Isca, the fortress of the 2nd Augustan Legion. *Daily 0930-1730 (winter Sundays 1400-1700). Free.* �🏛

25c Caldicot Castle (tel. 0291 420241). Collection of furniture and 18th century costumes; art gallery in the Woodstock Tower. *March to October daily PM.* ♣🎪

27a Haverfordwest: **Pembrokeshire County Museum,** The Castle (tel. 0437 3708). Display of local history from earliest times, including a fascinating poaching section; art gallery housing regular touring exhibitions; the Pembroke Yeomanry collection of military uniforms. *Monday to Saturday 1000-1730 (winter 1100-1600). Free.*

Library Hall, Dew Street (tel. 0437 2070). Frequent touring exhibitions, many sponsored by the Welsh Arts Council. *Monday to Saturday 1000-1700. Free.*

27b Picton Castle: **Graham Sutherland Gallery** (tel. Rhos 043 786 296). Valuable collection of about 130 paintings, sketches, etchings and lithographs donated by the artist. Most of the work was inspired by the local scenery. *April to end September: Tuesday to Thursday, weekends and Bank Holidays 1030-1230, 1330-1730. October to end March weekends 1400-1700. Free. (Castle is not open).* ♣✳︎

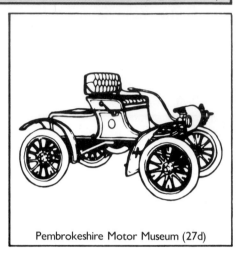

Pembrokeshire Motor Museum (27d)

27c Blackpool Mill (tel. Llawhaden 099 14 233). Small museum containing paperwork and documents connected with the old tidal mill. *Easter to September daily 1100-1800.* 🍺 ↓T

27d Pembroke Dock: **Pembrokeshire Motor Museum,** Garrison Theatre (tel. 064 63 3279). Traces the history of road transport since 1860, with early bicycles, an 1896 horse drawn fire engine, a 1903 Oldsmobile (used on the London to Brighton run), a replica of a 1920s country garage, period costumes, toys, an amphibious car and a hovercraft. *Easter to 30 September: Sunday to Friday 1000-1800.*

28g Tenby: **Castle Hill Museum** (tel. 0834 2809). Notable collections of geology, archaeology, natural history, maps, pictures, etc., all from the area; collection of marine shells; small art gallery. *Daily 1000-1800 (1600 in winter; closed Fridays and Sundays in winter).*

North Beach Art Gallery. *Daily in summer.*

29f Llanelli. See 20c.

30d Llanelli. See 20c.

30h Swansea. See 21e.

31b Dan-yr-Ogof Caves: **Geological Museum** (tel. Abercrave 063 977 284). Minerals, fossils and exceptional photographs of caves and cave preservation. *Easter to end October daily from 1000. Free.* 🍺🍴ℹ︎☆

31h Welsh Miners' Museum, Afan Argoed Country Park (tel. Cymmer 063 983 564). Simulated coal faces, plus collections of photographs and documents illustrating the history of Welsh coal mining. Also guided walks, film shows and lectures. *April to October: daily 1030-1830; rest of year weekends only 1200-1700.* 🍺♣🍴

32e Cyfartha Castle Museum and Art Gallery (tel. Merthyr Tydfil 0685 3112). Collection of 19th century paintings, items from the Roman occupation, valuable silver, coins and medals, plus some natural history and local objects. *Weekdays 1000-1300, 1400-1800 (1700 in winter); Sundays 1400-1700. Free on Monday to Saturday.* 🐘

33c Abergavenny: **Castle Museum,** Castle Street (tel. 0873 4282). Charming little museum in a 19th century cottage, with local crafts, a farmhouse kitchen, costumes, old prints and agricultural tools. Children's quiz corner. *Monday to Saturday 1100-1700; also March to October Sundays 1430-1700.*

The Welsh Gallery, above W H Smith, 18 Cross Street (tel. 0873 4023). Permanent display of hand made furniture in oak and ash; exhibitions of Welsh painting and sculpture; also regular one man shows by leading professional Welsh artists. *Monday to Saturday: 0900-1300, 1400-1730 (Thursdays AM only). Free.*

33i Cwmbran: Llantarnam Grange Arts Centre (tel. 063 33 3321). Local and visiting exhibitions throughout the year. *Only during exhibitions: Monday to Saturday 1000-1700; Sundays 1430-1700. Free.*

33i Newport. See 25a.

34a Abergavenny. See 33c.

34a Llanvapley: Rural Crafts Museum, on B4233 (tel. Llantilio 060 085 210). Collection of old agricultural and farmhouse tools, plus items used in country crafts. *February to November Sundays 1500-1800 (or dusk).* ↓T

34c Monmouth: Local History Centre, Market Hall, Priory Street (tel. 0600 3519). Displays depicting the history of Monmouth. Guide to local buildings available. *Monday to Saturday 0900-1700; Sundays 1415-1715 (later in summer). Free.*

Nelson Collection, at the same address, contains a selection of documents, equipment, models and pictures. *Monday to Saturday 1030-1300, 1400-1700; Sundays PM (later in summer).*

34f Wolves Newton Folk Museum (tel. 029 15 231). Collection of domestic and agricultural implements; complete Victorian bedroom; pottery collection; visiting exhibitions. Housed in unique cross-shaped barns. *Easter to end September daily 1100-1800; October to Easter Sundays 1400-1730.* ↓T

34g Cwmbran. See 33i.

34g Caerleon. See 25a.

34g Newport. See 25a.

34i Caldicot Castle. See 25c.

35d Tintern Abbey: Exhibition Gallery (tel. 029 18 251). Photographic display illustrating the history of the abbey and its preservation; collection of prehistoric bones and flints, plus some Roman remains found on the site; also items connected with visits to the abbey by Wordsworth, Turner and others. *Daily from 0930 (winter Sundays from 1400).* ✿ ✝

35g Chepstow: Museum, Bridge Street (tel. 029 12 5981). Displays of local history, including shipbuilding and agriculture; notable salmon fishery exhibition. Free children's worksheets. *March to October: Monday to Saturday 1100-1300, 1400-1700; Sundays PM.*

37h Scolton Manor: Country Park Museum (tel. Haverfordwest 0437 3708). Late Georgian manor housing large exhibition hall with displays of local and natural history. Study centre. *Summer only: Telephone for times. Free.* ✿ ✿ ⌂

37h Treffgarne: Nant-y-Coy Mill and Museum (tel. 043 787 686). Collection of farmhouse furnishings, Victoriana, ornaments and china. Nature walk

Tom Norton Bicycle Collection (50b)

with historical and geological interest. *June to August daily 1000-1700.* ☕ 🛈

39b Dre-fach: Museum of the Welsh Woollen Industry (tel. Velindre 0559 370453). Exhibition tracing the development of the industry from the Middle Ages to modern times, contained within a working mill. *1 April to 30 September: Monday to Saturday 1000-1700 (closed May Day). Free.* ↓T

39c Llandyssul: Maesllyn Woollen Mill Museum (tel. Rhydlewis 023 975 251). Working museum in a mill founded in 1881. Guided tours. Children's play area. *Monday to Saturday 1000-1800; Sundays 1400-1800.* ✿ ⌂

39i Abergwili: Carmarthen Museum, Old Bishop's Palace (tel. 0267 31691). Newly completed and well laid out, with displays of prehistoric, Roman and mediaeval history, Welsh costumes, geology, crafts and industry. *Monday to Saturday 1000-1630. Free.*

40g Abergwili. See 39i (above).

41i Dan-yr-Ogof Caves. See 31b.

42f Brecon: Brecknock Museum, Captain's Walk (tel. 0874 4121). Collections of local and natural history, archaeology, geology, agricultural and domestic items; library and archives; reconstructed Assize Court; costume gallery. Exhibits include a 1200 year old dug-out canoe. *Monday to Saturday 1000-1700. Free.*

The South Wales Borderers Museum, The Barracks (tel. 0874 3111 ext 310). Covers the history of the 24th Regiment from 1689 to 1969, with over 1000 medals awarded to members of the regiment, including 16 Victoria Crosses; other rooms devoted to relics and photographs; impressive Zulu War display. *Weekdays 0900-1300, 1400-1700; also April to September weekends and Bank Holidays 1100-1300, 1400-1900.*

43e Trefecca: Howell Harris Museum, Chapel Block, Trefecca College (tel. Talgarth 087 481 423 or 241) Collection of rare books, furniture, prints and other items (including a pulpit) associated with the 18th century religious revivalist whose community was based here. *Daily 1100-1700. Free.* ☕

44g Abergavenny. See 33c.

46i Blaenporth: Old School Studio Gallery (tel. Aberporth 0239 810482). Working studio with exhibition gallery and shop. *Daily 0930-1900.*

50b Llandrindod Wells: Tom Norton's Collection, Automobile Palace, Temple Street (tel. 0597 22147). Unique and valuable collection of cycles and tricycles dating from 1869 to 1938. *Monday to Saturday 0800-1800. Free.*

Llandrindod Museum, War Memorial Gardens, Temple Street (tel. 0597 2212). Archeological displays include items from nearby Castellcollen Roman Fort; also the Paterson Doll Collection, a Victorian Spa gallery with costumes and chemist's equipment, and a large dug-out boat. *Weekdays 1000-1230, 1400-1700; also May to September Saturdays. Free.*

52b Tre'r Ddol: Yr Hen Gapel, off A487. Branch museum of the Welsh Folk Museum, with displays depicting 19th century religious life in Wales. *April to September: Monday to Saturday 1000-1700. Free.*

52b Aberdovey: Outward Bound Sailing Museum, the waterfront. Small collection of maritime material, including sailors' tools, ropework, photographs, drawings, instruments, Lifeboat equipment and model ships. *Summer only — irregular hours (check at nearby information office).*

52d Aberystwyth: National Library of Wales, Penglais Road (tel. 0970 3816). One of Britain's 6 copyright libraries — they each receive a copy of every new book published — this extensive building now houses over 2 million books in many languages, especially Celtic and Welsh. Also on display are valuable manuscripts, prints, music, drawings and old deeds. Exhibitions (May to October) in the Gregynog Gallery and Central Hall. *Weekdays 0930-1800; Saturdays 0930-1700. Free.*

Aberystwyth Yesterday, St Paul's, Upper Great Darkgate Street (tel. 0970 617119). Everything in this Victorian Methodist Hall is connected with Aberystwyth, having been lovingly collected by a lifelong resident of the town. Among the star items are 300 hats, clothing and a complete Victorian shop (located 50 yards away) with price labels, etc. *April to October: Monday to Saturday 1100-2000. Children free.*

Arts Centre Gallery, University College of Wales, Penglais (tel. 0970 4277). Small display of museum ceramics, plus visiting exhibitions of painting and sculpture. *Daily 1000-1700. Free.*

Ceredigion Museum, 14 Vulcan Street (tel. 0970 7911). Mainly local items, including a reconstructed 1850 cottage interior, plus folk and industrial items. *Weekdays 1100-1300, 1400-1700; Saturdays PM.*

Welsh Folk Museum (23f)

Oriel 700 Gallery, Corporation Street. Workers' co-operative offering displays of members' art and crafts, plus that of others. *Summer: daily 1100-1700.*

53f Llanidloes: Museum of Local History and Industry, Old Market Hall. Half timbered 16th century building with museum on its upper floor. Displays include relics of the 1839 Chartist riots. *Easter week; then Spring Bank Holiday to 30 September daily; 1100-1300, 1400-1700. Free.*

54c Newtown: Davies Memorial Gallery, town centre (tel. 0686 26220). Touring exhibitions only. *Weekdays 0900-1700. Free.*

W H Smith, town centre. This branch of the famous newsagents and booksellers has been thoroughly restored to its original 1920 style, with solid oak facade, plus the 'Ladies' bookstall'. *Normal shop hours; early closing Thursdays. Free.*

Textile Museum, Commercial Street (tel. 0686 26243). Documents, pictures and maps, plus machinery and buildings depicting 19th century weaving. *April to October: Tuesday to Saturday 1400-1630 (AM by appointment).* ↓T

54d Llanidloes. See 53f.

56a Barmouth: RNLI Maritime Museum, Pen-y-Cei, The Quay (tel. 0341 280253). The story of lifeboats in Wales, with models, photographs, equipment, honours and records of rescue missions. *Easter weekend, then Spring Bank Holiday to mid September: Monday to Saturday 1100-1300, 1400-1600, 1900-2100; Sundays PM and evening. Free, but donations welcome.*

56e Abergynolwyn: Village Museum, 14 Water Street. Over 200 relics of the time when this village was a busy slate mining town. *Summer: Monday to Saturday and Bank Holidays 1100-1800.*

56h Aberdovey. See 52b.

59e Welshpool: Powysland Museum, A458 (tel. 0938 3001). Displays the history of the region through archeology, agriculture, crafts and domestic items. Star exhibits include an Iron Age shield and a model guillotine. *Weekdays 1100-1300, 1400-1700 (closed winter Wednesdays); Saturdays 1400-1630. Free.*

61b Llanystumdwy: Lloyd George Memorial Museum, A497 (tel. Criccieth 076 671 2654). Documents, awards and other memorabilia from the life of the famous Liberal peer, who was prime minister from 1916 to 1922. *Spring Bank Holiday to 30 September: weekdays 1000-1700.*

62a Porthmadog: Maritime Museum, The Harbour. Display of 19th century harbour life in a restored sailing boat. *April to September daily 1000-1800.*

62d Harlech: Theatr Ardudwy, A496 (tel. 076 673 667). Series of exhibitions in the foyer arranged by the Coleg Harlech Arts Centre. *Monday to Saturday 1000-1700. Free.*

65a Glyn Ceiriog: Memorial Institute, High Street. Small museum with memorial windows to 3 Welsh poets and a tablet commemorating Thomas Jefferson and the American Declaration of Independence. *Monday to Saturday 1300-2100. Free.*

67b Caernarfon: Segontium Museum, Llanbeblig Road, A4085. Displays of material from the site of the famous Roman fort, on whose site it stands; items include an impressive inscribed altar to Minerva. *Daily from 0930 (Sundays from 1400).* �m

Museum of the Royal Welch Fusiliers, Caernarfon Castle (tel. 0286 3362). Traces the history of the regiment since 1689 with a wide range of fascinating militaria, including a 16 lb

Russian gun, a collection of medals with 8 Victoria Crosses, the Keys of Corunna, portraits, clothing and a life size tableau. *Daily from 0930 (winter Sundays from 1400). Free after paying castle entry.* ▮

68f Blaenau Ffestiniog: Gloddfa Ganol Mountain Tourist Centre, A470 (tel. 076 681 664). Museum, Exhibition Hall, restored cottages, etc., showing life in the slate quarries of 1800 to 1960. *Easter to October: daily 1000-1730.* ☕ ↓T 🅿 ☆

Llechwedd Slate Caverns (tel. 076 681 306). Exhibition of Victorian photographs, audio-visual slide show and tableaux show life in these 19th century quarries. *March to October: daily 1000-1800.* ☕ ↓T 🅿

68g Porthmadog. See 62a.

69b Betws-y-Coed: Gallery (tel. 069 02 432). Specialises in landscapes by local artists, with work in water colour, oil, ink and pencil. *Daily 1000-1700 (later in summer). Free.*

71c Bwlch-gwyn: North Wales Geology Museum (tel. Wrexham 0978 757573). Includes a 'time tunnel' depicting the development of the region over 600 million years; also a display of dinosaurs, a 'stone garden' and geology trail. *Easter to October: weekdays 0900-1700; also weekends and Bank Holidays in summer 1100-1730.* ☕ 🍴 ↓T

71h Glyn Ceiriog. See 65a.

72d Wrexham: Library and Arts Centre, Rhosddu Road (tel. 0978 261932). Visiting exhibitions, some from the major London museums; also local art displays. *Weekdays 1000-1730; Saturdays 1000-1600. Free.*

75h Plas Newydd (tel. Llanfairpwll 0248 714795). National Trust Military Museum contains relics of the Marquess of Anglesey's campaigns, while the house itself contains much else of artistic and historical interest. *Easter to late October: Sunday to Friday and Bank Holiday weekend Saturdays; 1230-1700.* ☕ ❋ 🅟

75i Bangor: Museum of Welsh Antiquities, Ffordd Gwynedd (tel. 0248 51151 ext 437). Collection of prehistoric and Roman items, furniture, clothing, crafts, maps and prints; also exhibits connected with Thomas Telford. *Monday to Saturday 1030-1630.*

The Art Gallery, housed in the above building (tel. 0248 53368), has monthly exhibitions of modern paintings and sculpture. *Monday to Saturday 1030-1700. Free.*

David Windsor Gallery, 201 High Street (tel. 0248 4639). Permanent displays of 18th to 20th century paintings, also porcelain, etchings, lithographs, engravings and old maps. *Mondays, Tuesdays and Thursday to Saturday: 1000-1300, 1400-1730. Free.*

75i Menai Bridge: Museum of Childhood, Water Street (tel. 0248 712001). Fabulous collection covering 150 years of children's interests, with many rare and valuable items. There are 6 rooms containing: 1) toy savings boxes, some of which gobble up coins in complicated ways; 2) dolls, educational toys and games; 3) an art gallery with pictures, prints and needlework of and by children; 4) a selection of pottery, glassware and commemoratives; 5) mechanical toys, including clockwork cars and trains; 6) music boxes, magic lanterns and wonderful old arcade machines, which take modern coins—see the mummies and treasures of Egypt reveal themselves on the 1923 "King Tut's Tomb", for example. *Easter to end October: Monday to Saturday 1000-1730; Sundays 1300-1700. Other times by arrangement with the curator.*

Tegfryn Art Gallery, Cadnant Road (tel. 0248 712437). Private gallery displaying paintings and sculpture by prominent North Wales artists. *Daily 1000-1300, 1400-1800. Free.*

76d Bangor. See 75i.

76d Menai Bridge. See 75i.

76d Penrhyn Castle (tel. Bangor 0248 53084).

Collection of over 1000 dolls from all over the world in a marble castle with much else to offer. *April, May and October daily 1400-1700; June to end September and all Bank Holiday weekends 1100-1700.* ☕ ❋ ▮ 🅟 ↓T

77a Llandudno: Doll Museum, Masonic Street (tel. 0492 76312). Collection of over 1000 dolls, plus toys, prams and many other items depicting fashion through the ages. Working model railway in separate room. *Easter to end September: Monday to Saturday 1000-1300, 1400-1730; Sundays PM.*

Rapallo House Museum and Art Gallery, Fferm Bach Road, Craig-y-Don, east of town centre (tel. 0492 76517). Paintings, porcelain, sculpture, bronzes, Roman relics, arms and armour and a restored Welsh kitchen. Guided tours. *April to end October: weekdays 1000-1245, 1400-1600 (1700 in summer)* ❋

Mostyn Gallery, 12 Vaughan Street (tel. 0492 79201). Visual arts centre, with exhibitions of contemporary British and foreign works; also lectures and films. *Tuesday to Saturday 1100-1700. Free.*

77b Colwyn Bay: New Colwyn Gallery, 26A Penrhyn Road (tel. 0492 44302). Monthly exhibitions by North Wales artists; also prints. *Mondays, Tuesdays and Thursday to Saturday 1000-1300, 1430-1700. Free.*

77d Conwy: Visitor Centre, Rosehill Street (tel. 049 263 6288). Good starting point for tourists, with displays of the town's busy history; also film shows, Welsh crafts and a bookshop. *March to December: Monday to Saturday and summer Sundays 0930-1730 (2130 summer).*

Royal Cambrian Academy of Art, Plas Mawr, High Street (tel. 049 263 3413). Elizabethan town house with regular art shows, notably the academy's annual Summer Exhibition from June to September. *April to September daily 1000-1730; October to March daily 1000-1630* ☕

The Conwy Exhibition, Aberconwy House, at the junction of Castle Street and High Street (tel. 049 263 2246). The history of the borough from Roman times to the present day is depicted in this mediaeval house. *April to end September daily 1000-1730, but closed on Wednesdays in April and May; other dates by appointment.* 🅟

77g Llanrwst: Encounter—The North Wales Museum of Wildlife, From Ganol, School Bank Road (tel. 0492 640664). The British Empire Trophy Collection of big game victims; also examples of Snowdonia wildlife and rare birds from all over the world. *Easter to September: daily 1100-1600 (later in summer). Other times by appointment.* ☕ ☆

78e St Asaph Cathedral Museum, High Street (tel. 0745 583429). Collection of documents, silver, seals and ancient books; also weapons and tools unearthed locally; letters from Dickens, Darwin, Trollope Florence Nightingale and others. *Daily by request. Free.* ✝

78h Denbigh Castle Museum. Displays illustrating the campaigns and castles of Edward I. Denbigh in mediaeval times, mediaeval warfare, and the people and events of later years. *Daily from 0930 (winter Sundays from 1400). Free after paying to enter castle.* ▮

79d Holywell: The Grange Cavern Military Museum, The Holway (tel. 0352 713455). Large collection of vehicles and militaria in an underground setting. Amusements. *Daily 0900-1730.* 🄿

79g Mold: Daniel Owen Centre, Earl Road (tel. 0352 4791). Exhibition gallery and memorial room to the 19th century Welsh novelist, with manuscripts and personal items; also exhibitions by local artists and organisations. *Weekdays 0930-1900; Saturdays 0930-1230. Free.*

Theatr Clwyd (tel. 0352 56331). Modern Entertainment and arts complex with 3 theatres and exhibition areas with changing displays. *Daily.* ☕

Castles

Only complete military fortifications or substantially complete ruins are included here; lesser remains are listed as Historical Sites (pages 86-89). Where castles also have notable interiors, further details can be found in the section on Historic Buildings (pages 96-97).

20e Weobley Castle. Well-fortified manor house built in the 13th and 14th centuries with many different-shaped towers and high, crenellated walls. It was badly damaged during the rising by Owain Glyndwr, but was restored and modified in Tudor times. Attractive setting. *Daily from 0930 (Sundays PM).*

20f Penrice Castle. Largest of the Gower castles, although little remains inside the extensive curtain walls; two towers, the gatehouse, a number of bastions and the 3-storey keep form part of the walls, all dating from the 12th/13th centuries. *Written appointment only:* Mr C Methuen-Campbell, Penrice Castle, Penrice, Gower, West Glamorgan.

New Castle (tel. 044 122 207), nearby, is a Georgian mansion.

20f Pennard Castle. The most impressive castle in Gower, these extensive 13th century remains stand high on a windswept cragg, best seen from the north. Twin gate towers and 60 ft long great hall. *Any time. Free.*

21d Oystermouth Castle, Mumbles (tel. Swansea 0792 50821 ext 2815). Although the site was fortified long beforehand, the existing Norman castle dates from about 1280. It was visited by Edward I in 1284 during his subjugation of Wales, although the castle was badly damaged the following year when fighting broke out again. The castle was rebuilt, however, and some parts were added early in the 14th century. *June to August daily 1100-1730; rest of year weekdays 1100-1530.* ♠

23g St Donat's Castle. Built in the 14th century, but restored and converted to an international college (tel. 044 65 2530). Ex-home of American newspaper tycoon William Randolph Hearst. *Open occasionally.*

23h Beaupre Castle. Ruined Elizabethan manor house with Italian-style doorways. (tel. Cardiff 0222 62131). *Any reasonable time. Free.*

24a Caerphilly Castle. One of the major castles of Britain, covering 30 acres (only Windsor is larger). Built between 1271 and 1326, it is one of the finest examples of mediaeval defensive planning, with extensive water and land defences. Much of the castle is in fine condition and parts have been restored. It was built by the Normans to defend the approaches to Cardiff from the Welsh, and was militarily unimportant after the 14th century. The famous leaning tower was the result of attempts by Oliver Cromwell to blow up the castle in the 17th century, to prevent possible use by the Royalists. *Daily from 0930 (winter Sundays from 1400).*

24d Castell Coch. Although based on 13th century foundations, this small Gothic castle was designed by the imaginative Victorian architect William Burges and features a fairy-tale concoction of every feature one might expect in a real castle. The interior is richly decorated, much of it with scenes from Aesop's fables or Greek mythology. *Daily from 0930 (winter Sundays from 1400).*

24a Cardiff Castle (tel. 0222 31279). Like Castell Coch (24d), this is an elaborate creation of William Burges, with lavishly-decorated rooms reflecting Victorian ideas of mediaeval chivalry and romance. The castle also has historical significance, however: a Roman fort occupied the site before the Normans built a castle there in 1090, parts of which still stand, notably the keep. It played an important part in Welsh history when, in 1158, Ifor Bach kidnapped the Norman lord from the keep and held him until the local people had been

compensated for injustices by the Norman invaders. Conducted tours on the hour. *March, April and October daily 1000-1200, 1400-1600; May to September daily 1000-1230, 1400-1700; November to February 1100-1500.* ☕ ▣ ⌂

25b Penhow Castle (tel. 0633 400800). This compact fortified manor house, now the oldest inhabited castle in Wales, was built as a border fortress by the Normans early in the 12th century. Many later additions include the 15th century great hall. Magnificent views from ramparts. Now being fully restored. Guided tours. *Good Friday to September, Wednesday to Sunday 1000-1800.* ⌂

25c Caldicot Castle (tel. 0291 420241). Started by the Normans in 1100, it was completed by Thomas Woodstock, sixth son of Edward III, in 1396. Features from throughout those years remain, notably the 14th century great gateway, whose towers have been restored. Used by Prince Hal (later Henry V) when he was Lord of Monmouth. The castle now supplies an appropriate setting for Welsh mediaeval banquets. *March to October: castle open daily PM; banquets Monday to Saturday evenings* (tel. 0291 421425). ♠ ▣ ⌷

27f Carew Castle. One of the most attractive castles in Wales, the present structure was begun in 1270, replacing an earlier Norman fort. It was enlarged by the Tudors in the 15th century, was the scene of a great tournament in 1507, but was badly damaged during the Civil War. The massive fortifications are architecturally interesting. *Interior closed for restoration.* ⌂ ⌷ ⌇

27h Pembroke Castle (tel. 064 63 4585). This monument to mediaeval military architecture is impressively sited on a rocky spur above the town. The inner bailey was built in 1093, soon after which the Norman defenders withstood a long siege by the Welsh. Despite its substantial appearance, little remains of the interior, although the 75 ft high keep still stands, with its 16 ft thick walls, circular rooms and unusual domed stone roof. The massive castle was once the hub of a 14-miles-wide defensive system. It is the only castle in Britain built over a natural cavern, known as "The Wogan". Birthplace of Harri Richmond (later Henry VII, first of the Tudors). During the Civil War, its occupants changed sides and were thus attacked by both armies. *Easter to end September daily; October to Easter, Monday to Saturday.*

27i Manorbier Castle (tel. 083 482 394). Built in the 12th to 14th centuries, this impressive castle is still occupied. It was conceived by the Normans to defend their hold on south-west Wales and features exceptionally high curtain walls linking towers and the late-mediaeval gatehouse. The coastal location is attractive and the interior is enhanced by life-size wax figures. Birthplace in 1146 of Giraldus Cambrensis, famous for his descriptions of life in 12th century Wales. *Easter, then Whitsun to end September daily 1100-1800.*

29a Llanstephan Castle. Originally a small Norman outpost, it became important during the 13th century English conquest of Wales, mainly for its strategic location on the Towy, giving easy access to the sea. Main living quarters were in the Great Gatehouse (built 1280), which features impressive examples of contemporary military technology. *Any reasonable time. Free.* St Anthony's wishing well, ¼ mile west, is said to have medicinal properties.

29e Kidwelly Castle. On a site fortified early in the 12th century, the stone castle was built in the late 13th to early 14th centuries by the Normans. Its location enabled it to be supplied by sea during periods of siege by the Welsh. The main defences are remarkably well preserved, including a three-storey gatehouse, while a notable chapel projects over the river. One of the finest castles in Wales. *Daily from 0930 (winter Sundays from 1400).*

29i Weobley Castle. See 20e.

34a Clytha Castle. Gothic fortress built on the hilltop in 1790; now used for holiday accommodation.

34b Raglan Castle. Built in the late 14th and early 15th centuries, its design was affected as much by aesthetic as military considerations. The hexagonal Great Tower of Gwent with elaborate twin drawbridges is unique, while the Long Gallery is 126 ft long. The castle was extensively damaged during the longest siege of the Civil War. *Daily from 0930 (winter Sundays from 1400).*

34h Penhow Castle. See 25b.

34i Caldicot Castle. See 25c.

35g Chepstow Castle. Oldest known stone castle in Britain, begun in 1067, although little remains of the Norman original. Majestically sited atop a cliff overlooking the Wye, the castle was constantly improved until 1662 and thus shows defensive thinking from many periods of history. A Royalist

Penhow Castle (25b)

stronghold in the Civil War, it was captured by Parliament and dismantled in 1690. *Daily from 0930 (winter Sundays from 1400).*

38c Cilgerran Castle. Picturesque location above the River Teifi has inspired many famous artists, including Turner. The stone defenses date from the 12th and 13th centuries, although the site was fortified in Norman times. *Daily from 0930 (Sundays PM).*

41g Carreg Cennen. Legend has it that this was the site of a castle built by Sir Urien, one of King Arthur's knights; certainly, the spectacular limestone crag was fortified long before the present building was started in the late 13th century. The castle saw heavy fighting in the Anglo-Welsh wars and was taken in 1277 by the English. John of Gaunt and Henry Bolingbroke (who became Henry IV) were later occupants, and it was fiercely fought over during the Wars of the Roses. It was demolished in 1462 to prevent its use by robbers. Magnificent views of Brecon Beacons. *Daily from 0930 (winter Sundays from 1400).*

43b Maesllwch Castle. Built in 1829 on attractive site north of the River Wye.

44f Grosmont Castle. Built in 1201, a typical compact border castle. Attacked by the Welsh in 1233 and (under Owain Glyndwr) in 1405, the latter siege being raised by Prince Hal (later Henry V). The oldest remnant, the Great Hall, dates from 1210, most of the fortifications dating from 1220-40. *Any reasonable time. Free.*

44h White Castle. Best of the three 'trilateral' castles (with 44f Grosmont and 45g Skenfrith) built by the Marcher lords to subdue the Welsh early in the 12th and 13th centuries, it got its name from the white plaster coating, traces of which can still be seen on the masonry. Formidable defences, with moat and two rings of walls. *Daily from 0930 (Sundays PM).*

45g Skenfrith Castle. On the west bank of the River Monnow, commanding one of the main routes from England, this 13th century castle features well-preserved curtain walls—almost to their original height in places—and an unusual keep built on an earth mound to provide extra height, allowing the defenders to fire on attackers outside the main walls. *Any reasonable time. Free.*

59d Powis Castle (tel. Welshpool 0938 3360). Owned by the National Trust, it has been occupied constantly for over 500 years. The first castle on the site was destroyed by Llywelyn the Last in 1275; the foundations of the present building were laid before 1300 by one of Edward I's barons, but the castle suffered heavily when captured by Cromwell's forces in 1644. It was extensively refurbished in 1667, however, and the results of that work survive virtually unchanged. The walls are in red limestone and the castle is spectacularly sited on a high ridge. Impressive interior. *Easter weekend; then May to late September, Wednesday to Sunday 1400-1730; also Bank Holiday Mondays 1130-1730.*

61c Criccieth Castle. Standing on a rocky peninsula overlooking the town, this strategically placed castle was started in 1230 by the Welsh prince Llywelyn the Great. One of the towers and the inner gatehouse were added in 1260, as the struggle against England reached its climax, but Edward I nevertheless captured it in 1282, after which the defences were much strengthened by its new owners. Cracked stones and extensive scorchmarks are believed to date from the castle's next great battle, when Owain Glyndwr re-took it for the Welsh in 1404. Note the so-called Engine Tower, on the first floor of which stood a huge machine for hurling boulders. *Daily from 0930 (winter Sundays from 1400).*

Harlech Castle (62d)

62d Harlech Castle. After defeating Llywelyn in 1282, Edward I planned the castle as part of his subjugation of the Welsh. It was begun in 1285 and the 800 workmen finished the job in only five years at a cost of about £8500 (roughly £1m today). Rectangular in plan, it has no keep but instead a massive gatehouse—with 143 steps to the top for the energetic. Despite the apparent might of the defenses and its strategic location by the sea (which reached the base of the castle rock in the 14th century), Harlech became famous for failing to withstand attack. It first came under fire in 1294, when Madoc ap Llywelyn was repulsed by a garrison of only 37 men; it was captured in 1404 by Owain Glyndwr at the peak of the Welsh uprising; he in turn lost it to the English four years later. During the Wars of the Roses, it was besieged by the Yorkists in 1461, the eight-year siege that followed inspiring the famous march "Men of Harlech". It fell into ruin during Elizabethan times, but was still strong enough to be the last Royalist stronghold in Wales during the Civil War. *Daily from 0930 (winter Sundays from 1400).*

65b Chirk Castle (tel. 069 186 7701). The exterior is a uniquely unchanged example of an Edward I Marcher fortress, on a hilltop site with fine views to the Pennines. Completed in 1310, it has been inhabited ever since. In 1595 it was bought by Sir Thomas Myddleton, who sailed the Spanish Main with Walter Raleigh, and his ancestors remain in residence, although the estate is now publicly owned. *Easter to late October: Wednesdays, Thursdays, and weekends 1400-1700; June to end September Wednesdays and Thursdays and all Bank Holiday weekends 1100-1700.*

Chirk Castle (65b)

67a Fort Belan (tel. Llanwnda 0286 830220). Napoleonic fort built in 1775, with cannons still intact and fired twice a week. Now a tourist attraction, with miniature railway, etc. *Easter to September 1000-1700.*

67b Caernarfon Castle (tel. 0286 3094). The site was first occupied by the Normans, then captured by the Welsh in 1115. The present castle was built by Edward I between 1283 and about 1330 and cost £12,000 (about £1.2m today). It remains one of the mightiest and best preserved in Europe, covering 3 acres and including 13 towers and two major gateways. The whole atmosphere is military: the interior fittings were never completed, fiscal priority having gone to the defences. Birthplace in 1284 of Edward II, the first Prince of Wales; scene in 1969 of the investiture of Prince Charles, the present Prince of Wales. *Daily from 0930 (winter Sundays from 1400).*

67c Bryn Bras Castle (tel. Llanberis 028 682 210). Never sullied by military action of any kind, this elegant stately home was built as a Romanesque castle in 1830. *Spring Bank Holiday to mid-July 1330-1700; mid-July to end August 1030-1700; September 1330-1700; but closed Saturdays throughout.*

68c Dolwyddelan Castle. Traditional birthplace of Llywelyn the Great, parts of the castle date from the 12th century, although the rectangular Great Tower was reconstructed in the mid-19th century and is thus well preserved. *Daily from 0930.*

71a Ruthin Castle (tel. 082 42 2664). Late 13th century border fortress on 100 ft high sandstone ridge above the River Clwyd, but with many later additions, including an 1830 house. Now a luxury hotel, the whole site has been reconstructed to capture the spirit of the original castle, albeit not with total accuracy. *Non-residents welcome.* ☆

71i Chirk Castle. See 65b.

Conwy Castle (77d)

Caernarfon Castle (67b)

75i Beaumaris Castle. The most sophisticated concentric castle in Britain, it was built in the closing years of the 13th century as the final link in Edward I's chain of Welsh strongholds. Sited on level ground—the name means "beautiful marsh"—the designers had a free hand and created a range of defensive positions that would have made any attack a most unpleasant prospect. The outer walls are almost 30 ft high and there are 12 towers. When built, the harbour could handle ships of up to 40 tons. The fortifications were never put to the test, however, as the castle has never seen action. *Daily from 0930 (winter Sundays from 1400).*

76d Penrhyn Castle (tel. Bangor 0248 53084). Built 1827-40, this is the biggest and best of the 'replica' Norman castles. With seven miles of exterior wall, a 115 ft high keep and a 3-storey Great Hall, it outdoes anything the Normans actually did. Sumptuously furnished, it is run by the National Trust. *April, May and October daily 1400-1700; June to end September and all Bank Holiday weekends, daily 1100-1700.* 🍴 ❄ 🖪 🏢 ⬇T

76d Beaumaris Castle. See 75i.

76g Bryn Bras Castle. See 67c.

77d Conwy Castle. Designed by Master James of St George, the Savoy architect responsible for many of Edward I's Welsh fortresses, Conwy was one of his outstanding achievements. Standing on a narrow ledge commanding what used to be the site of the Conwy ferry, it is a linear castle with 8 round towers in the outer walls surrounding two inner wards. Although little remains of any interior fittings, the stonework is almost complete. When built, it was entirely limewashed, traces of white still being visible. *Daily from 0930 (winter Sundays from 1400).* m

77f Gwrych Castle (tel. 0745 822326). Gothic extravagance built in 1815 on a wooded hillside overlooking the sea. Battlements, 18 towers, pets corner, miniature railway, etc. *Easter to September daily.* 🍴 🏢

78a Rhuddlan Castle. Built in 1277 and used by Edward I as the base for his operations against the leading Welsh princes in the late 13th century, it is a good example of the concentric castle, with access to the sea via the River Clwyd, which was diverted to suit. The four-storey Gilot's Tower protected the dock gate. The castle was ruined during the Civil War, when it was attacked by Cromwell's forces in 1646. *Daily from 0930 (winter Sundays from 1400).*

78h Denbigh Castle. Built by the Earl of Lincoln in 1282, it stands on a 467 ft hill above the town. The gatehouse and 8 towers remain. The castle saw much action, involving such notables as Owain Glyndwr and Henry "Hotspur" Percy, and was fought over in the Wars of the Roses and the Civil War. *Daily from 0930 (winter Sundays from 1400).* 🖪

The Castles of Edward I

In order to fully appreciate the significance of the huge programme of castle building undertaken by Edward I during the last quarter of the 13th century, one must first understand the role of earlier castles. The use of stone fortifications was largely developed by the Normans, but their castles were never part of a co-ordinated strategy; they were built by individual lords as defensible homes and as refuges for their serfs and tenants in times of trouble. Most of these Norman castles began life as simple motte-and-bailey affairs, consisting of a motte, or mound, on which was sited a keep; and a bailey, a courtyard walled in stone or wood in which livestock could be protected. Because these castles were residential, however, they were constantly expanded and altered, often incorporating the latest defensive ideas, so that many such buildings evolved into sophisticated castles.

The castles of Edward I were totally different: they were never intended as homes and they were conceived and built as part of a unified programme the like of which has never been seen in Britain before or since. They were not even intended to be defensive structures, their role being offensive in nature: each castle was an instrument of suppression, part of Edward's desire to see the Welsh finally subjugated and incorporated into his kingdom. Thus each castle was an administrative centre, prison and, above all, a base from which would emerge punitive expeditions whenever the locals became too restive.

It was an enormous undertaking, involving no less than 17 castles, ten of them totally new; tens of thousands of workmen were conscripted from all over England and Edward employed one of the leading military architects of the time, Master James of St George, to oversee the design and construction. Master James, whose earlier works had included castles in France and Italy, did a thorough job designing each castle to suit its site: apart from much later restoration work, nothing significant was ever added to his basic designs.

The history of each castle is described in its gazetteer entry. Because the classification of castles is dependent on their physical condition rather than their historical significance, however, several of the more dilapidated sites (marked m below) appear in the section on Historic Sites on pages 86-89.

The first phase of Edward I's programme lasted from 1277 to 1282 and involved three new castles - Aberystwyth (m 52d), Rhuddlan (78a) and Flint (m 79e) - and the modernisation of Builth (m 50e). The scale of these fortifications so alarmed the Welsh that they rose under Llywelyn the Last, but were crushed after his death in 1282.

Encouraged by the success of those castles, Edward embarked on a further programme of even more ambitious construction, involving the massive castles at Harlech (62d), Caernarfon (67b), Ruthin (71a), Hope (71c, but nothing remains), Beaumaris (75i) and Conwy (77d). This phase lasted from 1283 to about 1330, and resistance by the Welsh was confined mainly to local chiefs - Caernarfon in particular was twice attacked during its construction, often the only time when the ill-equipped natives could hope for real success.

In addition to the castles mentioned so far, Edward I sanctioned the building of four new 'Lordship' castles at Chirk (65b), Holt (72b but nothing significant remains), Denbigh (78h) and Hawarden (m 79i); he also ordered major improvements carried out to three captured Welsh castles at Castell y Bere (m 56e), Criccieth (61c) and Dolwyddelan (68c).

The whole programme was so successful that many of the castles were ruins within 50 years of being built; and those that survived remained largely untested until the rising led by Owain Glyndwr some 120 years later.

Artist's impression of Conwy town and castle in the 13th century.

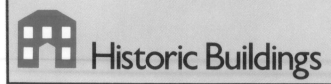

Historic Buildings

Including stately homes, historic houses and non-military buildings with interesting architectural features. Some castles which boast fine interiors have their rooms described here, although their military histories will be found in the section on Castles (pages 93-95).

23g Llantwit Major: Town Hall (tel. 044 65 3707). Mediaeval courthouse and market, mainly 17th century, but including some 12th century parts. Once known as Church Loft, it covers 2 floors and is used for local exhibitions and shows. *Weekdays 0900-1600; weekends by appointment. Free.*

24c Tredegar Park (tel. Newport 0633 62568). This 16th to 18th century brick house set in a country park is probably the finest example of its kind in Wales. The Gilt Room features wood panelling with gold leaf borders and inset paintings; the Brown Drawing Room has elaborate carved panels and a notable ceiling with candelabra. *April to end September Wednesday to Sunday and all Bank Holidays 1400-1800; other times by appointment.* 💬 🏺 🛍 🎏

24e Cardiff Castle (tel. 0222 31279). The subject of wholesale reconstruction during the late 19th century, the rooms of this castle were lavishly decorated to accord with Victorian ideas of mediaeval life. The Bachelors' Bedroom has walls inlaid with precious stones; the Summer Smoking Room is guarded by a chained dragon and a bronze model of the world adorns the floor; the mock Moorish Arab Room has a white marble chimney inset with lapis lazuli; the Banqueting Hall features murals of the life of Robert the Consul, son of Henry I; the Chaucer Room has stained glass windows showing scenes from "Canterbury Tales". Also: a dining room with gold leaf ceiling, entrance hall with stained glass portraits of monarchs who have owned the castle, impressive library and chapel. Much of the decoration is artistically overdone, but is none the less beautiful for that. Guided tours. *March, April and October daily 1000-1200, 1400-1600; May to September daily 1000-1230, 1400-1700; November to February 1100-1500.* 💬 🖼 ⛏

25b Penhow Castle (tel. 0633 400800). Compact fortified manor house built in 12th century and now the oldest inhabited castle in Wales. The interior, which is being completely restored, covers 800 years of history, including a 15th century Great Hall, 16th century Tudor wing, 17th century kitchen and a Victorian housekeeper's room. *Good Friday to September: Wednesday to Sunday 1000-1800.* ⛏

27h Lamphey Court (tel. Pembroke 064 63 2351). Georgian house with colonnaded facade.

28g Tenby: Tudor Merchant's House, Quay Hill (tel. 0834 2279). Fine example of mediaeval residence from the time when Tenby was an important port, with original 15th century floor beams, Flemish chimney and remains of wall paintings found under 28 coats of lime. Exhibition of Tudor period. Difficult stairs. *Easter Sunday to end September. weekdays 1000-1300, 1430-1800; Sundays PM.*

34c Monmouth: Great Castle House (tel. 0600 2935). Built by the 1st Duke of Beaufort in 1673, it became the headquarters of the Royal Monmouthshire Royal Engineers in 1875. Notable for its superbly decorated plaster ceilings. *By appointment only.* 🏛

34c Tre-Owen Wonastow (tel. Dingestow 060 083 224). Four storey manor house dating from 16th century, with impressive staircase. In use as a farm. *By appointment only.*

34e Cefntilla Court. Built in 1616 and restored in 1856, the home of Lord Raglan. His ancestor, the 1st Baron Raglan, fought in the Peninsular Campaign as ADC to Sir Arthur Wellesley (later the Duke of Wellington) and commanded troops during the Crimean War. *Not open.* ✿

34h Penhow Castle. See 25b.

43h Tretower Court. Well fortified manor house rebuilt in the 15th century, but retaining earlier, mediaeval design, with spacious rooms, oak timbers and an open first floor gallery looking onto a central courtyard. *Daily from 0930 (Sundays PM).* 🏛

44h Llanvihangel Court (tel. Crucorney 087 382 217). Gabled Elizabethan manor house, with front rebuilt in 1559 and interior remodelled in 1660. Yew staircase, interesting furniture and portraits. *1st, 3rd Sundays in June: all Sundays July and August; Easter, Spring and Summer Bank Holiday Sundays and Mondays: 1430-1800.* 💬

48d Gelly, Talsarn, Lampeter. Rare example of 17th century gentry house with oak staircase, leaded windows, original Welsh kitchen, thatched lodge and walled garden. The poet Dylan Thomas was a frequent guest. *By appointment only: The Hon John Vaughan.*

51c Presteigne: Radnorshire Arms (tel. 054 44 406). Like several of the buildings in Presteigne, this small hotel is of typical Marches black-and-white half-timbered construction. Also features round steps, a priest's chamber above the Tudor doorway and secret passages. 💬

52e Nanteos (tel. 0970 617756). Fine Georgian mansion built between 1739 and 1757, with carved oak staircase, period kitchen, Victorian morning room and delightful music room. Good example of the life enjoyed by Welsh nobility in the 18th and 19th centuries. The name means "valley of the nightingale". *Easter weekend, then June to September daily: 1300-1730.*

54b Maesmawr Hall (tel. Caersws 068 684 410255). Late example of a timber-framed house, thought to date from the early 18th century. Now a 28-bedroom hotel. 💬

55h Monk's House, Monaughty. Tudor mansion. *Summer weekdays.*

56b Ty Gwyn yn Y Bermo (White House in Barmouth); said to have been built for the Earl of Richmond, a Welshman who later became Henry VII of England after defeating Richard III at Bosworth. Near the quay.

57g Machynlleth: Royal House, said to be where the future Henry VII stayed in 1485.

Owain Glyndwr Centre, site of his Parliament House when Machynlleth was proclaimed capital of Wales in 1404.

Maengwyn Street contains 17th, 18th and 19th century houses.

59b Trelydan Hall (tel. 0938 2773). Extensive Tudor home with original timbers, attic priest hole and late Georgian drawing room housing rare collection of Victorian wedding dresses. Limited accommodation in four Tudor suites; intimate candlelight dinners every Friday/Saturday evening from late November. *Easter to December: daily 1200-1700.* 💬

59d Powis Castle (tel. Welshpool 0938 3360). Occupied for over 500 years, this 12th century castle was extensively refurbished in the 17th century. Fine plasterwork, woodwork, murals, tapestry, paintings and Georgian furniture can be seen, together with relics of Clive of India. Impressive state rooms. *Easter Weekend; then May to late September, Wednesday to Sunday 1400-1730; also Bank Holiday Mondays 1130-1730.* 💬 ✿ ⛏

60d Aberdaron: Y Gegin Fawr (The Big Kitchen) was once a 14th century rest house for pilgrims on their way to Bardsey Island; now a cafe and souvenir shop. 💬

60e Plas-yn-Rhiw (tel. Rhiw 075 888 219). Small manor house, partly mediaeval with Tudor and Georgian additions. Restored by National Trust. *By appointment only: April to end June Wednesdays and Thursdays 1500-1630.* ✿

62a Portmeirion (tel. Penrhyndeudraeth 0766 770228). A complete Italianate village created by architect Sir Clough Williams-Ellis on a 175-acre private peninsula on the shores of Cardigan Bay. Begun in 1926, it was inspired by the Italian village of Portofino and comprises a collection of reconstructed buildings and monuments dating from 1610 onwards. The architecture covers a wide range, from Jacobean to Oriental and includes Baroque and Romanesque buildings, a 17th century ballroom, the 18th century Bath House Colonnade, a barbican gatehouse, a lighthouse, cloisters and much more. The village provided the dramatic setting for the popular TV series "The Prisoner". It is run as a luxury hotel, but is open to non-residents, although the entrance toll, varied according to demand, can be expensive. *Easter to end October daily 0930-1800.* 💬 ✿

62e Glyn Cywarch. Welsh country house, the main part of which dates from about 1550. In 1616 it was extended by the unusual means of adding a complete second house alongside. This was thought to be a legacy of the local custom of dividing property among heirs instead of giving everything to the eldest son. Notable tall gatehouse, with off-centre entrance.

65b Plas-newydd, Butler Hill, Llangollen (tel. 0978 860234). This black-and-white timbered mansion was, for 50 years of the 18th century, the home of the "Ladies of Llangollen"—Lady Eleanor Butler and Miss Sarah Ponsonby—expatriate Irishwomen whose conversation and eccentricity drew scores of famous and talented guests, including the Duke of Wellington, Sir Walter Scott, William Wordsworth and Sheridan. The house has been beautifully preserved inside and out, with oak carvings, leather work and an exhibition room. *1 May to 30 September: Monday to Saturday 1000-1900; Sundays 1100-1600. October to April weekdays by appointment.*

65b Chirk Castle (tel. 069 186 7701). Unique Marcher fortress built in 1310 and always inhabited since. State rooms provide examples of 16th, 17th, 18th and early 19th century style. Neo-Gothic entrance hall, a restored 18th century dining room and a Tudor block containing a four poster bed in which Charles I slept. Many other superb rooms, a display of Civil War armour and fine paintings throughout. *Easter to late October. Wednesday, Thursday, Saturday and Sunday 1400-1700; June to end September Wednesdays, Thursdays, and all Bank Holiday weekends 1100-1700.* 💬 ⛏

67c Bryn Bras Castle (tel. Llanberis 028 682 210). Elegant stately home built in Romanesque style in 1830. Fine example of Victorian fantasy, with splendid ceilings, galleries, staircase, Louis XV suite, drawing room, morning room, library, etc. *Spring Bank Holiday to mid-July 1350-1700; mid-July to end August 1030-1700; September 1350-1700; but closed Saturdays throughout.* 💬 ✿ ⛏ ⛲

68h Portmeirion. See 62a.

69a Ty-mawr (tel. Penmachno 069 03 213). Birthplace in 1541 of Bishop William Morgan, first translator of the Bible into Welsh in about 1587. *Easter to late October daily 1000-1800; closed Saturdays.* 🍵

71a Ruthin: Exmewe Hall, now housing Barclay's Bank, the Square. Half timbered mansion built in 1500 and home of a Lord Mayor of London. It was restored in 1928. Outside is Maen Huail (Huail's Stone), on which King Arthur is said to have beheaded Huail, his rival in love. *Exterior any time; interior in banking hours.*

Nantclwyd House, Castle Street. Half timbered 14th century town house with oak carving and a gallery bearing 15th century crests. *Not open.*

Plas Coch, Well Street. 13th century residence destroyed during Owain Glyndwr's sacking of Ruthin in 1400. It was rebuilt with ship's timbers in 1613.

Lordship Court House, St Peter's Square. A 'replica' of the old court house and prison built in 1401, with gallows built into the wall (part of the gibbet can still be seen). This half timbered building also houses a bank. *Open as Exmewe Hall.*

Myddleton Arms, now part of the 18th century Castle Hotel (tel. 082 42 2479), is a timber framed building dating from the 14th century, with low roof and notable dormer windows.

71f Wynnstay Hall. The original hall burnt down in 1858 and was replaced by this modern replica of a Danish castle. The Great Hall, with intricate ceiling, contains a rare Snetzler organ of 1774. The premises are now part of a school. *By appointment only.* ♠

71f Erddig. Built between 1684 and 1687, this manor house was extended early in the 18th century. Now in the hands of the National Trust, it has been completely restored to its former glory. Although the exterior is unremarkable, the interior is beautifully furnished and includes a collection of the original 18th century silver and gilt furnishings which is among the best of any country house. Visitors enter through the outbuildings, which include a laundry, bakehouse, sawmill and blacksmith's, all in working order. Some rooms containing pictures and tapestry have no electric lighting and should be visited in daylight; the Tapestry and Chinese Rooms are open on Fridays and Saturdays only. *Easter to late October: Tuesday to Sunday and Bank Holiday Mondays 1200-1630.* 🍵 ✿ ⬆T

71h Plas-newydd. See 65b.

71i Chirk Castle. See 65b.

72d Erddig. See 71f.

75h Plas Newydd (tel. Llanfairpwll 0248 714795). Fine 18th century mansion standing in 170 acres of gardens and woodland. Designed in Georgian Gothic style, with some rooms in classical style. Magnificently furnished and decorated throughout,

notable attractions including the Rex Whistler Room, in which the famous painter produced his largest mural, of an Italianate coastal scene. Also: Music Room, impressive chapel and a stable block with arches and spires. Excellent views of Snowdonia. *Easter to late October Sunday to Friday and Bank Holiday weekend Saturdays; 1230-1700.* 🍵 ✿ ⬛

75i Beaumaris: The Tudor Rose, 32 Castle Street (tel. 0248 810203). Half-timbered building of about 1400, with upstairs minstrel gallery giving views of barrel braced ceiling and fine hall. Restored in 1945, it is now an antique shop with displays of work by local artists. *Monday to Saturday: 0900-1300, 1400-1730 (but closed winter Wednesdays PM).*

County Hall. Built in 1614 and modified in the early 19th century. Roof and many fittings are original and there is an 18th century canopied pew for the mayor and bailiffs. Also known as the Assize Court House, where the notorious "hanging judge" Jeffreys is reputed to have sat.

76d Penrhyn Castle (tel. Bangor 0248 53084). Not strictly a castle, and certainly not the Norman castle it appears to be, this 'replica' was constructed in 1827-40 by Thomas Hopper for G H Dawkins Pennant, who used the profits of Penrhyn slate quarries to pay for it. The interior is a richly appointed mixture of 18th century and Gothic with an understandable profusion of slate throughout: a full size billiard table in the library and a one-ton bed in the master bedroom are both carved from slate! The main interior feature, however, is the 3-storey Great Hall, vaulted, arched and with stained-glass windows depicting the signs of the Zodiac. Drawing room, Ebony room, chapel, dining room and bedrooms are all worth seeing. *April, May and October daily 1400-1700; June to end September and all Bank Holiday weekends, daily 1100-1700.* 🍵 ✿ ⬛ ⬆ ⬆T

76d Beaumaris. See 75i.

76g Cochwillan Old Hall, Talybont, Bangor (tel. 0248 4608). One of the finest surviving late-mediaeval houses in Wales, it was built in about 1450 for William ap Gruffydd, who fought at Bosworth and was later made High Sheriff for life of Caernarfonshire. Notable for fine woodwork in the roof, it was restored in 1971. *By appointment only; Mr and Mrs P Llewellyn.*

76g Bryn Bras Castle. See 67c.

77d Conwy: Aberconwy House (tel. 049 263 2246). Mediaeval house at the junction of Castle Street and High Street, now housing the Conwy Exhibition and a National Trust shop. One of the town's last 15th century timberframe houses, it is 3 storeys high with pretty, uneven frontage. *Easter to end September daily 1000-1730, but closed on Wednesdays in April and May; other dates by appointment.*

Plas Mawr, High Street (tel. 049 263 3413).

Imposing late 16th century house—the name means "great hall"—with exterior of local grey stone and famous interior of ornamental plasterwork. Watchtower has 52 steps and 365 windows. Also: wooden spiral staircases, Queens Parlour and haunted room. Finest surviving Elizabethan town house in Britain. *April to September daily 1000-1730; October to March daily 1000-1630.* 🍵 ⬛

"Smallest House" on quayside. 19th century cottage with mid-Victorian Welsh interior. With 6 ft frontage and a height of 10 ft 2 in, said to be the smallest house in Britain. *Easter to October 1000-1800 (2100 in August).*

77f Garthewin (tel. Abergele 0745 84213). This Georgian mansion was built in 1730 and altered in 1722. Period furniture, armorial china and family portraits. Nearby 18th century barn used as a small theatre.

77f Gwrych Castle (tel. 0745 822326). Gothic extravagance built in 1815, with many paintings, antiques and curios, including a chamber of horrors. Mediaeval jousting in summer. *Easter to September daily.* 🍵 ⚔

77g Llanrwst: Tu Hwnt I'r Bont. A 15th century stone building, once used as the local courthouse, later divided into two cottages. Restored by local subscription and now let as a tea room. *Easter to end of tourist season: Tuesday to Sunday. Free.* 🍵

77g Gwydir Castle, Llanrwst (tel. 0492 640261). Not a castle, but a Tudor mansion built between 1500 and 1600, some parts using mediaeval stonework and roof beams from the dissolved abbey at Maenan. The house is built around the even older (14th century) Hall of Maredudd, which forms the banqueting hall. Antique furnishings, a bedroom where Charles II slept and a priest's hole in a fireplace can also be seen. The house was burnt out earlier this century, but has been magnificently restored. *Easter to October daily 1000-1700, but closed Saturdays.* ♠ ✝

78b Bodrhyddan Hall, Rhuddlan (tel. 0745 590414). The site has been occupied since about 1280, but the oldest part of the current building dates from 1696, with later additions up to 1874. Paintings by Reynolds and Hogarth; an octagonal well-house thought to be by Inigo Jones and used for secret marriages; a collection of 18th century Chinese porcelain; and a superb collection of arms and armour, including two suits of armour used in the Wars of the Roses. *June to end September Tuesdays and Thursdays 1400-1730.* 🍵 ✿ ⚐

78g Henllan: Llindir. One of Wales' historic inns, built in 1229.

78h Denbigh: The Old Vaults, 40-42 High Street. Licensed since 1763, but the premises are even older.

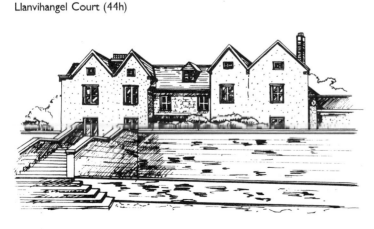

Llanvihangel Court (44h)

Bodrhyddan Hall (78b)

Religious Places

20b Pembrey. 13th century church with a fine timber barrel roof in the nave and chancel. Notable memorials in the churchyard.

20c Llanelli: St Elliw. Impressive 19th century church with 18th century monuments.

20d Burry Holms: St Cenydd. Remains of a mediaeval chapel linked to the hermit St Cenydd, who lived here for a few years in the 6th century. **m**

20d Rhosili: St Mary. Part Norman church with a fine ornate south door and lancet windows.

20e Llangennith: St Cenydd. 13th century church on the site of a 6th century monastery founded by St Cenydd and destroyed by the Danes in the 10th century.

20i Oxwich: St Illtyd. 11th/12th century church with a font said to have been installed by St Illtyd.

21c Neath Abbey. Ruins of a Cistercian abbey founded in 1130 and much enlarged in the 13th century. Fragment of the main gateway remains. *Daily from 0930 (Sundays PM).* ↓T

21d Mumbles: All Saints. Part 14th century church; burial place of Thomas Bowdler, who published an expurgated edition of Shakespeare thus giving rise to the verb 'bowdlerise'.

22b Margam Abbey. Founded for the Cistercians in 1147 by the Earl of Gloucester; the Norman church remains as part of the present parish church. The 12-sided chapter house is in ruins. Located in Margam Country Park. See♣ for times.

22f Ewenni Priory. Ruins of a Benedictine monastery, with military defences, established in 1141. The mid-12th century church is still used for services and also houses a small museum. The vault of the chancel is the best Norman work in the county. A number of mediaeval sepulchral slabs have Norman French inscriptions in Lombardic characters. *Weekdays 0800-1630.*

23d Coity: St Mary. 14th century church with much of interest.

23g Llantwit Major. 15th century church contains treasures which precede it: Christian memorial stones and crosses dating from 9th/10th centuries survive from a 5th century wooden Christian monastery where St David and St Teilo studied.

24c Newport: St Woolos Cathedral. Once the church of St Gwynllyw, it became the cathedral in 1949; it has fine Norman arches and a mediaeval tower. The magnificent east window was erected in 1963.

24d Llandaff Cathedral, Cardiff. The first church, built in the 6th century of wood, was replaced in the 12th century by Norman stone. Following extensive damage in World War II, the cathedral was completely renovated. The interior of the nave is dominated by Epstein's "Christ in Majesty", an aluminium sculpture. Nearby are the remains of the cathedral's 13th century bell tower which once housed the 5½ ton bell 'Great Peter'.

24e Cardiff: St John. The church, restored in 19th century, has a notable 15th century tower. Much of the building displays 13th and 15th century work; Renaissance screenwork in the north chapel.

St David's Cathedral. The Roman Catholic cathedral contains a fine altar of alabaster and marble.

25c Runston. Evocative ruins of a Norman chapel.

25d Goldcliff. 17th century church which has a plaque high on one of the walls showing the height to which water rose in the Great Flood of 1606.

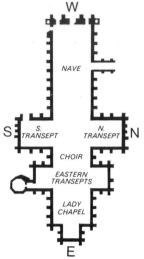

Glossary of Terms

Shown here is the ground plan of a typical mediaeval cathedral. Most of the cathedrals and churches described here were started and/or completed during the mediaeval period, and their general layout will be similar.

Apse. Vaulted recess, usually at one end of the choir.
Barrel Vault. Semi-circular vault in the roof; also known as a tunnel vault.
Fan Vault. Chamber whose supporting ribs spread out in the shape of an open fan.
Lancet Window. High narrow window with sharply pointed arch.
Lady Chapel. Usually named for its dedication to the Virgin Mary. See plan.
Misericord. Small hinged wooden seat, used in the choir stalls to give some support to a person standing up; often elaborately carved.
Rood Loft. Loft or gallery built above a rood screen (see below).
Rood Screen. Separates the nave from the chancel or choir; incorporates a large rood (crucifix).
Tympanum. A triangular space above the main door, usually highly decorated.
Vault. Arched room or passageway, often underground.

Memorial stones at Llantwit Major (23g)

27a Haverfordwest: St Mary. 13th/15th century church with fine Early English lancet windows.

Priory of St Mary and St Thomas, south of town centre. Ruins of an Augustinian priory founded in 1207.

27d Milford Haven: St Katherine. 19th century church where Lord and Lady Hamilton are buried. Nelson laid the foundation stone and gave the church a Bible and prayer book.

27d Llanstadwell. Parish church possesses the oldest Norman work in the area.

27f Carew Cheriton: St Mary. 14th century church with detached chantry chapel in the churchyard and a 9th century cross which is 14 ft high and intricately carved.

27h Monkton. Ruins of an 11th century Benedictine priory.

27h Pembroke: St Mary. 13th century church much restored during the 19th century.

27h St Govan's Chapel. Tiny 14th century chapel with stone-vaulted roof, set in a cleft in the cliffs which can be reached only by a path from above. At the side of its original stone altar is a doorway leading to a small chamber in the rock.

28b Whitland Abbey. Ruins of Cistercian abbey founded in 1143; the wars of Owain Glyndwr and Henry VIII's dissolution of the monasteries took their toll on the buildings.

28g Tenby: St Mary. 13th/15th century church much restored by the Victorians.

28g Penally: St Nicholas. 13th century stone-vaulted cruciform church with a square embattled tower; contains a highly decorated Celtic cross in the south transept.

28g Caldey Island. 12th century Benedictine priory, now occupied by Cistercians. The stone-vaulted chapel contains a stone with an inscription in Ogham, an 8th century script. Boats run from Tenby. *Summer only.* ♣

29e Kidwelly: St Mary the Virgin. Ancient church with much of interest.

Priory. 12th century Benedictine priory, the finest example of the Decorated style in west Wales.

29e Pembrey. See 20b.

29f Llanelli. See 20c.

29h Burry Holms. See 20d.

29h Llangennith. See 20e.

30d Llanelli. See 20c.

31g Neath Abbey. See 21c.

33b Blaenavon: St Peter. 18th century church having many links with the local iron industry, including an iron font, iron tomb covers and memorials to local iron pioneers.

33c Abergavenny: St Mary. 14th century cruciform-shaped church with central tower, once part of a 12th century Benedictine priory. Contains canopied choir stalls and 13th and 14th century monuments.

33d Rhymney: St David. Built for the Rhymney Iron Company, its 'sad bells' are recalled in "Gwalia Deserta", a poem by the local poet Idris Davies.

34a Abergavenny. See 33c.

34d Betwsnewydd. Church retains an elegant Perpendicular rood screen with its original gallery decorated with open-tracery work.

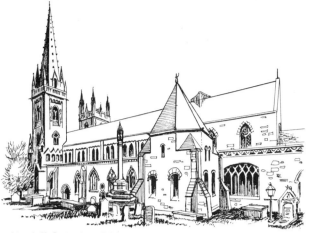

Llandaff Cathedral (24d)

Tintern Abbey (35d)

34e Usk: St Mary. 13th century church with a 15th century screen across the whole width of the building; the 17th century pulpit and organ came from Llandaff Cathedral (24d). Also a 13th century priory gatehouse.

34i Runston. Evocative ruins of a Norman chapel.

35d Tintern Abbey. Ruins of a Cistercian abbey set in the beautiful Wye valley. It was founded in the 1131 and enlarged in the 13th and 14th centuries; the well-preserved abbey church is almost intact, with its soaring east end and rose window. *Daily from 0930 (winter Sundays from 1400).*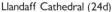

35g Chepstow: St Mary. Large Norman church with a west tower (1706), which replaced the original tower that collapsed in 1700. Also a 16th century canopied monument and a 17th century organ from Gloucester Cathedral.

36h St David's Cathedral. 12th to 14th century cathedral built of purple sandstone, quarried locally; it is a magnificent example of mediaeval architecture. Notable features: fascinating misericord carvings on the choir stalls; fine Irish oak roof in the nave; delicate fan vaulting above the Holy Trinity Chapel; and the shrine of St David, the patron saint of Wales.

36h St Non's Chapel. Ruins of a chapel, holy well and shrine to St Non, St David's mother, stand above the rocky bay.

38a Nevern: St Brynach. Norman church with original tower and two stones with inscriptions in the 5th century Gaelic script Ogham. The churchyard contains St Brynach's Cross with notable Celtic carvings; a wayside cross is cut in the rock face nearby, marking a 6th century stopping place for pilgrims; the nearly 'Bleeding Yew' drips a blood-like sap.

38c Manordeifi. Church with permanent 'escape coracle' by the Afon Teifi.

38i Whitland Abbey. See 28b.

39a Newcastle Emlyn: Holy Trinity. 19th century church with slate quarried at nearby Cilgerran (38c) used in the interior.

39c Llandyssul: St Tyssul. Norman church, restored in the 19th century, with an embattled tower.

39i Carmarthen: St Peter. 13th/14th century church with fine stained-glass windows.

40f Talley Abbey. Ruins of an abbey founded in the 12th century, probably by Rhys ap Gruffydd, for the Premonstratensian Order, originally from Prémontré in France. *Daily from 0930 (Sundays PM).*

40i Llangathen: St Cathen. Fine 13th century church.

41b Llandovery: St Dingat. 14th/15th century church with a Gothic font built around the original Norman one.

Llandovery College (tel. 0550 315). The school contains a chapel with a painting of the Crucifixion by Graham Sutherland. *By appointment only.*

42f Defynnog: St Cynog. 15th century church with a 5th century pillar embedded in the tower and inscribed in Latin and Ogham; ancient font bears the only Runic inscription in a Welsh church.

42f Brecon Cathedral: Priory Church of St John the Evangelist. Partly 13th century fortified cathedral, cruciform-shaped, with a mainly Gothic tower and five-lancet east window. The building was restored in late 19th century by Sir Gilbert Scott.

43b Llowes. The churchyard contains the remarkable Great Cross of St Meilig: 11 ft long, it is incised with a 7th century cross and one of the 11th century.

43b Maes-yr-Onnen Chapel. A Nonconformist meeting house founded in 1696. The interior is little altered except by the lowering of the pulpit.

43b Llanelieu. Church, 800 ft up the slopes of Rhos Fawr, with a wooden porch and a door with original mediaeval ironwork.

43c Hay on Wye: St Mary. 12th century church rebuilt in the 19th century.

43i Crickhowell. 14th century church with elaborate tombs.

44d Llanthony Priory. Ruins of a priory founded in 1108 for Augustinian canons, although the present buildings date from the early 13th century; much of the church remains.

44g Partrishow. Small, isolated church, mainly 15th century, with a magnificent rood screen; it retains its gallery and delightful open-work tracery decoration.

44g St Dogmaels: Abbey of St Mary the Virgin. Remains of an abbey founded in 1115 for monks of the French order of Tiron, who were inspired by the austere life of St Benedict. Fine carvings.

St Thomas the Martyr. 19th century church on the site of a Celtic monastery; contains an Ogham stone which helped scholars to interpret this 5th century script in 1848.

46h Mount Church. Charming 14th century white-washed church.

48f Llanddewibrefi. The church is sited on a mound and dominates the village; the churchyard has many crosses and early Christian monuments.

49a Strata Florida Abbey. The remains of a remote Norman abbey founded for the Cistercians. The west doorway has unusual moulding and there are some mediaeval tiles. *Daily from 0930 (winter Sundays from 1400).*

50a Llanwrthwl: St Gwrthwl. The churchyard has an ancient stone said to have been used as an object of worship before the Roman occupation.

50c Llanbadarn-fawr. The church contains a Roman inscribed stone, a Celtic stone carving and a fine Norman arch and tympanum.

50c Llandegley: The Pales. Tiny Quaker Meeting House dated 1745; it is a simple rectangular building divided into a schoolroom and meeting-room. Most of the seating is original and the roof is still thatched.

50i Aberedw. Restored 14th century church with a fine porch and rood screen.

51c Presteigne. The parish church has notable Saxon and Norman work and a 16th century Flemish tapestry.

51e Old Radnor: St Stephen. 14th century church considered to be one of the finest in Wales; boasts the oldest organ case in Britain (dating from about 1500) and a font formed from a Bronze Age altar stone.

51g Llowes. See 43b.

51h Hay on Wye: St Mary. 12th century church rebuilt in the 19th century.

52d Llanbadarn-Fawr: St Padarn. 12th century church on the site of a 6th church which was destroyed by the Danes; contains fine Celtic crosses.

53f Llangurig. Fine monastic 14th century church; although restored, it still has much mediaeval work of interest.

54h Abbey Cwmhir. Ruins of the second largest Cistercian monastery in Wales. Founded in 1143, all that remains are some traces of the outside walls, the bases of several nave piers and fragments of the north and south transepts.

54i Llananno. Small church with a skilfully carved 16th century rood loft and screen; the gallery has a row of canopied niches containing carved figures.

54i Llanbister. The church has an unusual tower at the eastern end of the building.

56a Llanaber: St Mary. Completed in 1250 after 50 years work, the church is one of the finest examples of Early English architecture in North Wales. Has a large collection of early Christian monuments.

56c Cymer Abbey. Ruins of a tiny 12th century Cistercian abbey; the general layout can be seen as well as part of the south cloister and the frater (refectory).

56d Llanegryn. Church with a magnificent rood screen still retaining its original wide gallery on top, decorated with a wealth of delicate carving (dating from about 1520); also a Norman font.

56g Tywyn: St Cadfan. Norman church, restored in the 19th century, contains the 7 ft tall Stone of Cadfan. *Daily. Free.*

57b Mallwyd. The church has the date 1641 inscribed on the porch door, but the foundations are thought to be much older.

60c Pistyll: St Beuno. 6th or 7th century church used by pilgrims en route for Bardsey Island.

60c Nefyn: St Mary. Ancient ruined church with a narrow tower topped by a disproportionately large weather vane in the form of a ship.

60d Aberdaron. Church dating from the 6th century and perched on the edge of the sea, protected by a stout breakwater; its floor is below sea level at high tide.

60f Llanengan: St Einion. Large 6th century church with a double nave, a wonderful rood screen, a fine tower dated 1534 and a solid oak coffer where 'St Peter's Pence' were stored.

60g Bardsey Island: Abbey of St Mary. The existing ruins date from the 13th century, but the first abbey was founded by St Cadfan in the 6th century.

Because of the 2 miles of treacherous sea separating the island from the mainland, Bardsey became a refuge for persecuted Christians; many stayed and are buried there giving Bardsey the name: 'Isle of 20,000 Saints'.

62d Llandanwg. 15th century church containing inscribed stones, probably dating from the 6th century; the surrounding dunes have started to encroach and bury the church.

62g Llanenddwyn. 16th century church with an Inigo Jones chapel attached to it; the circular churchyard is an early Christian successor to Bronze Age stone circle monuments.

62h Llanaber. See 56a.

62i Cymer Abbey. See 56c.

64e Pennant Melangell. Remote church whose patron saint, St Melangell, was the playmate of wild hares.

65a Llanarmon Dyffryn Ceiriog. Unusual church with no chancel, no choir stalls and no apse but—almost uniquely—two pulpits; also a memorial to the bard 'Ceiriog' (John Hughes).

65b Llangollen: St Collen. Church has a fine roof carved with beasts and flowers which probably came from Valle Crucis Abbey (71e).

66c Ty-Cwfan: St Cwyfan. This 7th century church, restored in 1893, stands on an islet linked to the mainland by a causeway, covered at high tide. Services held once a year in June. *Daily at low tide.*

66c Llanddwyn Island. This ruined 15th century church replaced an oratory built 1000 years earlier by St Dwynwen; holy well nearby.

67b Brynsiencyn: St Nidan. Well preserved 15th century church, built on the foundations of a 7th century church, set in a wooded glade.

67g Clynnog Fawr. 15th century collegiate church, with carved rood screen and fine timbered roof, joined to the 7th century St Beuno's Chapel by a cloister; holy well nearby was famous for its curative powers.

69b Betws-y-Coed: St Michael Archangel. This 14th/15th century church is now only used for weddings or funerals.

70f Derwen. 13th century church with a fine rood loft and screen; the churchyard contains an excellent elaborate Celtic cross.

70f Rug Chapel. Private chapel built in 1637 by a local eccentric, William Salisbury; it was sometimes known as 'Envy Chapel' because of some conflict between the owner and the rector of Corwen. The carved painted frieze and the furnishings are interesting.

71a Ruthin; St Peter. 14th century church which has oak roofs with 500 elaborately carved bosses, given to the church by Henry VII; also several brasses and monuments.

71b Llanarmon-yn-Ial. The church has two naves separated by an unusual 18th century arcade; it also contains an effigy of a 14th century crusader and the tomb of a 17th century cavalier.

71e Valle Crucis Abbey. Cistercian abbey, founded in 1202 by Madoc ap Gruffydd Iorwerth, Prince of northern Powys, it is one of the most interesting ecclesiastical ruins in Wales: the extensive remains include the Early English west front, 14th century lancet windows and the eastern cloister. *Daily from 0930 (winter Sundays from 1400).*

71e Llangollen. See 65b.

71f Ruabon. The church contains a restored 14th century fresco; also many interesting monuments of the 18th century.

71g Llanarmon Dyffryn Ceiriog. See 65a.

72a Gresford: All Saints. 15th century church with fine stained glass; the peal of bells are one of the ancient Seven Wonders of Wales. A yew tree in the churchyard is said to be 1400 years old.

72d Wrexham: St Giles. 14th century church with 15th and 16th century additions and a Decorated-style interior. The 135 ft high pinnacled steeple is one of the Seven Wonders of Wales. It is rich in 18th century monuments and Elihu Yale, one of the Pilgrim Fathers (after whom Yale University in the United States was named) is buried here. The wrought-iron gates are also notable.

72e Overton. 13th century church; in the churchyard is a splendid group of yew trees which were considered one of the Seven Wonders of Wales.

74c Llanbadrig. Cliff-top church said to have been founded by St Patrick in the 5th century, after his ship was wrecked on the Middle Mouse rocks.

74d Holyhead: St Cybi. Cruciform-shaped church with 13th century chancel.

75b Porth yr Ychain: Llaneilian. 15th century church on the site of a 5th century one. Relics include a pair of 'dog tongs', used to evict animals that started fighting during services.

75e Hen Capel Lligwy. Although nothing remains of the roof of this ancient chapel, the walls are complete to gable height.

75i Beaumaris: SS Mary and Nicholas. 14th century church with fine choir stalls; contains the stone coffin of Princess Joan, daughter of King John.

75i Menai Bridge: St Tysilio. Church stands on a grassy islet and is linked to the mainland by a causeway; best viewed at high tide. This is the church mentioned in the full name of Llanfair P.G. (see ☆).

75i Bangor Cathedral. Originally Norman, this small cathedral was rebuilt during the 13th and 14th centuries and was much restored by Sir Gilbert Scott in 1870-8. Cruciform-shaped building with central and west towers; 15th century font and stone with 14th century relief.

76b Penmon: Priory Church of St Seriol. Church dates back to the 6th century but the present building is 12th century and later: the nave dates from 1140, the square tower and transept from around 1160 and the chancel is 13th century. The church has some of the best preserved Romanesque detail in North Wales, notably the crossing arches, wall arcades and font.

76b Puffin Island. Remains of a 12th century monastery. Boat excursions from Llandudno pass the island; permits to land from Baron Hill Estate Office, Beaumaris.

76d Beaumaris. See 75i.

76d Menai Bridge. See 75i.

76d Bangor. See 75i.

77b Rhos-on-Sea: St Trillo. 16th century chapel, the smallest in Wales (12 ft long and 6 ft wide), on the promenade overlooking the beach where the remains of a fishing weir once used by monks is visible at low tide.

77d Conwy: St Mary. 14th century church built on the site of the 12th century Abbey of Aberconwy.

77e Bryn-y-maen: Christ Church. Known as 'The Cathedral on the Hill', the church's tower offers a panoramic view of the district.

77e Llanelian-yn-Rhos. Fine church with a rare rood loft.

77g Gwydir-uchaf. Former private chapel of Gwydir Castle. Dating from 1673, it is noted for its rare 17th century Welsh painted roof.

77g Llanrwst. 15th century parish church, rebuilt in the 17th century, which possesses fine rood screen from Maenan Abbey with its original gallery; notable 17th century mausoleum.

78c Maen Achwyfan: Wheel Cross. Fine example of pre-Norman Welsh Christian art with interlacing designs (10th/11th century); the tallest monument of its kind in Britain.

78d Bodelwyddan: Marble Church. Built between 1856 and 1860 by Dowager Lady Willoughby de Broke as a memorial to her husband; beautiful, elegant spire is 202 ft high.

78e St Asaph Cathedral. The smallest cathedral in Britain, founded in 537AD, the existing building is largely 13th century, cruciform in style. Restoration work was done in the 19th century by Sir Gilbert Scott. The north aisle contains the 'Greyhound Stone' which has long baffled heraldic experts. There are some good 15th century stalls; stained glass (mostly 19th century); fine views of the Vale of Clwyd from the massive central tower.

78f Carmel. Model of the Grotto of Lourdes in a quarry behind the Franciscan monastery.

78h Denbigh: Leicester's Church. Ruined church, dubbed 'Leicester's Folly', which was planned to become cathedral of the diocese (in place of St Asaph) soon after the Reformation. *Daily from 0930 (Sundays PM).*

Denbigh Friary. Ruins of a 13th century friary, one of the simpler monastic houses in Wales.

79a Greenfield: Basingwerk Abbey. Ruined Cistercian abbey, founded in 12th century and later serving as a base for Edward I while Flint Castle was being built. *March to September: any time.*

79d Holywell: St Winifred's Well. Known as the 'Lourdes of Wales', this well chapel and chamber, built in the late 15th century, has been the goal of numerous pilgrimages. The well forms the basement of the chapel and consists of a large stone basin with steps for pilgrims to descend into the water. Another of the Seven Wonders of Wales. *April to September: Fridays and Saturdays 1100-1900.*

79g Mold: St Mary. Spacious Perpendicular church, with a west tower rebuilt in 1773. Contains a remarkable fresco of animals and many monuments; Richard Wilson, the 18th century landscape painter, is buried here.

Vale Crucis Abbey (71e)

Bird Watching

These pages list the most popular bird watching sites and those of ornithological significance. Birds in captivity are included in the section on Wildlife in Captivity (page 102).

20e Whiteford Burrows. Nature reserve; extensive sand dunes with saltings. Important for wintering and passage wildfowl and waders including brent geese.

20g Tears Point—Worms Head Nature Reserve: rocky peninsula with breeding auks and gulls, also noted for offshore passage.

20i Oxwich Burrows. Nature reserve with varied habitats. Winter wildfowl abundant; spring and autumn waders.

22b Eglwys Newydd Reservoir. Limited access, permits from Steel Company, Port Talbot. Winter wildfowl; small passage of waders.

22e Kenfig Pool. Freshwater pool amongst sand dunes. Best in winter for wild swans; small number of autumn waders.

24f Peterstone and St Brides Wentloog. Mud flats which are good for winter waders.

24h Penarth Flats. Holds a large number of waders and sea duck (winter).

24h Lavernock Point. Good viewpoint for spring migration of seabirds, including gannets.

24i Flat Holme. Rocky shore noted for large gullery. Administered as a bird sanctuary by the Kenneth Allsop Trust. Accessible only by boat.

25c Caldicot Level. Flat grazing land that floods in winter and spring and hosts a large variety of wild swans, ducks and waders.

26d Skomer Island. Nature reserve of 752 acres inhabited by many seabirds, including Manx shearwaters and puffins, as well as buzzards and ravens. Visits arranged by West Wales Naturalists' Trust at Dale Fort Field Centre, Haverfordwest. ♣

26e St Brides. Short stretch of coast giving an excellent variety of birds.

26e Dale—Gann River Mudflats holding waders in winter passage.

26e St Ann's Head. Good viewpoint for offshore seabirds such as fulmars and gannets (summer); divers and grebes (winter).

26f Angle Bay. Divers and grebes to be found in winter especially in rough weather.

27b Cleddau Rivers. Wintering and passage wildfowl and waders seen on mudflats.

27c Canaston Wood. Variable woodland habitat for birds like warblers, nightjars and redstarts.

27e Cresswell River. Mudflats good for watching winter and passage waders.

27g Pembroke River holds a number of wintering wildfowl and waders. Mudflats.

27g Stack Rocks, Flimston. Limestone cliffs holding good colonies of seabirds.

28g St Margaret's Island. Nature reserve; breeding ground for many seabirds, including cormorants and guillemots. Restricted access.

29d Taf, Towy and Gwendraeth Rivers. Communal estuary noted for wintering duck and a variety of waders (autumn).

29i Whiteford Burrows. See 20e.

32b Llwyn-on-Reservoir. Summer population, such as herons, buzzards and ravens, augmented by passage waders (autumn) and by winter wildfowl.

34d Llandegfedd Reservoir. Important inland water noted for abundant duck and grebes.

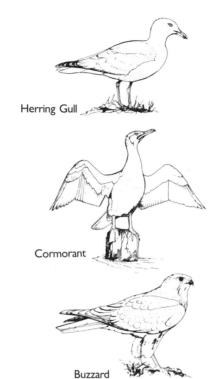
Herring Gull

Cormorant

Buzzard

36g Ramsey Island. RSPB reserve: 650 acres with high cliffs on which choughs breed. Boat and permit from Lifeboat Station, Porth Stinian.

37a Strumble Head. Steep cliffs and offshore stacks hold large numbers of seabirds, including choughs and auks.

37c Dinas Head. High cliffs give good view of offshore seabirds. Also seen are ravens and buzzards.

37f Gwaun Valley. Old oak woods lining the valley give a good variety of upland birds, including buzzards and redstarts.

41h 41i Black Mountain. Upland area of oakwood valleys which hold the usual upland birds. Occasional grouse also seen.

42g→43i Brecon Beacons. Moorland in summer brings a great variety of birds, like the buzzard and wheatear. Wooded valleys contain the typical upland birds.

43b Llyswen—Dderw Pool. Farmland pool holding a diversity of wintering wildfowl and waders, including whooper and Bewick's swans.

43e Llangorse Lake. Large natural lake with extensive reed-beds supporting a big colony of reed warblers. Also good for migrating birds, especially sand martins.

43g Talybont Reservoir. Major haunt of winter wildfowl; small passage of waders.

44g Neuadd—Llanthony Valley. Steep hillsides and oak woods with the typical upland birds.

46g Teifi Estuary. Inter-tidal area with small number of wintering ducks and waders, especially widgeon.

47d New Quay Head. Birds Rock is a breeding sanctuary for many varieties of seabird.

48c National Nature Reserve, Cors Goch. Marshy area where wildfowl are frequent visitors. Buzzard and grouse also seen. Permit required. ♣

49g Cefn Gwenffrwd. RSPB reserve (permit needed). Upland valleys and old oak woods with usual upland birds. Area of protection for the red kite.

49g Craig Clyn-gwyn—Dinas RSPB Reserve (tel. Rhandirmwyn 055 06 228). Oakwood gorge with a wide variety of native and migratory birds; red kite flies over the area. Resident warden; binoculars for hire from information centre.

51d Radnor Moors. Large area of bleak moorland where birds such as grouse, ravens, ring ouzels and dippers can be seen.

52b Dovey Estuary. Extensive mudflats and saltings; an important feeding and roosting area for wintering wildfowl and waders.

52b Cors Fochno (Borth Bog). Marshy area with numerous duck and geese.

52c Ynyshir. RSPB reserve (permits needed). Old oak woods full of the usual birds, such as pied flycatchers and redstarts.

56b Mawddach Estuary. Inter-tidal sand holding wintering wildfowl, like duck and whooper swans, and common waders.

56c Penmaenpool. Observatory for Mawddach estuary (see above) in an old signal box. ♣

56e Craig-yr-Aderyn (Bird Rock): impressive crag where cormorants and guillemots nest.

56g Broad Water. Small tidal estuary which has a small population of wildfowl and waders. Summer haunt of buzzards. △

56h Dovey Estuary. See 52b.

56i Ynyshir. RSPB reserve. See 52c.

57d Dovey Forest. Planted conifers and oak and birch woods which support upland birds and many buzzards.

57g Dulas Valley. Wooded valley where buzzards, redstarts, wheatears, ring ouzels and other upland birds can be found.

60g Bardsey Island Bird Observatory. Varied breeding population of seabirds, like shearwaters and petrels, and passage migrants, including rarities (such as the melodious warbler). Access by boat only, by permission of Bardsey Island Trust (tel. 076 671 223).

62a Traeth Bach. Inter-tidal area with varied habitats. Good population of wintering waders and wildfowl, such as whooper swans and eider.

62b Coed Llyn Mair. Small lake visited by black-headed gulls, mallards and little grebes, with occasional whooper swans in winter. ♣

62c Snowdonia provides good birdwatching for a wide variety of upland birds, including buzzards, ravens, ring ouzels and occasional grouse on the open moors; dippers and pied flycatchers in the wooded valleys. Whooper swans can be seen on the lakes during winter. See later entries.
    Vale of Ffestiniog. Oak woods with pied flycatcher.

62d Mochras (Shell Island). Nesting ground for many birds, including shelduck, herons, buzzards and sandpipers. Private land, but open to public on payment of a toll. Access only at low tide.

62f Coed-y-Brenin. Forest on both sides of A470 with planted conifers and natural oak woods containing a large variety of birds, including buzzards and dippers. ♣ ⌂ ◼

62h Mawddach Estuary. See 56b.

62i Penmaenpool. See 56c.

64g 64h Lake Vyrnwy. Reservoir with wooded shores. Birds include usual upland species with moorland species above the tree line. ◢

67a Malltraeth Sands. Estuary which is part of Newborough Warren Reserve. Frequented by throngs of wildfowl and waders.

    Newborough Warren Nature Reserve. 1,566 acres of open dunes and slacks housing a large variety of wildfowl and waders. One of the best bird watching areas in Wales.

67d Foryd Bay. Wilderness of mud and shingle holding many wintering wildfowl and waders.

67i Moel Ddu. Good area for buzzards. See also 62c Snowdonia.

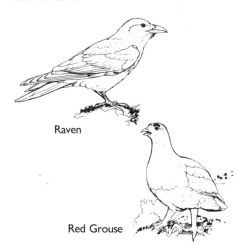

Raven

Red Grouse

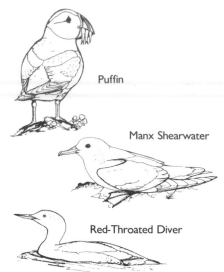

Puffin

Manx Shearwater

Red-Throated Diver

68b Ogwen Valley. Wheatear and ring ouzel can be seen. See also 62c Snowdonia. ♣

68c Llyn Mymbyr. Whooper swans often seen here. See also 62c Snowdonia.

68c Pont Cyfyng. Oak woods containing many birds. See also 62c Snowdonia.

68e Llyn Dinas. Whooper swans wintering area. See also 62c Snowdonia. ◢

68e Moel Ddu. Good area for buzzards. See also 62c Snowdonia.

68h Traeth Bach. See 62a.

68i Vale of Ffestiniog. See 62c.

74b Cemlyn Bay. National Trust bird sanctuary where waders nest (April to June). Do not walk along the spit during this time.

74d South Stack. Cliffs teeming with many seabird species, particularly gulls, puffins and guillemots. May to mid-July. ♣ ◢ ▲ ☆

74f Llyn Llywenan. Inland water with reed-beds noted for breeding ducks. Large winter population of wildfowl.

74i Llyn Coron. Important roost for winter wildfowl, especially widgeon.

75i Bod-gylched—Bulkeley Lake. Extensive reed-beds and sedges hold a mixed colony of marsh birds.

76b Puffin Island. Cliffs provide a breeding site for an excellent variety of seabirds, including auks. Boats from Beaumaris.

76b CG—Penmon Point. Cliffs which hold a large number of seabirds, particularly razorbills, guillemots and kittiwakes.

76d Bod-gylched—Bulkeley Lake. See 75i.

76d 76e Penrhyn—Lavan Sands. Mudflats and sands are good for waders (late autumn) and duck (Ogwen estuary).

76h Nant Ffrancon Valley (A5). Good for dipper and wagtail. See also 62c Snowdonia.

77a Great Orme's Head. High cliffs with large colonies of breeding seabirds; good viewpoint for offshore passage in autumn. ♣ ⬛

77b 77c Colwyn Bay. Rhos Point is an excellent spot to watch migrating waders (autumn); Abergele and Llanddulas are good for sea duck, including scoter.

77d Conwy Estuary. Large number of waders and ducks with rarer grebes frequent this area in autumn.

78i Clwyd Hills. Significant area for such birds as buzzard, ring ouzel, wheatear, grouse and other upland species.

79e Shotton Pools. Freshwater with extensive reed-beds providing a roost for a large number of swallows in August; also good for waders on passage.

Lesser Spotted Woodpecker

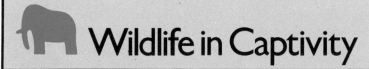

Wildlife in Captivity

Including zoos, aviaries, aquaria and outdoor safari parks. Animals in the wild are included in the sections on Countryside (pages 80-84) and Bird Watching (pages 101-102).

23i Zoological Gardens: Welsh Hawking Centre, Weycock Road (tel. Barry 0446 734687). Specialises in birds of prey, with flying displays every hour; exhibition area; adventure playground. Daily 1030 to dusk.

24c Tredegar Park (tel. Newport 0633 62275): 8-acre country park including children's farm with rare breeds; aquarium; insect, mammal and reptile houses; pony and donkey rides. Easter to end September Wednesday to Sunday and all Bank Holidays 1100-1800. ⬛ ♣ ⌂ ◣

27f Manor House Wildlife & Leisure Park, St Florence (tel. Carew 064 67 201). Covers 12 acres, with apes, monkeys, otters, deer and birds; also children's amusements and working model displays. Pets' corner; adventure playground. Easter to September 1000-1800. ⬛ ♣

28d Manor House Wildlife Park. See 27f.

31d Penscynor Wildlife Park, Cilfrew, Neath (tel. 0639 2189). This 15-acre site is mainly devoted to

birds, but the animal collection is fairly extensive, including otters, foxes, badgers, deer, llamas, donkeys, monkeys, sea lions and some fish. Features include Chimp House, Gibbon Island and a children's play area. Daily 1000 to dusk. ⬛ ◣

32e Cyfartha Castle (tel. Merthyr Tydfil 0685 3112): small aviary in park containing much else of interest. April to October: Monday to Saturday 1000-1300, 1400-1830 (1700 in April and October); Sundays 1400-1700. ♣ ◼

34g Llandegfedd Farm Park (tel. Usk 029 13 2692). Collection of rare breeds; pets' corner; old farm machinery. Daily 1100-1900.

38c Cardigan Wildlife Park, near Cilgerran (tel. Llechryd 023 987 662). Specialises in Welsh animals past and present; also many European breeds. All set in 250 acres of natural habitat with nature trails, industrial archeology, local crafts and coracle fishing displays. Daily 1000-1800. ⬛ ♣

46h Cardigan Wildlife Park. See 38c.

47b Aberaeron Marine Aquarium, The Quayside (tel. 0545 570445). Illustrates the marine life of Cardigan Bay. Easter to mid October: daily 1000-1800.

62d Llanbedr: Maes Artro Craft Village (tel. 0341 23437). Site includes a marine aquarium and a model village with a small zoo. Easter to October: daily 0900-2100.

68e Nantmor: small wildlife sanctuary at Cae Ddafydd Pottery (tel. Beddgelert 076 686 213). Easter to October: daily 0930-1800. ◣

77b Welsh Mountain Zoo, Flagstaff Gardens, Colwyn Bay (tel. 0492 2938). Unusual zoo in beautiful location, with animals, birds and reptiles. Displays of free-flying falcons, hawks and vultures; restaurant above lion compound; penguin pool with underwater observation room. April to October 0930-1900; October to March 1000-1600. ⬛ ❀

78a Rhyl: children's zoo in the Royal Floral Hall, East Parade (tel. 0745 31515). Easter to early October: daily 1000-1900. ❀

Industry Past and Present

From industrial archeology to the latest nuclear power stations, including open-air museums, craft workshops, modern factories and collieries. Preserved railways offering rides to the public are, however, detailed in the section on Tourist Railways (pages 108-109).

20c Trostre: British Steel Tinplate Works (tel. Llanelli 055 42 2260). Restored Welsh farmhouse housing a museum of the tinplate industry, including a large working model of the process. Contained within Britain's largest tinplate works, covering 270 acres. *By appointment only; Mr D C Williams, works manager. Free.*

20c Llanelli: Parc Howard Museum, off A476 to Llandeilo (tel. 055 42 2029). Mansion house with displays of the tinplating process and materials used. *Daily 1000-1600 (1900 April to October).* 🖼

21b Clydach: John Player & Son (tel. 0792 3330). Tinplate works (still in operation) with steam engine, office furniture and machinery from the 19th century. *By appointment only: Mr John Bellingham, manager.*

21b Llansamlet: Scotts Pit. Restored remains of the steam engine house built in 1817 to drain the pit workings.

21b Morriston: 3 mile town trail illustrating local industrial history. Leaflet available locally. Takes about 2 hours.

21c Neath Abbey Furnaces (tel. 0639 3665). Remains of two huge 70 ft high blast furnaces established by Quakers in 1792 on a site which made much heavy industrial machinery in the 19th century. *By appointment only:* Matt Price & Sons Ltd garage office.

21e Swansea Valley Industrial Trail. Covers 2½ miles between the symbols shown. Starts in dockland at the Royal Institution of South Wales, with its small museum, and runs north via 19 viewpoints to Landore Quay on the River Tawe. The sites, most of which are marked with plaques, span 250 years of industrial history. Leaflet available locally. Takes about 3 hours. 🖼

21e Swansea: Maritime and Industrial Museum, South Dock (tel. 0792 50351). Converted warehouse containing complete working woollen mill, plus exhibits connected with the Port of Swansea and with transport. Steam locomotives run on some Saturdays. *Monday to Saturday 1030-1730. Free.* 🖼

22a Cwmavon Copperworks Flue. Stone culvert running up the 1200 ft high Foel Fynyddau to a chimney; was used to clear toxic fumes from copperworks in the valley.

23a Gilfach Goch Industrial Trail. Coal mining town which was the scene of Richard Llewelyn's book "How Green Was My Valley"; parts of the TV serial were also filmed here. 2 miles, with information panels en route. Takes about 1½ hours.

23b Tre-hafod: Hetty Shaft. Winding House, Ty Mawr Colliery, housing 1875 steam engine.

23c Nant-garw Colliery. Modern working pit offering conducted tours of the surface; includes exhibition room with complete miniature coal face. Travel by open top bus from Cardiff (tel. 0222 396521 for timetable). *Easter to end September.*

23c Pontypridd: 1755 Bridge. Single stone arch spanning 140 ft over the River Taf.

Nightingale's Bush. Romantically named section of the old Glamorganshire Canal, with locks, cottages and bridge. Now a local nature reserve. *Any time.*

23f St Fagans: Welsh Folk Museum (tel. Cardiff 0222 569441). Extensive site with many reconstructed buildings in fine condition. An 18th century woollen mill and 19th century corn mill, both rebuilt stone by stone after being brought here from their original locations, are in working order and use

water power to produce car rugs and corn meal. *Monday to Saturday 1000-1700; Sundays 1430-1700.* 🐷🖼⚒

24a Nant-garw Colliery. See 23c.

24a Caerphilly Railway Society, Harold Wilson Industrial Estate, Van Road. Former locomotive works of the Rhymney Railway, now housing a collection of six steam locos undergoing restoration, including the only surviving standard gauge Welsh loco, an 1897 Taff Vale Railway 0-6-2 tank. *April to September: six steam days (advertised locally); otherwise by appointment only.* 🐷

24a Ystrad Mynach: Mill and Smithy. Working blacksmiths and corn mill undergoing restoration. *By permission:* Mr John West.

24b Rudry: several sites here and to the south east. Remains of colliery workings and of a tramway to Rudry Brickworks. 🚶

24c Rogerstone: Fourteen Locks. Restored section of the Monmouthshire Canal with historical information at new centre. *Canal and walks: any time. Centre: Easter to September Thursday to Monday; rest of year by appointment only* (tel. Cwmbran 063 33 67711 ext 657); *1000-1730.* 🚶

24d St Fagans: Welsh Folk Museum, See 23f.

24d Melingriffith Tinplate Works. Remains of an undershot water wheel which drove a pump via rocking beams. Substantial buildings being restored. A model of the water pump can be seen in the National Museum of Wales (24e Cardiff). 🐷

24e Cardiff: Welsh Industrial and Maritime Museum, Bute Street (tel. 0222 371805). Housed in purpose-built premises on a 4 acre site that includes the old West Bute dock basin. The emphasis is firmly on working machinery, with steam, gas and diesel engines, compressors, alternators, etc. to be seen indoors; cranes, a canal boat, a restored sailing cutter and a steam loco (children can climb aboard) outside. Also a Bristol Channel tugboat. *Monday to Saturday 1000-1700; Sundays 1430-1700. Free.*

Chapter Workshops, Market Road, off Cow bridge Road East (tel. 0222 396061). Craftsmen to be seen at work include potter, instrument maker and those working with video and photography *Monday to Saturday and Bank Holidays 1000-2200. Free.* 🐷🖼

24g Barry: Woodham's Scrapyard. Famous site chosen by British Rail to dump over 250 steam locomotives, over 100 of which have since been rescued and restored. The remainder will not be scrapped while the yard has other work. *Visible from trains between Cardiff and Barry Island; visits by appointment.*

24h Lavernock Point. Scene in 1897 of the first wireless message over water, sent by Marconi from Flat Holme island.

25a Newport Transporter Bridge. One of only three in Britain, it was opened in 1906 and carries 6 cars or about 120 tons in its cable-car-like carriage between towers 242 ft high. It can operate in winds over 100 mph. Much of the regular traffic now uses a conventional bridge up river. For a small charge, the energetic can cross the river on the top span, affording marvellous views. *Monday to Saturday 0530-2300; Sundays 1300-2300. Free.*

27c Blackpool Mill (tel. Llawhaden 099 14 233). Unique restored tidal mill, with original 1813 wooden machinery in working order. *Easter to September daily 1100-1800.* 🐷🖼

27d Neyland: Promenade Limekiln on B4325. Single kiln built into the bank.

27d Hobbs Point. Dock used by the Irish packet ships in the 19th century; also, until the Haven bridge, landing place for the Neyland ferry. It was used as an RAF Sunderland seaplane base from 1935-57, and as an Admiralty dockyard. Nearby is the new Celtic Sea oil terminal.

27f Carew: French Mill. 3 storey corn mill worked by tidal water stored in mill pond. *April to September Monday to Saturday 1000-1800, Sundays 1400-1800.*

28g Tenby: Kiln Park. Impressive row of Nash-designed limekilns. *By permission only:* owners of Kiln Park Caravan Site.

29e Kidwelly Tinplate Works. Two chimneys, ruined buildings, various machines. The foundry was established in 1719 and a plaque claims it is "the oldest in the kingdom". Llanelli Council plan to turn the site into a museum. *Can only be viewed from the road at present.*

29f Llanelli. See 20c.

30d Trostre: British Steel. See 20c.

30d Llanelli. See 20c.

30f Clydach. See 21b.

30i Llansamlet. See 21b.

30i Morriston. See 21b.

30i Swansea. See 21e.

31e Cefn Coed Coal and Steam Centre, off A4109 (tel. 0792 42044). Preserved steam winding engine, boilers and pithead gear, plus a small haulage engine; main gallery with exhibition of coal mining history in the Dulais Valley. *Thursday to Monday: April to October 1030-1800; November to March 1100-1600.*

31e Resolven. Neath & Tennant Canal. Partly restored section, with iron aqueducts and lock chambers. Various walks, up to 4 miles long. Nearby pub. *Any time.* 🐷

Melin-cwrt Iron Forge, south of Resolven. Ruins of a charcoal blast furnace of 1708, closed in 1808. *By permission of the owner:* Gwilym Farm.

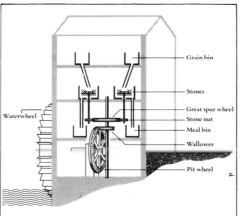

This diagram shows the main working parts of a typical water-powered corn mill.

— Grain bin

— Stones

— Great spur wheel

— Stone nut

Waterwheel

— Meal bin

— Wallower

— Pit wheel

31e Tonna: Dulais Iron Works. Weir, wheel pit and sluices of water-worked forge on a site industrialised in 1584.

Aberdulais Canal Basin. Fine 1823 aqueduct over the River Neath, slipway, canal basin and some buildings from the Neath & Tennant Canal. Start of the Tonna Trail, a 2 mile walk. Leaflet available locally.

31f Neath Canal. Another section of the Neath & Tennant canal undergoing restoration, with lock, limekiln and boathouses.

31f Cwm Gwrach Iron Works, Heol Wenallt. Remains of plant built in 1842. Former manager's house now lived in by farmer. *Visible from road, but access by permission of the farmer.*

31g Neath Abbey. See 21c.

31h Cwmavon. See 22a.

31h Welsh Miners' Museum, Afan Argoed Country Park, Cymmer (tel. 063 983 564). Simulated coal faces and real miners' equipment demonstrate the harshness of pit life in South Wales. *April to October daily 1030-1830; rest of year weekends only 1200-1700.* ⛴♦◳▣⌂

32 Merthyr Tydfil. One of the most important industrial towns in Welsh history, Merthyr has connections with iron, coal and railways. Dowlais was once the largest ironworks in the world, employing 10,000 men; Richard Trevithick carried out his early steam locomotive trials on the tramway to Abercynon; and in the 19th century coal became a major industry, with pits throughout the immediate area. As a result of all this activity, there are too many sites of industrial significance for them all to be marked on the map. What follows is a summary of the more interesting locations, beginning with the town centre and progressing clockwise around the town. Where a site is marked, its reference is given.

Town Centre Chapel Row, next to bus garage off A470. Row of two-storey terraced houses. No 4 was the birthplace in 1841 of Joseph Parry, the prolific Welsh composer: this house has been restored and a small museum incorporated.

Town Centre: Robert and Lucy Thomas Fountain, at junction of A470 and A4102. Ornate cast iron canopy built in 1907 as a memorial to the pioneers of South Wales steam coal.

Town Centre: Ynysfach Ironworks, next to College of Further Education. Remains of a sandstone engine house with limestone arches, bricked-up furnaces and blast culvert. *Any reasonable time.*

32b Cefncoedycymer: Cefn Viaduct. The third longest in Wales, at 725 ft, it carried the Brecon Railway over 15 arches built of bricks clad in stone. It was completed in 1866 and is up to 115 ft high.

32b Pontsarn Viaduct, near Vaynor, Smaller than that at Cefn, but also built in 1866 for the Brecon Railway. It is 45 ft long and its 7 arches rise to 90 ft. You can walk between both viaducts along the disused railway line.

32c Dowlais Stables. Built in 1820 to house the horses of Dowlais Ironworks, then the world's biggest. Attractive two-storey building, part of which was once a school.

32f Penydarren Tunnels, at the rear of Baker's Garage, east of A470. Part of the Penydarren Tramroad, along which Trevithick drove the world's first high-pressure steam locomotive in 1804. A model of the train can be seen in the Cyfartha Museum (See page 90).

32e Cyfartha Ironworks. Little remains of this once-huge plant, apart from blast furnace ruins; *View from A470.*

Pont-y-Cafnau Bridge, just north of the old ironworks, is a cast iron bridge thought to date from 1792, possibly the first in the world.

32c Bute Town. Three parallel terraces of typical company houses, built in 1802 for workers at the nearby Union Ironworks. They were thoroughly restored in 1975. *Exteriors: any time. Interiors: By appointment with the owners.*

32d Dare Valley Country Park. Landscaped area which once contained six collieries and is now a major tourist attraction. Four Industry Trails cover many sites, including a wooden viaduct by Brunel and the modern pithead gear of Bwllfa No 2 Colliery. *Any reasonable time.* ♠

32e Roberts Town: Cast Iron Bridge built in 1811 to carry a tramroad over the River Cynon. Ribbed walkway along the centre to prevent horses slipping. *Any time. Free.*

Glamorganshire Canal. Recently restored head of the Aberdare Canal branch, where iron and coal was transferred to the tramway. *Any time. Free.*

32f Mountain Ash: Waddle fan, Abergorki Colliery. Curious parallel-disc ventilation system common in 19th century pits, one of only two left in south Wales. *By appointment only:* NCB Area Estates Manager, Coal House, Cardiff.

32h Gilfach Goch Industrial Trail. See 23a.

32i Abercynon Miners' Institute. Dwarfing the surrounding pit cottages, this was the centre of cultural life for local miners. Interior not worth seeing. Exterior can be seen *any time.*

32i Quakers Yard: Penydarren Tramroad. Built to by-pass Glamorganshire Canal locks in 1802, it was the scene two years later of Trevithick's steam locomotive experiments (see 32 Merthyr Tydfil). About 1 mile of the route can be followed, as far as Pontygwaith Bridge.

32i Tre-hafod: Hetty Shaft. See 23b.

31i Pontypridd. See 23c.

33a Ebbw Vale: British Steel. The incredible sight of a factory 2½ miles long, which produced sheet steel and tin plate. Now closed.

33a Tredegar: Sirhowy Ironworks (tel. Cwmbran 063 33 67711 ext 657). Started in the late 18th century, using local coal, iron ore and limestone, it once produced 7000 tons of iron per year, but closed in the late 19th century. Recently excavated. *Weekdays 0800-1600.*

33b Bunkers Hill: Blaenavon Ironworks. Blast furnaces, water lift and workers' cottages dating from 1789-1860. Being restored prior to opening as a museum. Viewing and information platform. *Weekdays 0800-1600.*

Big Pit. The first complete coal mine opened to the public. *From Spring 1981.*

33b Forgeside Works, south west of Blaenavon. Working forge with heavy hammer. *Any reasonable time by permission.*

33d New Tredegar: Elliot Colliery, opposite Health Centre. Stone engine house of 1891 containing steam winding gear. Viewing of the engine—a twin tandem compound—by arrangement with the National Museum, Cardiff (see page 90).

33d Bedwellty House. Private residence for the managers of the Tredegar Iron and Coal Company in the 19th century, it has been well preserved, with many old photos and beautiful grounds containing a 15-ton block of coal cut for the 1851 Exhibition. *Weekdays 0800-1600.*

33e Abertillery: Town Trail, starting from Aberbeeg Road and taking in 6 view points illustrating the industrialisation of a once-rural valley. Leaflet from town museum (see below).

Museum, County Library. Exhibits showing development of iron and coal industry and of local tramroads. *Tuesdays and Thursdays 1400-1630; Saturdays 0930-1300, 1400-1630.*

33e British: Cwmbyrgwm Pit Headgear. Last surviving example of pre-1820 balance gear, which used tanks of water to lift loaded trams. *Any reasonable time.*

33f Pontypool: The Valley Inheritance Centre (tel. 049 55 52063). Newly opened in former stables, this industrial museum describes the history of the eastern valleys with exhibits and audio-visual material. *Daily 1000-1700 (Sundays 1400-1700).*

Pontymoile Aqueduct, just south of town centre. Carries the Monmouthshire Canal over the River Lwyd. Toll cottage and gauging stop, where boats halted to discover what toll was to be paid, now houses a small exhibition of canal history (tel. 0495 790437). *Daily 1400-1700. Free.*

33g Gelli-groes Mill. Water powered corn mill used to grind animal feed and basically unchanged since built in the 16th century, although the water wheel is cast iron. *View from road only. Any time.*

33g Hengoed: Maesycwmmer Viaduct. Built in 1857 to carry the Newport, Abergavenny and Hereford Railway, with 15 stone arches. *Any time. Free.*

Maesycwmmer Mill. Attractive corn mill converted to a woollen mill and still used as a wool sorting house. *Not open.*

33g Ystrad Mynach. See 24a.

33i Llantarnam: start of the Eastern Valley Trail, which runs to Blaenavon (33c) via the industrial sites described at Pontypool, Abersychan and Forgeside. Llantarnam itself is notable for having remained an agricultural village after the 18th century, while most surrounding towns became heavily industrial.

33i Rogerstone: Fourteen Locks. See 24c.

33i Newport. See 25a.

34a Llanvapley Rural Crafts Museum (tel. Llantilio 060 085 210). Collection of tools used in agriculture, thatching, smithing and milling. Over 500 exhibits. *February to November Sundays 1500-1800 (or dusk).*

The Tinplating Process

This diagram, showing the basic stages in the process, is part of an informative display at the Parc Howard Museum, Llanelli (20c).

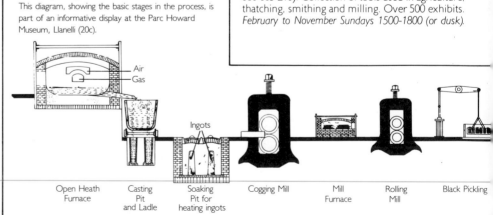

| Open Heath Furnace | Casting Pit and Ladle | Soaking Pit for heating ingots | Cogging Mill | Mill Furnace | Rolling Mill | Black Pickling |

34f Wolves Newton Folk Museum (tel. 029 15 231). Collection of craft and agricultural implements in 18th century barn. Entertainment evenings, craft courses, exhibitions, children's work sheets. *Easter to end September daily 1100-1800; October to Easter Sundays 1400-1730.* 🔲

34g Newport. See 25a.

35g Coed Ithel Furnace. One of many sites in the area, including tramways, bridges, old mills, tinplate works, a wire drawing mill and river docks, all used during the 16th to 18th centuries. Map at Tintern information centre (see page 122).

36i Solva Limekilns. In the 19th century some two dozen ships were needed to supply limestone for the two kilns whose remains are on the hillside.

36i Middle Mill. Woollen mill opened in 1907 and still producing tweeds, tapestries and carpets in traditional patterns. *Monday to Saturday 0930-1730.*

37d Tregwynt Woollen Mill. Worked since the 18th century. Pleasant location. *Weekdays 0900-1700.*

37i Wallis Woollen Mill (tel. Clarbeston 043 782 297). Founded in 1800, six looms produce quality Welsh weaving. The original water power equipment has been restored. *Weekdays and Bank Holidays 1000-1800.*

38c Llechryd. 17th century bridge of 6 arches over the River Teifi.

39a Cwmcoy: Felin Geri Flour Mill (tel. Newcastle Emlyn 0239 710810). One of the last remaining water-powered mills grinding wholemeal flour for sale to the public. It was built in 1604 and visitors can see every stage of production. Water powered saw mill; shop and bakery; small museum. *Daily 1000-1800 (1600 weekends).* ☕

39b Dre-fach: Museum of the Welsh Woollen Industry. A branch of the Welsh Folk Museum, it occupies part of the working Cambrian Mills, with a collection of textile machinery and exhibits showing the history of the industry since the Middle Ages. *1 April to end September Monday to Saturday 1000-1700 (closed May Day). Free.* 🔲

Dre-fach—Felindre Factory Trail. Circular route based on the museum (above) and taking in the Cambrian Mill, several disused mills, terraced cottages built for weavers, a smithy and an old waterwheel.

39c Llandyssul: Maesllyn Mill and Museum (tel. Rhydlewis 023 975 251). Founded in 1881 and now a working museum with many of the original machines still operating. Guided tours. Children's play area. *Monday to Saturday 1000-1800; Sundays 1400-1800.* ☕ 🚻

39c Capel Dewi: Rock Mills (tel. Llandyssul 055 932 2350). Founded in 1890, this is one of the few remaining water powered woollen mills, with much of the original machinery intact and producing fine goods for sale. *Monday to Friday 1000-1800; Saturdays AM.*

39e Cynwyl Elfed: Cwmduad Woollen Mill (tel. 026 787 337). Small museum of life in the village and at the mill, which worked from 1840 to 1960. Demonstrations of handloom spinning and weaving. *Summer: daily 0930-1930 (1830 Sundays). Winter: Monday to Saturday 0930-1700.*

40a Capel Dewi. See 39c.

46h Llechryd. See 38c.

47g Troedyraur: Curlew Weavers (tel. Rhydlewis 023 975 357). Thriving little modern mill by the River Ceri, specialising in tweeds and furniture fabrics. *Weekdays 0800-1700.*

47g Maesllyn Mill. See 39b.

49i Llanwrtyd Wells: Cambrian Factory (tel. 059 13 211). Royal British Legion mill opened in 1918 to cater for disabled World War I servicemen. Now thriving as a modern business producing a large range of patterns in tweed and wool. *Weekdays 0815-1700 (1545 Fridays).* 🏴

50g Llangammarch Wells: Lake Hotel. Disused pump house and barium chloride well connected with the town's history as a spa, with supposed cures for heart disease and gout.

51g Clyro: Wye Pottery (tel. Hay-on-Wye 049 72 510). *Monday to Saturday 0900-1800.*

52c Eglwysfach: Dyfi Furnace. Looks like an old watermill, but the 31 ft water wheel drove bellows in a blast furnace built in the mid 18th century.

52e Capel Bangor: Rheidol Hydro Electric Power Station. Run by the Central Electricity Generating Board and offering guided tours. *Easter, then Whitsun to 30 September daily 1100-1630.* 🏴

52f Cwmsymlog Lead Mine. Started as a silver mine in the 17th century supplying the Royal Mint. Remains of its mining village can also be seen.

52f Llywernog Silver-Lead Mine (tel. Ponterwyd 097 085 620). Fascinating water powered mine of 1740-1910, restored to working order and laid out as an open-air museum covering 6½ acres. Three working water wheels, floodlit underground workings, the only lead mine roll crusher left in Wales and a complete range of buildings laid out to show what life was like for the miners in the 19th century. Guide books, waymarked trails, audio-visual shows. Plenty for all the family, but wear sensible shoes. *Easter to end September 1000-1800 (1630 in September).* ☕ ♣ 🚻 ℹ

52g BBC Television transmitter mast, west of A487, is 550 ft high.

53b Dylife Lead Mine. Desolate village (although the pub survives) with remains of lead mining buildings. *Best viewed from road.*

53c The Van Lead Mine. Remains, including houses, chimneys, chapels and pit buildings, of what was once the most profitable mine in mid Wales.

53f Llyn Clywedog: Bryn Tail Mine. Cleared site of small lead mine at the foot of the dam, with waymarked trail and information board. *Any time.*

53g Cwmystwyth Lead Mine. Jagged landscape with remains of offices, workshops, mill, tramways, etc. Several dangerous shafts on site, so view from road. *Any time.*

54a The Van Lead Mine. See 53c.

54c Newtown: Royal Welsh Warehouse, beside the railway station. Once owned by Pryce Jones, who in 1859 started the world's first mail order business, selling Welsh flannel products. *Easter to October: Tuesday to Saturday 1400-1630.*

Menai Suspension Bridge (75i)

Newport Transporter Bridge (25a)

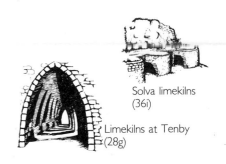
Thomas Telford (1757-1834), the Scottish civil engineer who played such a prominent part in the development of transport in Wales, designing bridges for road, rail and canal traffic.

Textile Museum, Commercial Street (tel. 0686 26243). Machinery and building frontages from the 19th century. Guided tours. *April to October Tuesday to Saturday 1400-1630.* 🔲

Town trail. Starts on A483 and covers 1¾ miles via many types of building. Takes about 1 hour. Leaflets locally.

55b Bacheldre: water mill (tel. Church Stoke 058 85 489) dating from 1747 and still working. *Any time after 1430.*

56a Barmouth: Weavers Loft (tel. 0341 280779). Modern working mill. *Weekdays 0900-1700 (Fridays 1500).*

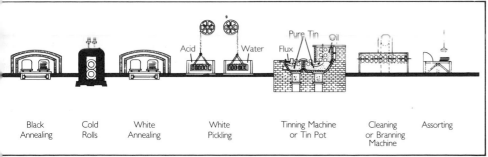

Black Annealing | Cold Rolls | White Annealing | White Pickling | Tinning Machine or Tin Pot | Cleaning or Branning Machine | Assorting

Solva limekilns (36i)

Limekilns at Tenby (28g)

56b Bontddu: Clogau Gold Mine. Famous mine which provided the gold for royal wedding rings, etc. Information board and short walk.

56c Dolgellau: Y Tanws (the tannery) on the 1638 bridge in the town centre.

56g Tywyn: Narrow Gauge Railway Museum, Wharf Station, A493 (tel. 0654 710472). Locomotives, rolling stock and other items connected with the little trains of Britain and Ireland, with natural emphasis on the Talyllyn Railway, in whose station yard it resides. *Easter to end October daily 1000-1700 (1800 July and August). Other times by arrangement.* ☕ 🏠

56i Eglwysfach: Dyfi Furnace. See 52c.

57b Minllyn: Meirion Mill (tel. Dinas Mawddwy 065 04 31). Full scale production mill founded in 1947 and occupying former railway station. *April to October: daily 1000-1630. Telephone first in winter. Free.* ☕

57d Corris Railway Museum, 300 yards from A487 Relics of the Corris Railway, which carried slate to Machynlleth on narrow gauge tracks between 1890 and 1948, housed in 19th century railway buildings. Old wagons on rails outside. Children's play area. *July and August: Tuesday to Friday and Bank Holiday weekends 1300-1730. Free.*

57d Llywyn-gwern: Centre for Alternative Technology (tel. Machynlleth 0654 2400) Self contained research area in old slate quarry with no mains services. Wind power, solar energy and pollution prevention experiments. Children's play area. *Daily 1000-1700 (dusk in winter).* ☕ ☆

57h Dylife. See 53b.

58b Lake Vyrnwy: 1881 dam holding 5 square mile reservoir which supplies Liverpool. Used in "The Dambusters" film. Old chapel houses visitor centre with display of the lake's history. *Easter to Spring Bank Holiday: weekends; then daily until end September.*

59b→59e Montgomery Canal: the marked symbols show the extent of the restored section, with locks, bridges, tow path, lock-keepers cottages, etc

59g Berriew: interesting aqueduct and disused lock of the Montgomery Canal.

59h Bacheldre. See 55b.

61c Criccieth: Roy Williams' Slate Works, Beach Bank. *Weekdays 0900-1700.*

61c Brynkir Woollen Mill (tel. Garn Dolbenmaen 076 675 236). Founded in 1830, this modern mill is famous for its wide range of produce. Old waterwheel on site. *Weekdays 0800-1600.*

62a Brynkir Woollen Mill. See 61c.

62a Porthmadog: Festiniog Railway Museum, Harbour Station (tel. 0766 2384). Former goods shed converted to show the history of the line since its conception in the 1830s. Includes an 1869 model steam engine, maps and an unusual hearse. *February to December weekends and when the railway is operating (see page 108).* ☕ 🏠

Maritime Museum, The Harbour. Displays of harbour life aboard a preserved sailing ketch. *April to September daily 1000-1800.* ☆

Pottery, Snowdon Street (tel. 0766 2785). Try your hand at making a pot. *Weekdays 1000-1630; summer weekends.*

62b Penrhyndeudraeth: Saltings Pottery (tel. 076 674 662). Attractive range for sale. *Monday to Saturday 0930-1730.*

62b Maentwrog: Plas Tan-y-Bwlch (tel. 076 685 324). Spacious country house housing the National Park Study Centre, whose weekly and weekend courses include a range of industrial archeology courses, all of which offer site visits as well as classroom instruction. ♠

Trefor Glyn Owen's Crochendy Twrog is an active local pottery. *Daily 1000-1830.*

62c Llyn Trawsfynydd Nuclear Power Station (tel. 076 687 331). Britain's first inland nuclear station, which takes 35 million gallons of water per hour from the lake to cool its reactors. *Conducted tours by arrangement.*

62c Ffestiniog: Celmi Candles, Cynfal House (tel. 076 676 2675). Candle-making demonstrations. *Weekdays 0900-1700.*

62d Llanfair: Old Quarry Slate Caverns (tel. Harlech 076 673 247). Man made caverns blasted out of the hills in the quest for slate, now floodlit. Guided tours; miners' helmets supplied; temperature underground usually only 50°F. *Easter to mid October daily 1000-1730.* ☕

62f Pont Dolgefeiliau: Forest Information Centre (tel. Ganllwyd 034 140 210). Display of local gold mining machinery. *Easter to October daily 1000-1700.* ♣ ℹ️

62i Bontddu. See 56b.

62i Dolgellau. See 56c.

63d Rhaeadr Mawddach: Gwynfynydd Gold Mine. Dressing mill, strong room and water powered machinery remains in very scenic location. Park at picnic site (62f). ♣

64h Lake Vyrnwy. See 58b.

65a Glyn Ceiriog: Chwarel Wynne (tel. 069 172 343). Small slate mine with guided tours around life size tableaux, displays of tools and machinery; nearby Glyn Valley Hotel has photographic exhibition about the local tramway. *Easter to September: daily 1000-1700.*

65c Chirk: Aqueduct carrying the Llangollen canal over the River Ceiriog in a cast iron trough 70 ft up. To the north, the canal runs through the 460 ft long Chirk Tunnel.

Viaduct carrying the Shrewsbury & Chester Railway over the same valley, with 16 brick arches.

65h Montgomery Canal. See 59b.

66i Porth y Nant: remote, lonely bay with old quarry workings and ruined piers.

67a Belan (tel. Llanwnda 0286 830220). Old forge, maritime museum and do-it-yourself pottery in tourist castle. Miniature steam railway. *Easter to September daily 1000-1700.* ☕ 🏠 ☆

67b Caernarfon: Maritime Museum, Victoria Dock. Coal-fired steam dredger *Scout II* is part of this new museum, covering the port's history of slate exporting. Exhibition in dockside building. *Easter to September: daily 1000-1700.*

67c Gilfach Ddu: North Wales Quarrying Museum (tel. Llanberis 028 682 630). The workshops of a former quarry converted to show how slate was blasted, then worked by hand; also shows the many ancillary trades needed to keep the quarry going—smith, foundry, repair shops, etc. Also machinery, rolling stock and famous 54 ft Dinorwic water wheel. Film shows. *Easter Saturday to end September daily 0930-1700 (1900 in summer).*

Vivian Quarry Trail. 1 hour walk through Padarn Country Park showing slate quarrying buildings, including Quarry Hospital, now an interpretative centre. *Any reasonable time.* ♣ 🏠

67f Drws-y-Coed Copper Mines. Worked from 1761-1918, remains of mine buildings and cottages can be seen from the road.

67i Brynkir Woollen Mill. See 61c.

68a Gilfach Ddu: North Wales Quarrying Museum. See 67c.

68a Drws-y-Coed. See 67f.

68b Snowdon: remains of the Britannia Copper mine and its 1853 causeway over Llyn Llydaw. Access via the railway or the Miners Track. 🏠 ▲

68e Beddgelert: Sygun Copper Mine, in the hills east of town. Remains of an impressive causeway and mine entrances. Site was used for filming "The Inn of the Sixth Happiness".

68e Nantmor: Beddgelert Pottery, Cae Ddafydd (tel. 076 686 213). Aromatic pomanders filled to secret recipes. *Easter to October: daily 0930-1800.* 🏠

68f Blaenau Ffestiniog: Gloddfa Ganol Mountain Tourist Centre, A470 (tel. 076 681 664). The largest slate mine in the world, with 42 miles of tunnels, massive machinery restored to working order, furnished quarrymen's cottages and museum/exhibition centre. Conducted tours by Land Rover, with helmets and miner's lamps supplied. Craft shop. *Easter to October daily 1000-1730.* ☕ 🖼️ 🏠 ☆

Llechwedd Slate Caverns (tel. 076 681 306). Complete 19th century slate mine with lifelike tableaux and machinery seen in electric tram rides through deep caves, including the 200 ft high Cathedral Cave. Exciting moment when floodlights are turned off, leaving only miners' 'candles'. Also reconstructed slate splitting mill, with working demonstrations, and audio-visual show covering 1700 years of slate mining. Only 50°F underground, so bring warm clothes. *March to October daily 1000-1715.* ☕ 🖼️ 🏠

68f Stwlan Resr: Ffestiniog Pumped Storage Power Station. Guided tours of this impressive hydro-electric scheme. Special buses from Blaenau Ffestiniog. *Easter; then Whitsun to end September; 0900-1630.*

68f Tan-y-grisiau: Moelwyn Mill. Water powered 18th century fulling mill with interesting machinery. Recently restored. *Wednesdays and Thursdays during school holidays: 1430-1630.*

68g Brynkir Woollen Mill. See 61c.

68g Porthmadog. See 62a.

68h Penrhyndeudraeth. See 62b.

68i Maentwrog. See 62b.

68i Llyn Trawsfynydd. See 62c.

69a Cyffty Lead Mine. Reservoir, some buildings and other remains. Reached by walking from Ty-hyll or Miners Bridge. 🚶

69b Waterloo Bridge. Designed in 1815 by Thomas Telford, with single arch of cast iron carrying A5.

69b Betws-y-Coed: Conwy Valley Railway Museum, Old Goods Yard, BR Station (tel. 069 02 568). Standard gauge locos and rolling stock, plus collection of large models. Refreshments from buffet car. *Easter to end September daily; October weekends; 1400-1700 (1030-1730 in summer).* ☕

69e Penmachno Woollen Mill, B4406 (tel. Betws-y-Coed 069 02 545). Weaving and spinning of colourful Welsh produce. *Weekdays 0900-1700 (weekends in summer).*

69f Pentrefoelas: rare working water mill, producing wholemeal bread and biscuits. *Office hours.*

69g Ffestiniog. See 62c.

71c Bwlch-gwyn: North Wales Geology Museum (tel. Wrexham 0978 757573). Colliery winding gear and beehive tile kiln among many exhibits. Trail in adjacent silica quarry. *Easter to October: weekdays 0900-1700; also weekends and Bank Holidays in Summer 1100-1730.* ☕ ♣ 🏠

71c Minera Lead Mines, viewed from B5426 south of village: beam engine house, chimneys and other buildings visible. Actual sites have dangerous shafts. Minera is the start of the Bersham Industrial Trail (see 71f).

Britannia Railway Bridge (75i)

71e Llangollen: Railway Station (tel. 0978 860951). Restored Great Western station with steam locomotives, rolling stock, etc. *Daily 1000-1730. Free.*

Canal Exhibition Centre, The Wharf (tel. 0978 860702). 19th century warehouse housing display of barges, machinery and models showing life on the canals. Also realistic coal mine display; audio-visual shows. *Easter to end September 1100-1700.*

71f Froncysyllte: Pontcysyllte Viaduct. Built in 1794-1805 by Thomas Telford, it carries the Shropshire Union Canal 127 ft above the Dee Valley on 19 arches and is 1007 ft long. Still used by holiday craft.

71f Bersham Industrial Trail. Runs 8 miles from Minera (71c) to Erddig (71f), but its main sites are here at Bersham. The town was an ironmaking centre from about 1670 until the mid 19th century, reaching a peak in the late 18th century, when the New Bersham Company made a wide range of products, including armaments, cylinders for James Watt's early steam engines and lead piping. The many interesting sites at Bersham include workers' cottages, blast furnace remains, weirs, the Ballistics Bank (into which new cannons were test fired), Corn Mill Building (containing a huge cast iron water wheel) and the odd Octagonal Building (thought to have been a cannon foundry with a centrally mounted crane). Guide available from Shire Hall, Mold.

71f Felin Puleston Agricultural Museum. Remains of a water powered mill dating from about 1620, now housing a National Trust museum showing the evolution of farm machinery during the 19th century. *Easter to end October: Tuesday to Sunday 1200-1730.*

71f Erddig. Restored manor house with restored 18th century outbuildings including laundry, bakehouse, sawmill and smithy, all in working order. *Early April to late October: Tuesday to Sunday and Bank Holiday Mondays 1200-1730.* 🍽 ❋ 🏠 ○

71h Glyn Ceiriog. See 65a.

72a Rossett: Rossett Mill. Black and white half timbered building dating from about the 14th century, with wood and cast iron water wheel. *Exterior at any time.*

Marford Mill, opposite, has been converted to offices. *Exterior any time.*

72d Bersham Industrial Trail. See 71f.

72d Felin Puleston. See 71f.

72d Erddig. See 71f.

74c Wylfa Head: Nuclear Power Station (tel. 040 789 471). One of the largest in the world, producing enough electricity for the whole of North Wales and Liverpool. The warm cooling water is used to breed edible eels. Observation tower. *Guided tours by arrangement.* ♣

75a Amlwch Port: remains of quay, dock gates and dry dock from the port's days as a copper shipping terminal for the mines on Parys Mountain (see below). The harbour is now used by an oil company.

A contemporary 19th century view of the Menai Suspension Bridge (75i)

75a Parys Mountain: spectacular copper mining site, once the largest in Europe, employing 1500 men, women and children in 1790. Now a deserted, lunar-like landscape, well worth seeing, but full of dangerous shafts. To the north is a disused windmill used to help pump water from the diggings.

75e Bodeilio Weaving and Craft Centre. Local craftsmen and artists at work. Courses arranged. *Summer: daily 1000-1830. Winter: by arrangement.*

75i Britannia Railway Bridge, built by Robert Stephenson in 1846-50 to carry Holyhead-London expresses over the Menai Strait at a height of 200 ft. The twin tracks were enclosed in wooden tubes but these were damaged by fire in 1970 and have been replaced by open steelwork. The bridge now carries a new road linking Anglesey to the mainland. Note the giant lions at each end of the bridge.

75i Menai Suspension Bridge. Built by Thomas Telford in 1819-26 to carry A5 over the Menai Strait. When opened, it was the longest single span in the world, at 579 ft. The 100 ft headroom was demanded by the Admiralty.

76d Menai Suspension Bridge. See 75i.

76d Penrhyn Castle Industrial Railway Museum (tel. Bangor 0248 53084). Norman castle now run by the National Trust and containing a collection of locomotives connected with the Welsh slate industry, some of them in working order. *April, May and October daily 1400-1700; June to end September and all Bank Holiday weekends 1100-1700.* 🍽 ❋ ▣ 🏠 🏛

Llanfair-ym-Muallt Pottery, in the castle grounds, has items for sale.

76h Penrhyn Slate Quarries, Bethesda. Up to 1000 ft deep, producing slate in blue, red, grey and green. *April to September: guided tours by arrangement.*

77d Conwy: Telford Bridge. Designed and built by the famous engineer in 1826, its design is similar to that of Menai (75i), except that the towers match those of nearby Conwy Castle. It has been replaced by a 1959 road bridge, but preserved by the National Trust. *Pedestrians only. Any time. Free.*

Railway Bridge: next to the road bridge is a 410 ft tubular bridge built by Robert Stephenson in 1846-8.

Old Toll House: National Trust shop with Telford exhibition. *April to late September daily 1000-1700.*

77d Pentre felin: Felin Isaf (tel. Colwyn Bay 0492 65646). A 17th century flour mill with restored buildings and 1730 machinery. Milling demonstrations and wholemeal flour for sale. Waymarked walks. *April to October: Tuesday to Saturday 1030-1700; Sundays 1430-1700.*

77g Llanrwst: Transport Museum, Goods Warehouse, Station Yard (tel. Deganwy 0492 82394). Diesel locomotives, rolling stock, 3-wheel lorries and a single-deck bus, plus many smaller exhibits. *First Sunday of each month 1000-1630. Free.*

77g Trefriw Woollen Mills (tel. Llanrwst 0492 640462). Water driven mill founded in 1859 producing a renowned range of tapestry and clothing. The complete processing of raw wool to woven product can be seen. *Weekdays 0745-1200, 1300-1645.*

78f Nannerch: old water mill, now a craft workshop with enamelling and pottery demonstrations. The Afonwen Tweed Company woollen mill is nearby. *Daily 0900-1700.*

78h Pentre: Yr Hen Felin (tel. Llanynys 074 578 239). Local mill converted to museum and crafts shop with hand tools and original water wheel. *See below.*

Yr Hen Gegin Gymraeg — the Old Welsh Kitchen— is next to the mill and is furnished as a typical Victorian Welsh cottage, with guide wearing traditional Welsh costume. *Both premises: Easter, then Spring Bank Holiday to end September Monday to Saturday 1030-1730.*

79d Holywell Textile Mills, Greenfield Street (tel. 0352 712022). One of the few large-scale mills in Wales, specialising in Jacob Sheep wool tweed. *Weekdays 0900-1730.*

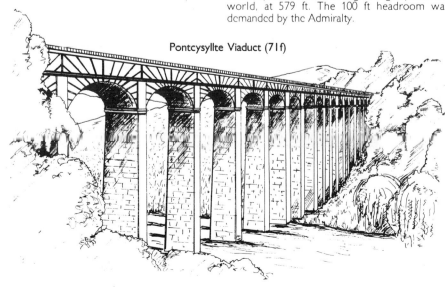

Pontcysyllte Viaduct (71f)

![steam locomotive icon] Tourist Railways

These are railways on which the public can ride and include both standard and narrow gauge lines, together with some of the most impressive miniature systems. Where trains can only be watched, they are listed under Industry (pages 103-107).

30i Swansea: Heart of Wales Line (tel. 0792 50808). The town is the southern terminus for this British Rail line which, although not strictly a tourist railway, is well worth considering as it is one of the most spectacular in Britain, taking in magnificent scenery and some impressive railway architecture, including two major tunnels and several viaducts. From Swansea, trains run north via Ammanford (30b), Llandeilo (40i), Llandovery (41b), Llanwrtyd Wells (49i), Builth Road (50e), Knighton (55h), continuing east to Shrewsbury in England. The whole trip takes about 3½ hours, but you can break your journey at several places without paying extra; indeed, there are many special fares available. *Four trains daily, from about 0530 to 2230.*

32c Brecon Mountain Railway. Newest Welsh narrow-gauge line, opened in 1980. Will eventually run 8 miles over former Brecon & Merthyr Railway route, including Torpantau Tunnel, the highest (1313 ft) in Britain. Much of the route runs through the scenic Brecon Beacons National Park. First 1¾ miles open. 2 ft gauge; steam traction, using tank locos, mostly ex-South African. Access at Pant Terminus only. (Tel. 0685 4854). *Easter to end October: daily 1100 to dusk.* ☕

39i Gwili Railway. The only standard gauge steam passenger line in Wales, using part of the ex-Great Western Carmarthen-Aberystwyth route. It is planned to run 8 miles from Abergwili to Llanpumsaint, but only 1½ miles are currently open, with road access at Bronwydd Arms only. Steam traction, using ex-GWR and industrial tank locos and GWR carriages. Timetables from Great Western Chambers, Angel St., Neath (tel. 0639 2191). *Bank Holidays 1100-1730; July to September weekends PM; some summer weekdays.* ☕ 🚃

52d→i Vale of Rheidol Railway. British Rail's only all-steam-powered line covers the 12 miles from Aberystwyth (tel. 0970 612377) to Devil's Bridge in just over one hour, climbing 680 ft. The scenery at the eastern end is spectacular, including the Rheidol Falls and the 400 ft Mynach Falls. 1 ft 11½ in gauge; steam traction by three 2-6-2 tank locos, including *Prince of Wales*, built for the line's opening in 1902. *Easter to early October daily 1000-1735.* ☕ ♣ ☆

52d Aberystwyth: Cliff Railway. Cable cars from Cliff Terrace, at the northern end of the Promenade, climb 400 ft to the top of Constitution Hill. *Easter, then May to September: daily, every few minutes.*

Cambrian Coast Line (tel. 0970 612378). The

Talyllyn Railway (56g)

town is one terminus for this British Rail line which, although not actually a tourist railway, is worthy of inclusion here as one of Britain's most scenic routes. Diesel multiple units run north to Dovey Junction (56i), where they join similar units from the line's other branch, which runs north to Morfa Mawddach (56b). The two trains then combine to travel east via Machynlleth (57g), Newtown (54c) and Welshpool (59e), before leaving Wales and continuing east to Shrewsbury. The northern branch also serves Barmouth (56a), Harlech (62d), Porthmadog (62a) and Pwllheli (61a), but through trains were suspended late in 1980 due to the poor condition of the wooden viaduct over Afon Mawddach south of Barmouth—until this is repaired special buses link Machynlleth and Barmouth to connect with the isolated northern portion of the route. The whole line is useful to railway enthusiasts in that it offers direct connections with several of the narrow gauge tourist railways: the Vale of Rheidol at Aberystwyth (52d), the Talyllyn at Tywyn (56g), the miniature railway at Fairbourne (56b), the Festiniog at Minffordd (62b) and Porthmadog (62a) and the Welsh Highland, also at Porthmadog. *Six trains daily.*

55h Knighton: Heart of Wales Line, from Shrewsbury to Swansea. See 30i Swansea.

56b Fairbourne Station: Fairbourne Railway (tel. 0341 250362). Miniature, 15 inch gauge line covering 2¼ miles to Ferry Station in 20 minutes.

Steam traction, including a scale Atlantic 4-4-2 built in 1924. Open and closed passenger coaches. *Easter, then April to May Sundays, then May to mid October daily.* ☕

56g→e Talyllyn Railway. Operated continuously since 1866, it was the first in the world to be restored by enthusiasts, who took over in 1951. Now well-preserved, with much new equipment, it runs 7¼ miles from the modernised Wharf Station in Tywyn (tel. 0654 710472) to Nant Gwernol. Spectacular scenery includes Cader Idris and the Dolgoch Falls (alight at Dolgoch station). The round trip takes about 2 hours. 2 ft 3 in gauge; steam traction, including *Talyllyn*, an 0-4-2 saddle tank built in 1864. *Easter to September daily; October Tuesday to Thursday and weekends.* ☕ ♣ 🍴

58f→59d Welshpool & Llanfair Railway. Currently runs 5½ miles from Llanfair Caereinion (tel. 093 882 441) to Sylfaen, but a 3-mile extension to a new station at Raven Square, Welshpool, is under construction. The line first opened in 1903, was closed by British Railways in 1956 and re-opened for tourists in 1963. Notable for its steep gradients, requiring powerful locos, which have been acquired from Austria, Africa and the West Indies, as well as Britain. 2 ft 6 in gauge; steam traction. *Easter, Spring Bank Holiday, then June to September daily; September to October weekends.* ☕

59d Welshpool & Llanfair Railway. See 58f.

62a Welsh Highland Light Railway. Opened in 1979, currently runs from near Porthmadog BR station to Pen-y-Mount Halt (1 mile). Extension to Pont Croesor (3 miles) under construction; plans to take line north of Beddgelert (68f) along the route of the unsuccessful Welsh Highland Railway of 1923-36. 1 ft 11½ in gauge; steam traction, including an ex-WHR 2-6-2 tank loco *Russell*, built in 1906, plus some unusual rolling stock. *Every weekend.* ☕

62a→c Festiniog Railway. The oldest and most famous narrow-gauge line in the world, built in 1836 to carry slate. Passenger services started in 1865 and ended in 1939. Preservation started in 1954, since when the 1 ft 11½ in gauge line has been constantly improved and extended, currently offering a 70-minute, 12-mile run from Porthmadog (tel. 0766 2384) to Tanygrisiau (68f). Under construction is an extension to connect with British Rail in Blaenau Ffestiniog (68f). The Festiniog has 11 steam engines, the oldest being *Prince* and *Princess*, both 0-4-0 tanks dating from 1863; but the line is best known for its double-ended articulated Fairlies, built by the Festiniog's own workshops at

Festiniog Railway (62a)

Boston Lodge. The latest double-ender, *Earl of Merioneth*, was completed in 1979, making it the newest passenger-hauling steam loco in Europe. There are also 7 diesels, used for some winter services. Bus connection to/from Blaenau Ffestiniog; picnic area and nature trail at Tanygrisiau. *End March to early November daily; rest of year weekends.*

63c Bala Lake Railway. Once part of British Railway's scenic line from Ruabon across North Wales to Barmouth, it was closed under Beeching in 1965. Re-laid in 1965 to 1 ft 11½ in 'Festiniog gauge', it now runs 4½ miles from Llanuwchllyn (tel. 067 84 666), where the station is that built for the Bala and Dolgellau Railway in 1867, to Bala (tel. 0678 520226), taking 30 mins each way. Steam traction, including two 1902 locos, plus 10 diesels. *Easter to end September daily; weekends to mid-October.* ●

Snowdon Mountain Railway (67f)

64a Bala Lake Railway. See 63c.

67c Llanberis Lake Railway. Follows the route of the old Padarn Railway, but with 1 ft 11½ in gauge track from nearby Dinorwic Quarries. Runs 2 miles from Gilfach Ddu, Llanberis (tel. 028 682 549) to Penllyn, with picnic sites at Cei Llydan halt. Five steam locos include 0-4-0 saddle tank *Elidir*, built in 1889; also 9 diesels. *Easter to October daily 1030-1730.* ● ♣ ↓|

67f Snowdon Mountain Railway. Runs 4¾ miles from Llanberis (tel. 028 682 223) to within 60 ft of the top of Snowdon, climbing 3200 ft on gradients as steep as 1 in 5½. 2 ft 7½ in gauge; all stream traction, using 7 Swiss-built 0-4-2 tank locos each pushing one 60-seat coach. Britain's only rack railway, trains travel at only 5 mph and take one hour to complete the climb. No trains in severe weather or high winds. Long queues on fine days. Expensive. *Easter to October daily 0900-1700.* ● ▲

68a Llanberis Lake Railway. See 67c.

68a→b Snowdon Mountain Railway. See 67f.

68f Blaenau Ffestiniog: Llechwedd Slate Caverns (tel. 076 681 306). Battery-powered train/tram rides into restored underground slate quarry; also new incline railway, Britain's steepest underground passenger line. *March to October daily 1000-1715.* ● ▣ ↓T ☆

68f→i Festiniog Railway. See 62a-c.

69i Bala Lake Railway. See 63c.

70g Bala Lake Railway. See 63c.

71e Llangollen Railway Society. Restored Great Western station (tel. 0978 860951) with occasional trips behind 0-6-0 saddle tank *Kitson*. Plans to extend the standard gauge line 10 miles west to Corwen. *Steam days on public holidays and first week of July.* ● ↓T

76g Llanberis Lake Railway. See 67c.

77a Great Orme Tramway. Built in 1903, it climbs almost 650 ft from Llandudno (tel. 0492 76749) to the top of Great Orme Head. Two sections, each ½ mile long, with gradients of 1 in 4 and 1 in 10; passengers must change cars half way up. Electrically driven cable traction. *1 May to early October daily 1000-1800.* Also cabin lift from Happy Valley to summit.

77a Rhyl Monorail (tel. 0745 31771). Continuous loop on steel pillars covering 1 mile along the promenade to the Sun Centre. Passengers carried in 40 seat electric train sets. *Easter to end September: daily 1000-2300; also winter weekends.*

 # Cruising by Boat

Includes all kinds of boat trips: sea cruises, island visits, river and canal boats, on all of which you can relax while someone else does the driving. Self-drive boating is dealt with on pages 111-112.

21e Swansea: steamer trips to Ilfracombe in north Devon, operated by P & A Campbell's White Funnel fleet (tel. Cardiff 0222 20255). *April to September: daily.*

21h Mumbles Head: pleasure cruises to many ports on both sides of the Bristol Channel depart from the pier near the lifeboat station; they include day trips to Ilfracombe in north Devon, operated by P & A Campbell's White Funnel fleet (tel. Cardiff 0222 20255). *April to September: daily.*

22e Porthcawl: regular cruises along the coast; also trips to the other side of the Bristol Channel.

24h Penarth: steamer trips to many Bristol Channel ports, including Weston-Super-Mare in Avon and Ilfracombe in north Devon; all operated by P & A Campbell's White Funnel fleet (tel. 0222 20255). *April to September: daily.*

27d Hobbs Point: the old car ferry pier is the departure point for cruises on Milford Haven in the Motor Vessel *Tudor Prince.*

27d Milford Haven: cruises to many of the remote spots in Milford Haven itself; also boat trips to Skomer and Skokholm islands (26d).

28g Tenby: pleasure cruises along the Welsh coastline in both directions; also launches to Caldey Island (*Summer only.* ♣ ✝).

33c Coed-y-Person: day trips by canal bus along the Monmouthshire & Brecon Canal. Organised by B & M Charter, Willsbrook, Raglan (tel. 0291 690201). *May to October.* ▵

36h Porth Stinian: boat trips around Ramsey Island leave from here.

43e Llangorse Lake: water bus trips on the lake. *Summer.* ▵

46g St Dogmaels: boat trips down river to Cardigan Island. *Summer.*

46i Aberporth: pleasure cruises along the coast. *Summer.*

47e New Quay: pleasure trips from the sheltered bay visit inaccessible parts of this otherwise rocky coastline. *Summer.*

52d Aberystwyth: boat trips around the bay depart from the main beach. *Summer.*

The Llangollen Canal (71e)

56a Barmouth: cruises up the Mawddach Estuary leave from Merioneth Yacht Club. ▣ ▵ ♪

60c Porth Nefyn: pleasure trips along the coastline. *Summer.*

60d Aberdaron: boat trips to Bardsey Island. No landing in bad weather. *Summer.*

60f Abersoch: boat trips to St Tudwal's islands.

67b Caernarfon: pleasure cruises from the quay near Caernarfon Castle to Fort Belan (▥ ↓T ☆). Operated by Menai Cruises (tel. Llanwnda 0286 830220).

71e Llangollen: trips by horse-drawn barge on the restored Llangollen Canal. Normal cruises run from Llangollen Wharf (tel. 0978 860702) to Pentrefelin, but large parties can arrange trips to Froncysyllte (71i). ↓T ▵

74d Holyhead: boat trips to The Skerries, although the lighthouse there is not open to the public. *Calm weather only.*

75e Traeth Bychan: pleasure cruises along the Anglesey coast. *Summer.*

75i Bangor: pleasure cruises along the North Wales coast.

76d Bangor: See 75i (above).

77a Llandudno: pleasure cruises to Douglas (Isle of Man) and Liverpool, operated by The Isle of Man Steam Packet Company (tel. Llandudno 0492 76837 or Douglas 0624 3824). *Summer.*

77b Colwyn Bay: speedboat trips.

77d Conwy: pleasure cruises into Conwy Bay; also up river to Tal-y-Cafn (3½ hour round trip).

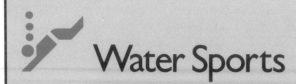

Water Sports

Swimming pools; waterskiing clubs and tuition centres; sub-aqua/diving clubs. Any sea area outside bays can be used for waterskiing but in bays, harbours, estuaries and creeks the local by-laws and speed restrictions (up to 6-8 nautical mph) must be adhered to.

The coastline is one of the great natural assets of the region, one which can be enjoyed free of charge by everyone, although car drivers must expect to pay parking fees almost everywhere. The maps in this atlas will enable you to choose which part to visit: sandy beaches, many of them surprisingly secluded even in summer, have been prominently marked in yellow.

Wherever you take to the water, however, do be careful. Each year, scores of holidaymakers are drowned at the seaside, almost always as a result of easily avoidable accidents. In order to avoid becoming one of the annual statistics:

DO Swim between the red and yellow flags where these are flying. These indicate that the area is patrolled by lifeguards.

DO Check the water before allowing children to bathe. Look for dangerous ledges, etc. and make sure any currents are not too strong for them.

DO Keep an eye on children in the water at all times, even if lifeguards are on duty. Swimming accidents tend to happen very quickly.

DO NOT Swim when red flags are flying, however tempting the beach may appear.

DO NOT Swim on an empty stomach or for one hour after a meal - both these states can cause cramps.

DO NOT Swim alone. Always swim near others or at least where you can be seen by others.

DO NOT Let small children go too far in. Unless they are proficient swimmers, they should not go past the point at which the water comes to their waist.

DO NOT Use inflatable airbeds, rings or other such toys in the sea, especially if there is an offshore wind or the tide is ebbing. Not only are these inflatables easily carried out to sea, but most of them are easily overturned by wind or swell.

In an Emergency
Do not panic. If you are in difficulty, tread water gently and raise one arm vertically as a signal for help. If you see someone else in difficulty, it is usually best to shout for help and/or to telephone 999 and ask for the coastguard, whose duties include alerting the appropriate rescue forces.

20c Llanelli. Jubilee swimming pool. 33.3 metres long; cafe overlooking the pool.

21d Mumbles. Popular waterskiing area. Note: a byelaw makes it an offence to ski within 40 yards of swimmers.

21e Swansea. Morriston Park (tel. 0792 71244) heated open-air swimming pool *(May to September)*; Swansea Leisure Centre has heated indoor pools and a surf-making machine.

21f Port Talbot. Afon Lido has an Olympic-standard swimming pool.

22a Port Talbot. See 21f (above).

23c Pontypridd. Ynsangharad Park open-air swimming pool.

24e Cardiff. Wales Empire Olympic-standard swimming pool, Wood Street, was built for the 1958 Commonwealth Games. There are open-air pools at Llandaff Fields and Splott Park, plus another indoor pool at the National Sports Centre, Sophia Gardens.

24g Barry. Open-air seawater swimming pool. *May to September.*

24h Penarth. Two indoor seawater swimming pools. *April to October.*

25a Newport. Stow Hill Baths (tel. 0633 51167).

27a Haverfordwest. Swimming pool in Dew Street.

27d Milford Haven. Outdoor seawater swimming pool. *May to September.*

27d Wear Point. Very good waterskiing area.

27e Burton. Waterskiing centre.

28d Saundersfoot Sailing Club (tel. 0834 812492). Sub-aqua facilities. *April to end September.*

28g Tenby. Sub-aqua school where underwater swimming gear is for hire. Also swimming pool (tel. 0834 3575).

29f Llanelli. See 20c.

30d Llanelli. See 20c.

30i Swansea. See 21e.

31g Port Talbot. See 21f.

32e Aberdare. Swimming pool at the Michael Sobell Sports Centre (tel. 0685 874323).

32i Pontypridd. See 23c.

37i Llys-y-fran Reservoir. Facilities for sub-aqua enthusiasts.

42f Brecon. Penlan indoor heated swimming pool in Cerrig-cochion Road.

50b Llandrindod Wells. Temple Street swimming pool.

50e Builth Wells. Groe Park swimming pool.

56a Barmouth: Welsh Windsurfing Centre. (tel. 0341 280494). Tuition; no experience needed, wet suits provided. Unaccompanied children over 15 years. *April to October.*

56g Tywyn. Indoor heated swimming pool.

59e Welshpool. Indoor heated swimming pool.

60e Berth-cur. Sub-aqua centre.

60f Abersoch. Popular waterskiing centre.

62d Harlech. Heated indoor swimming pool.

67b Tal-y-Gwynedd: Mermaid Inn. Waterskiing club operates from the jetty; lessons can be arranged.

Surfing Beaches

Surfing beaches indicated are good for both malibu and belly-board surfing; where the use of malibu boards is restricted, surfing lanes are denoted by flags on the beach. Good surf depends on the weather and the direction the beach faces; it will be best two or three tides after a major blow, on an incoming tide with an offshore wind. Most of the larger beaches are patrolled by life-guards in summer and most will have malibu boards for hire. Surfing in winter is possible but dangerous.

67b Caernarfon. Outdoor seawater swimming pool. *May to September.*

70f Corwen. Swimming pool with sun bathing patio.

71a Ruthin. Indoor heated swimming pool.

71f Acrefair: Plas Madoc Leisure Centre (tel. Wrexham 0978 821600). Lagoon-type swimming pool; also solarium and sauna.

72d Wrexham. Indoor swimming pool.

74d Holyhead: Scimitar Marine Leisure Centre, Porth-y-felin. Sub-aqua courses. Indoor heated swimming pool (tel. 0407 4112).

74d Trearddu Bay. Popular waterskiing and scuba/sub-aqua swimming area.

75a Amlwch. Heated indoor swimming pool.

75e Moelfre. Waterskiing centre.

75g Llangefni. Swimming pool at the Plas Arthur Sports Centre (tel. 0248 722966).

75i Beaumaris. Outdoor seawater swimming pool.

75i Bangor. Heated indoor swimming pool.

76d Beaumaris. See 75i.

76d Bangor. See 75i.

77a Llandudno. Swimming pool, Mostyn Broadway.

77b Rhos-on-Sea. Open-air seawater swimming pool. *Spring Bank Holiday to September.*

77b Colwyn Bay. Specialist sub-aqua shop: North Wales Divers, 85 Conwy Road, West End (tel. 0492 31806). Popular for waterskiing.

78a Rhyl. Open-air seawater swimming pool. *May to September.* Sun Centre (tel. 0745 3177) with heated indoor swimming pool, tropical lagoon and indoor surfing pool.

78b Prestatyn. Open-air heated seawater swimming pool. *Easter to September.*

78h Denbigh: Indoor heated swimming pool.

79e Connah's Quay. Indoor heated swimming pool, with learner pool and sauna bath.

79g Mold. Swimming pool.

Sailing and Boating

Sailing clubs and schools where temporary membership and/or other facilities are available to the short term visitor. Also: windsurfing, canoeing, rowing and power boating centres; and places where you can hire - for long or short term - canal boats, yachts, dinghies, motor boats and beach craft.

20b Burry Port Yacht Club, The Harbour (tel. 055 46 3635). Temporary membership available (free for RYA and WYA members).

21d Mumbles Yacht Club, Mumbles Road, Southend (tel. 0792 69321). Temporary membership available (free for RYA members). Racing from April to October.

The Bristol Channel Yacht Club, Southend (tel. 0792 66000). Cruiser racing; temporary membership available.

21e Swansea: Celtic Sea Charters, 8 De La Beche Street (tel. 0792 41503). Self-skipper yacht charter with instruction; equipment provided; maximum of 7 adults per boat; minimum age 21 for skipper. *1 April to 30 September.*

21f Port Talbot Small Boat Club (tel. Porthcawl 065 671 8141). Temporary membership for visitors.

22a Port Talbot. See 21f.

22e Porthcawl Harbour Boating Club, Jennings Buildings, The Harbour. 3 berths available for visitors; dinghy parking. *May to November.*

24e Cardiff Yacht Club, Roath Basin, Cardiff Docks (tel. 0222 387697). Races for cruisers only at weekends, plus evenings (tides permitting). Moorings on application. *April to October.*

24g Barry Yacht Club, The Harbour, Pier Head (tel. 0446 735511). Visitors welcome (RYA members free). Racing April to December.

24h Penarth Yacht Club, The Esplanade (tel. 0222 708196). Races for Enterprise class at evenings and weekends; dinghy parking. ☕

25a Uskmouth Power Station: Newport and Uskmouth Sailing Club (tel. 0633 71661). Short term membership available. *Clubhouse open April to November: weekends and Tuesdays.* ☕

26e Dale Yacht Club, Fort Road (tel. 064 65 362). Races for cruisers (weekends) and GP 14, Mirror and Handicap (Thursdays and Sundays). *April to October; Sunday and Thursday evenings; mid-July to early September: daily.* ☕

26f Gelliswick Bay: Pembrokeshire Yacht Club, Hakin (tel. Milford Haven 064 62 2799). Races for keelboats and GP 14, Mirror and Laser on Tuesdays, Thursdays and Sundays. No moorings but fair anchorage in bay and plenty of parking spaces.

27a Haverfordwest. Boats for hire to explore the upper reaches of the Western Cleddau River.

27d Neyland Yacht Club, The Promenade (tel. 064 64 600 or 267). Races Tuesdays, Thursdays and weekends for GP 14, Mirror and Laser. Temporary membership available. Dinghy parking; moorings.

27d Llanstadwell: Haven Multihulls, Church Road, St Anthony (tel. Neyland 0646 600578). Fully equipped catamarans for charter. Dinghy sailing experience necessary; unaccompanied children over 16 years. *May to September.*

27d Pembroke Dock: Pembroke Haven Yacht Club, Hobbs Point (tel. 064 63 4403). Dinghy parking and moorings; temporary membership available. Racing from April to November. ⛵

27e Lawrenny: Beacon Yacht Charters (tel. 0446 743122). Yachts available for self-drive hire.

Celtic Sea Charters (tel. Swansea 0792 41503). Self-skipper yacht charter; minimum age for skipper 21 years. *April to end September.*

Lawrenny Yacht Station. 130 swinging moorings in deep water; free car parking; laying-up facilities.

28d Saundersfoot Sailing Club, The Harbour (tel. 0834 812492). Races for GP 14, Mirror, Osprey and Graduate at weekends and on Mondays, Wednesdays and Fridays during summer. Windsurfing; dinghy parking; temporary membership for visitors.

West Wales Sailing School, Port Tack, High Street (tel. 0834 812212). Residential courses for advanced sailors and beginners; minimum age 8 years, 12 if unaccompanied; all equipment provided. *May to end September.*

28g Tenby Sailing Club, The Harbour (tel. 0834 2762). Racing for GP 14, Mirror Handicap and Redwing: May to September Wednesdays and weekends; October and November Sundays AM. Moorings; dinghy parking; temporary membership available. *April to November daily; December to March weekends.* ☕

29a Ferryside: River Towy Yacht Club (tel. 026 785 366). Races when tides are suitable; canoeing; dinghy parking; temporary membership available.

29i Burry Port Yacht Club. See 20b.

30b Ty-isaf Adventure Centre (tel. Warwick 0926 41961). Canoeing holidays organised; no experience needed; unaccompanied children over 10 years. *July and August.* ♣ ▲ ◡

30i Swansea. See 21e.

33c Coed-y-Person: Monmouthshire & Brecon Canal. Barges for hire for Gofilon Wharf (tel. Gilwern 0873 240) or The Boathouse, Llanfoist (tel. Abergavenny 0873 3877). The restored section of this waterway runs north through one of the most scenic areas of the Brecon Breacons National Park (map 43).

33f Goetre Wharf: Red Line Boats (tel. Nantyderry 0873 880516 or 880522). Fully equipped boats available for self-drive. *Easter to October.*

34a Goetre Wharf. See 33f.

34d Llandegfedd Reservoir: Sailing Club (tel. Usk 02913 2917) numerous launching points around the lake. *March to October.*

37b Fishguard Bay Yacht Club, The Quay, Lower Fishguard (tel. 0348 872866). Racing on Wednesdays and weekends (open events); temporary membership available. *April to September. Free dinghy parking and mooring.*

37i Llys-y-frân Reservoir. Canoeing and sailing boat park; boats for hire. 🏞 ✏ ⌇

Slipways

No details of individual slipways are given, but the location of all those with public access is accurately marked. Please note that in some cases permission may be needed and/or a small fee may have to be paid for access; also that launching times may be restricted by the tide. Check locally before using any slipway.

39c Pontwelly: Afon Teifi. Ideal canoeing river: fast and turbulent.

40i Ty-isaf Adventure Centre. See 30b.

43d Llanfrynach: Road House Holiday Hire (tel. Abergavenny 0873 830240). Fully equipped narrow boats for hire on the Monmouthshire & Brecon Canal. *Daily.*

43e Llangorse Lake Sailing Club. Racing for Fireball, GP 14, Mirror, Laser, Handicap, and Flying Fifteen; canoeing; dinghy parking and moorings. *March to November.*

PGL Young Adventure (tel. Ross-on-Wye 0989 4211 or 4217). RYA approved sailing courses and 3-in-1 adventure holidays, involving sailing, canoeing and riding; residential for weekends or one week; minimum age 7 years. *March to October.*

43h Cwm-crawnon: Sovereign Marine Holidays (tel. Tewkesbury 0684 292187). Fully equipped narrow boats for hire. *March to end November.*

46h Cardigan: Teifi Boating Club, Patch Gwbert Road (tel. 0239 3846). Racing, cruising and sports boat racing. Dinghy parking; moorings; temporary membership. *Visiting yachts free.*

47b Aberaeron: Sailing Club, The Harbour (tel. 0545 570077). Popular sailing centre based around the southern harbour wall.

47e New Quay: Sailing Club, Pier Buildings. Popular, sheltered sailing area. Regatta in August. *June to September.*

50b Llandrindod Wells: Cecil Lodge, The Centre of Adventure, Spa Road (tel. 0597 3292). Activity and sports holidays, including sailing and canoeing, for children aged 11-17 years.

52b Aberdyfi: Dovey Yacht Club (tel. Yockleton 074 384 266). Races for GP 14, Mirror and Solo; cruising; canoeing; dinghy parking. For moorings consult Harbourmaster (tel. Aberdovey 065 472 626).

Outward Bound (tel. 065 472 464). Holidays involving sailing and canoeing arranged for 12, 14 or 21 days. All equipment provided; no experience necessary; unaccompanied children from 14 years. ▲

52d Aberystwyth Sea Angling and Yacht Club, The Harbour (tel. 0790 612158). Handicap racing for keel boats and a few dinghies at weekends; dinghy parking; moorings; temporary membership for up to 1 week. ⌇

53c Llyn Clywedog: Clywedog Sailing Club (tel. Llanidloes 055 12 2631). Racing for GP 14, Mirror, Hornet and Flying Fifteen; dinghy parking and mooring. *Easter to October.*

56a Barmouth: Merioneth Yacht Club, The Quayside (tel. 0341 280000). Racing at weekends; cruising; dinghy parking; moorings. *April to October.* ▣ ⚓

Snowdonia School of Adventure (tel. 0341 280494). One week courses in sailing, canoeing and other outdoor sports. *April to October.*

Welsh Windsurfing Centre (tel. 0341 280494) Instruction in windsurfing; wet suits provided; no experience necessary; minimum age 12 years, unaccompanied children over 15 years.

56g Broad Water: Dyffryn Dysynni. Good canoeing where the river meets the sea; best time 2 hours after high water.

56g Tywyn: Outward Bound Wales (tel. 0654 710521). A variety of one week activity courses available, including canoeing; minimum age 10 years.

56h Aberdyfi. See 52b.

56i Derwen-las: River Dovey. Canoeing on the main stretch of the river; access from Ynyshir Hall Hotel (tel. Glandyfi 065 474 209). ☕

60f Llanbedrog. Canoes for hire from the beach for canoe-surfing.

60f Abersoch: South Caernarfonshire Yacht Club, The Headland (tel. 075 881 2338). Racing and cruising. Races at weekends all year and weekdays during August. Temporary membership for those arriving by sea only. ☕

61a Pwllheli Sailing Club, The Outer Harbour (tel. 0758 2219). Racing at weekends; cruising; moorings; dinghy parking. Visitors welcome. *April to October: daily.* ☕

Marina Boat Club, The Outer Harbour (tel. 0758 2271). Dinghy/boat parking; temporary membership. *June to September: daily.* ☕

62a Porthmadog: Porthmadog and Trawsfynydd Sailing Club, Greaves Wharf (tel. 0766 3546). Racing at weekends (daily during school holidays) for dinghies; cruisers on Saturdays. Dinghy parking; moorings; temporary membership. *May to September.*

62d Llanbedr: The Ranch Adventure Centre (tel. 034 123 358). Series of activity courses include sailing, boating and canoeing; minimum age 11 years; equipment provided.

63c Bala Lake: Bala Sailing Club (tel. 0678 520464). Racing and cruising; regattas for all classes on Bank Holiday weekends. Dinghy parking and mooring; temporary membership. ☕

67b Port Dinorwic Sailing Club. Popular yachting base in the summer; during the quieter months it serves as a dock for large ocean going yachts.

Mermaid Marine Enterprises, Glan Heulyn (tel. 0248 670915). Yachts for charter, equipped for cruising. RYA certificate required for skipper (experienced skipper available for hire); minimum age 7 years, unaccompanied 16 years. *March to October.*

67d Dinas Dinlle. Canoes for hire for canoe-surfing from the beach.

68c Capel Curig: Plas y Brenin, National Centre for Mountain Activities (tel. 069 04 214 or 280). Residential courses in canoeing available; equipment provided. ⵣ ▲

68g Porthmadog. See 62a.

69c Llyn Aled Sailing Club (tel. Denbigh 074 571 2690). Racing on Wednesdays, Sundays and Bank Holidays. Temporary membership available. *Easter to end October. Free dinghy parking.*

69i Bala Lake. See 63c.

70a Llyn Aled. See 69c.

70a Llyn Brenig Sailing Club, Cerrigydrudion (tel. Chester 0244 28012). Races on Sundays; dinghy parking; temporary membership. *Easter to end October.*

70g Bala Lake. See 63c.

71e Llangollen: Hoseasons Holidays (tel. Lowestoft 0502 67511). Self-drive canal narrow boats available for hire. *Mid-March to 1st week of November.*

Canoeing on a laid out white water course on the River Dee; International Slalom and Rapid River events in autumn.

74d Holyhead Sailing Club, Newry Beach (tel. 0407 2526). Racing on Wednesdays and weekends; annual regatta in August; moorings and dinghy parking; temporary membership.

Scimitar Sailing School, Porth-y-Felin Road (tel. 0407 2094 or 3178). Courses in all aspects of sailing and seamanship. Unaccompanied children over 8 years. *April to October.*

Ocean Youth Club, Town Hall, Newry Street (tel. 0407 2709). Cruising in a 71 ft Bermudan ketch under the tutelage of a professional skipper. For ages 15 to 21 years.

74d Trearddu Bay Sailing Club (south side of island). Racing in coastal waters during August. Temporary membership.

75e Moelfre. Sailing centre with boats for hire.

75e Traeth Bychan: Red Wharf Bay Sailing Club. The sheltered bay offers some of the best sailing in Angelsey. Boats for hire. ☕ ⛵

76d Beaumaris: Royal Anglesey Yacht Club, 6/7 Green Edge (tel. 0248 810295). Offshore keelboat and dinghy races (open events); mooring and dinghy parking; temporary membership available.

North West Venturers Yacht Club, Gallows Point. Dinghy parking and moorings; free membership for short term visitors. *April to October.*

Cornely Manor, Activity and Study Centre (tel. Llangoed 024 878 255). Residential courses in sailing and canoeing. Minimum age 8 years if unaccompanied; suitable for both beginners and experienced.

76e Llanfairfechan Sailing Club, The Promenade (tel. 0248 680301). Races on Sunday, mainly handicapped. Dinghy parking; temporary membership for visitors. *April to September daily.*

Towers Adventure Centre (tel. 0248 680012). Holidays arranged which involve sailing, windsurfing and surfing. No experience needed; minimum age 8 years. ⵣ ▲ ☀

76f Penmaenmawr Yacht Club, The Promenade (tel. 049 265 2565). Racing in coastal waters on Sundays; dinghy parking; regatta in August. *Easter to September.*

77a Llandudno Sailing Club, Irving Road (tel. 0492 76083). Dinghy races in the bay throughout summer.

77a Degannwy: Conwy Yacht Club, Station Road (tel. 0492 83690). Racing at weekends; cruising in coastal waters; dinghy parking and temporary membership available. ☕

77d Conwy: North Wales Cruising Club, Lower High Street (tel. 049 263 3481). Racing on Sundays; cruising in coastal water; moorings and temporary membership available. Regatta and Round Anglesey Race in August. *March to November daily.*

78a River Clwyd. Canoeing on tidal part of the river below Rhuddlan.

78b y-Ffrith. Boat park; motor boats for hire.

Sail marks

These are some of the more popular types. Details of each class and its rules can be obtained from the local sailing clubs

A	Albacore	**M**	Mirror Dinghy
C	Cadet	**18**	National 18
D	Dragon		Osprey
E	Enterprise	**R**	Redwing
	Finn		Scimitar
●	Fireball		Scorpion
	Flying Fifteen		Seabird
FB	Folkboat	**s**	Shearwater
	GP14	**SII**	Silhouette
G	Graduate		Skipper
	Gull	**T**	Tempest
H	Heron	**30**	Thirty Square Metres
	Hornet	**W**	Wayfarer
	Kestrel	**w**	Westerly
▲	Merlin Rocket	**DB**	YW Dayboat

Fishing

Game, coarse and sea fishing available to the general public, either free or on purchase of a permit. The species of fish mentioned are those most frequently caught in the area marked. If in doubt about what bait or tackle to use, consult the local tackle shops or angling associations.

20c Upper Lliedii Reservoir: brown trout. Permits from office on site. Boat fishing available.

20d Rhosili Bay. Offshore: dabs, plaice, dogfish, ray, tope, porbeagle. Nearest launching Burry Port. See 20b and 29f.

20f Salthouse Point. Shore: excellent flounder (*November to February*), occasional bass.

20g Worms Head. Shore: bass, tope (*July-September*), excellent whiting (*autumn*).

20h Port Eynon Point — Helwick Shoals. Offshore: first class for surface-shoaling bass.

20i Oxwich Point. Offshore: bass. Fish right hand side of bay in early morning or late evening low water.

21a Dulais River: salmon, sea trout, brown trout. Permits from Williams the Ironmonger, Pontarddulais (tel. 0792 882321).

21a Loughor. Shore: bass. From road bridge, popular with local fishermen.

21b Tawe River: salmon, sea trout, brown trout. Permits (weekly only) from Rowlands Sports shop (tel. Swansea 0792 75993).

21d Mumbles. Shore: bass. Spin for schools in the narrows with shiny toby lure.

21e Swansea Bay. Offshore: tope, ray, small conger (*summer*); whiting and occasional cod (*winter*).

22e Sker Point. Shore: thornback ray, dogfish, flatfish.

22f Porthcawl to Ogmore River. Shore: bass and flatfish are the main catches.

23g St Donats Bay. Shore: excellent bass, rockling and wrasse.

23h The Leys. Shore: bass, cod and good mullet. Popular summer and winter mark.

23i Whitmore Bay. Shore: popular conger (*summer*) and cod whiting (*winter*) venue.

24c Pant-yr-eos Reservoir: 16 acres of trout, fly only. Permits from Reservoir Superintendant at site.

24c Gwastad Mawr — Ynysyfro Reservoirs: brown trout, rainbow trout. Permits from office at site.

24c Tredegar House Lake. Coarse fishing by permit during season (tel. Newport 0633 62568)

24g Sully Island. Shore: bass, cod, dogfish, pouting. Approach only by causeway (when dry).

24g Whitmore Bay. See 23i.

24g Barry. Shore: bass, flatfish, whiting, codling. Both harbour and immense breakwater are popular.

24h Orchard Ledges. Shore: cod, whiting. Permission needed from British Docks Board.

24h Penarth. Offshore: good cod and whiting (*winter to spring*).

25d Gold Cliff. Shore: flounder, silver eel, pouting, whiting, cod and occasional bass, plaice and sole.

26b St Bride's Bay. Offshore: tope, good sole, large bull huss and the occasional shark. Launching from Little Haven or Broad Haven (26c).

26c Broad Haven. Shore: good-sized bass plus mackerel, flatfish and whiting. Fish from rocks 3 hours before high water.

26d Skokholm Island. Offshore: heavy pollack and big tope as well as coalfish, conger, monkfish and the occasional bass.

26e Marloes Sands. Shore: mainly first-rate bass. Position near or on Gateholm Island.

26f Chapel Bay. Shore: excellent bass.

26f Sawdern Point to Popton Point. Shore and offshore: sizeable bass. Launching at Angle, Milford, Dale or Pembroke Dock.

26i Freshwater West. Shore: classic storm beach for bass. Beware of treacherous undertow and occasional huge waves.
Offshore (The Turbot Bank): turbot, ray, tope and big whiting. Best fished from large craft because of very fast tides.

27c Canaston Bridge — Eastern Cleddau River: salmon, sea trout, brown trout. Permits from Hunters Lodge, Narberth (tel. 0834 860270) or Bush Inn, Roberston Wathen.

27d Wear Point. Shore: bass, flatfish, dogfish.

27d Carrs Rock and Hobbs Point. Shore: dogfish and excellent conger at times.

27e Garron Pill. Shore: bass, flounder and, surprisingly, thornback ray on fish baits.

27e Carew. Shore: very good mullet and some bass (try float with ragworm).

27h Bosherton Fish Ponds: tench and pike predominate, in addition to good perch, roach and eels. Permits from local tackle shops.

27h Barafundle Bay. Shore: large tope, monkfish, bull huss, dogfish and skate. Fish from rocks on south side of bay.

27h Pembroke Mill Pond. Saltwater lagoon in town centre: very large mullet and occasional bass.

28b Whitland — Taf River: salmon, sea trout and brown trout. Permits from Rees Garages, Whitland (tel. 099 44 304).

28c St Clears — Taf River: good early salmon, sea trout, brown trout. Permits from Dark's Tackle Shop, Carmarthen and Davies Newsagents, Kidwelly.

28d Monkstone Point. Shore: bass from the point at low tide (*spring and autumn*); dabs and the odd skate from the beach.

28e Marros Sands. Shore: splendid bass beach (*May-Nov*) with hope of small turbot and tope. Approach entails arduous climb.

28g Giltar Point. Shore: good bass and mullet.
Offshore: superb bass, good tope, thornback ray and bull huss.

29a River Towy. Shore: flounder and occasional summer bass. Beware roaming weed.

29a River Taf. Shore: good autumn bass and excellent winter flounder.

30d Upper Lliedi Reservoir. See 20c.

30e Dulais River. See 21a.

30f Tawe River. See 21b.

30g Loughor. See 21a.

30g Salthouse Point. See 20f.

31b Caves — Tawe River: mainly brown trout. Permit from Dan-yr-Ogof Caves Office, Penycae (tel. Abercrave 063 977 284).

31b Afon Tawe. See 31d.

31d Afon Tawe. River fishing for 20 miles upstream of this point (Ynysmeudwy Arms); also on Afon Twrch and Nant Llynfell rivers (31a) upstream from the Tawe to the National Park boundary: mainly brown trout. Permits from Craig-y-nos Park Office (tel. Abercrave 063 997 395) or from Tawe Sports, Ystradgynlais (tel. Glantawe 0639 2166).

32b Cantref Reservoir: 42 acres of brown and rainbow trout. Permits from Llwyn-on Reservoir. Fly only, no boat.

32b Llwyn-on Reservoir: 150 acres of brown and rainbow trout. Permits from the Filter House and ticket machine on site. Fly only; no boats.

32b Cefncoedycymer — Taf-fechan River: brown and rainbow trout for 2½ miles from confluence at Cefncoedycymer. Permits from Merthyr Tydfil Angling Association, 2 Wesley Close, Dowlais.

32c Pont-sticill — Bryn Cae-Owen Lakes: carp (to 20 lbs), tench, roach, bream, perch and trout. Permits from Merthyr Tydfil Angling Association, 2 Wesley Close, Dowlais.

32f Taf River, from Merthyr to south of Aberfan: brown and rainbow trout (to 2 lbs). Permits from Merthyr Tydfil Angling Association, 2 Wesley Close, Dowlais.

33c Abergavenny — Usk River: trout, salmon for 1 mile, both banks. Permits from P.M. Fishing Tackle; Fussells Sports Ltd. and Town Hall Abergavenny.

33i Pant-yr-eos Reservoir. See 24c.

33i Cwmbran Boating Lake: coarse. Tickets from boat house.

33i Gwastad Mawr — Ynysyfro Reservoirs. See 24c.

34c Monmouth — Monnow River: mainly brown trout. Permits from Monmouth Angling Society, Brook Cottage, Rockfield. Limited to 12 rods.

34c Jingle Street — Trothy River: brown trout (to 1½ lbs). Permits from Monmouth Angling Society, Brook Cottage, Rockfield.

34d Usk River: brown trout and coarse. Permits from Sweet's Tackle Shop, Usk (tel. 029 13 2552) for trout only and Bridge Inn, Chain Bridge, nr. Usk.

34d Llandegfedd Reservoir: 435 acres of brown and rainbow trout. Self service ticket machine at site or at Water Treatment Works.

34g Cwmbran Boating Lake: coarse. Tickets from boat house.

34h Wentwood Reservoir: 41 acres of brown trout (3-3½ lbs), rainbow trout (2½-3 lbs). Permits from Superintendent at site. Boats available.

35a Newton Court — Wye River: salmon, trout and coarse. Permits from District Council Offices, Monmouth.

36f Porth Gain. Shore: mainly pollack and mackerel (from rocks) with wrasse, tope and bass.

36f Aber Eiddy Bay. Shore: pollack, mackerel, wrasse, tope and bass.

36g North Bishop. Offshore: excellent pollack, tope and blue shark. Fish only in relatively calm conditions.

36g 36h Ramsey Island and Sound. Offshore: sizeable pollack, bass, mackerel, skate and plaice. Use powerful, reliable engine.

36h Whitesand Bay. Shore: popular beach for bass *(March-May)*.

36h Porth Stinian. Shore: first rate pollack Approach by foot from lifeboat station (limited parking).

36h Porth Glais. Shore: excellent pollack and mackerel.

36i Solva. Shore: mullet, bass and flatfish. Good marks: small quay (north bank) and rock promontry (south bank).

36i Scar Rocks/St Bride's Bay. Offshore: thornback ray (14-20 lbs), tope, spur-dog as well as brill, dabs and plaice. Launching from Solva.

36i Newgale. Shore: good bass, plaice and flounder with, in winter, whiting and codling. Classic shallow storm beach.

37a Strumble Head Lighthouse. Shore: excellent sport with pollack and bass. Only easy access mark on Pencaer peninusla.

37b Fishguard Bay. Offshore: tope, ray, skate, conger, gurnard, reasonable pollack *(summer)*; cod and whiting *(winter)*. Superb, sheltered venue.

37b Fishguard. Shore: conger, plaice, dabs with odd ray, wrasse and pollack. Best marks; Castle Point, Green and Red Light in harbour and base of breakwaters.

37c Dinas Head to Trwyn y Bwa (Newport Bay). Shore: tope, skate, ray, monkfish, turbot, gurnard as well as blue sharks and porbeagle. Trwyn y Bwa and Dinas Head are the best marks.

37c Newport Sands. Shore: shoaling bass and sea trout (river licence needed).

37d Abermawr to Aberbach. Shore: bass, plaice, flounder and pollack. Bay shelves to 40 ft of water close in.

37f Rosebush Reservoir: 39 acres of brown trout. Permits from Water Bailif, Blaenpant, near New Inn. Fly only.

37h Western Cleddau River: salmon, sea trout, brown trout. Permits from Hunters Lodge, Narberth (tel. 0834 860270). Seven miles of fishing.

37i Llys-y-fran Reservoir: brown and rainbow trout. Permits from site. Boats for hire plus 3 miles of bank fishing.

38a Newport Sands. See 37c.

38a Nevern River (between the two symbols): salmon, sea and brown trout. Permits from Nevern Angling Syndicate, Fishguard (tel. 0348 873215) and Beynon's Fishing Tackle, Newport (tel. 0239 820265).

38c Stradmore—Teifi River: 9 miles from here upstream to the old railway bridge at Llandyfriog (39b). Salmon, trout, sea trout. Permits from Emlyn Arms Hotel, Newcastle Emlyn (tel. 0239 710317).

Cych River: upstream to Pen-rhiw bridge. Salmon, trout, sea trout. Weekly permits from Teifi Trout Association, Newcastle Emlyn (tel. 0239 710405) or local tackle shops.

38d Rosebush Reservoir. See 37f.

39a Cenarth: Fishing Museum, the only one of its type in Britain.

39a Teifi River: salmon, sea and brown trout. Permits (weekly only) from local tackle shops. (See also 38c).

39b Llandyfriog—Teifi River: 9 miles downstream from the old railway bridge to Stradmore (see 38c). Salmon, trout, brown trout. Permits from Teifi Trout Association, Newcastle Emlyn (tel. 0239 710405).

39c Teifi River: salmon, sea trout and brown trout. Permits from Llandysul Angling Association, Siop-y-Jones (tel. 055 932 2317) and Megicks Corner Shop, Lampeter (tel. 0570 422226). 14 beats.

39f Llanllawddog Lake: fly fishing for rainbow trout. Permits from Home Farm (tel. 026 784 436), book in advance.

39i Cwm Gwili—Gwili River: sea trout and trout. Permits from Dark's Tackle Shop, 16 Chapel Street, Carmarthen and Davies' Newsagents, Bridge Street, Kidwelly. *Weekly tickets only.*

39i Abergwili—Gwili River: sea and brown trout. Permits from Carmarthen Amateur Angling Association (tel. 0267 7997).

39i Llangunnor—Tywi River: salmon (to 20 lbs), sea trout (to 5 lbs). Permits (weekly only) from Dark's Tackle Shop, 16 Chapel Street, Carmarthen.

40d Llanllawddog Lake. See 39f.

40g Glan Towy-Ian—Tywi River: sea and brown trout. Permits from Carmarthen Amateur Angling Association (tel. 0267 7997).

40g Llanegwad—Cothi River: salmon, sea trout and trout. Permits from Carmarthen Amateur Angling Association (tel. 0267 7997), Cothi Bridge Hotel (tel. Nantgaredig 026 788 251) and Carmarthen Angling Club, 25 Park Hall, Carmarthen.

41a Dolau Cothi—Cothi River: salmon (late season), sea trout (to 5 lbs), brown trout. Permits from Dolaucothi Arms Hotel. Pumpsaint (tel. 055 85 204). Residents have priority.

41b Tywi River: salmon, sea trout, trout. Permits from Tonn Farmhouse, Llandovery (tel. 0550 20276). Fish Middle Water.

41e Llandovery—Tywi River: 1¼ miles from symbol (south of town) upstream to A40 bridge. Salmon, sea trout, trout. Permits from Llandovery Angling Association (tel. 0550 20267). Reductions for juniors.

Bran River: 2 miles from Llandovery to Pen-y-bont (41b). Fish and permit details as for Tywi (above).

Gwydderig River: various stretches between the two symbols. Fish and permit details as for Tywi (above).

41f Usk Reservoir: 290 acres of brown (to 5½ lbs) and rainbow trout (to 2½ lbs). Permits from Reservoir Keeper at site. Boats for hire. Permit entitles holder to fish 14 reservoirs.

41i Caves—Tawe River. See 31b.

42h Ystradfellte Reservoir: 59 acres of brown trout fishing in moorland setting. Permits from Reservoir Keeper's House.

42i Beacons Reservoir: 52 acres of brown and rainbow trout. Permits from Reservoir Keeper's House. Fly only, no boats.

41i Neuadd Reservoirs: brown and rainbow trout. Permits from Pontiscill Reservoir Depot or ticket machine at site. Upper Neuadd: no boats; fly only. Lower Neuadd: no boats.

42i Cantref Reservoir. See 32b.

43d Brecon—Usk River: salmon and trout. Permits from R. Denman, Brecon (tel. 0874 2071).

43e Llangorse Lake: excellent pike and perch, as well as carp and roach. Welsh Water Authority licence only needed. Boats for hire.

43g Maes-mawr—Caerfanell River: trout only. Permits from Maesmawr Farm and Usk Hotel, Talybont-on-Usk (tel. 087 487 251).

43g Tal-y-bont Reservoir: 318 acres of brown and rainbow trout. Permits from Superintendent on site (tel. Talybont-on-Usk 087 487 237). Mainly fly but spinning in certain areas. Boats for hire.

43h Usk River: salmon and trout. Permits from Gliffaes Hotel, Crickhowell (tel. 0874 730371) and P.M. Fishing Tackle, Abergavenny (tel. 0873 3175).

45g Woodside—Monnow River: mainly brown trout. Permits from Birmingham Anglers' Association (tel. 021 622 2904 or 1025). Small stretch by Garway Mill.

46f 47b Aberporth to Aberaeron. Offshore: abundant mackerel, pollack, large monkfish, gurnards, dabs and rays among many. Launching from Aberaeron, New Quay, Llangrannog and Aberporth.

46f Penbryn. Shore: bass *(spring-autumn)*, tope, small rays and dogfish.

46g Cardigan Island and Estuary. Offshore: large bass and pollack, underfished by locals because of quality salmon and trout fishing available.

46g Towyn Warren — Poppit Sands. Shore: excellent bass, also mullet, mackerel and sea trout (River Division licence needed). Salt water lagoon above Cardigan Bridge is a holding ground for bass and mullet.

47c Llanrhystud. Shore: bass. Featureless beach, difficult to fish.

47c Llansanffraid. Shore: good bass. These featureless beaches are difficult to fish. Best to use a light bass rod.

47d New Quay. Shore: good bass and flatfish, whilst at high tide the harbour is excellent for small pollack and mackerel. Fishing trips bookable.

48a Llanrhystud. Shore: bass. Featureless beach, difficult to fish.

48f Teifi River: 12 miles of good salmon pools and abundant trout, from the confluence with the Camddwr River north of Pen-y-bont (48c) downstream to near Bremia Roman Fort (48e). Permits from: Caron Stores, Tregaron; Post Office, Llanddewibrefi; Megicks Stores, Lampeter; Barclay's Bank, Tregaron. Maps available.

49a Llyn Egnant and Teifi Pools: brown trout (to 3 lbs), rainbow trout (to 4 lbs) and American Brook trout (fly only—report catch on forms provided). Permits from Welsh Water Authority. Llanelli (tel. 055 42 57031) or local licence distributors.

49b 49c Elan and Claerwen reservoirs: 1,600 acres of brown trout and American Brook trout (report catch on forms provided). Permits from Estate Office, Elan Village (tel. Rhayader 0597 810449).

49g Twyi River. See 41b.

49i Cefngorwydd—Dulas River: salmon *(late summer)* and brown trout. Permits from Neuadd Arms Hotel, Llanwrtyd Wells (tel. 059 13 236).

50a Rhayader—Wye River, for 3 miles upstream: salmon and trout. Permits from Elan Valley Hotel, Elan Village (tel. Rhayader 0597 810448) and Vulcan Motel, Doldowlod (tel. Llandrindod Wells 059 782 438).

Freshwater eel

50a Doldowlod—Wye River: trout, fly only in season. Permits from Birmingham Angler's Association (tel. 021 622 2904 or 1025).

50b Llyn Gwyn Lake: 16 acres of rainbow trout. Permits from Elan Valley Hotel, Elan Village (tel. Rhayader 0597 810448).

50b Ithon River: 4 miles from A4081 bridge south to Disserth (50e). Mainly trout. Permits from Llandrindod Wells Angling Association (tel. 0597 2397) and Birmingham Anglers' Association (tel. 021 622 2904 or 1025).

50b Llandrindod Wells Lake: carp (to 20 lbs) plus most coarse. Permits from Selwyn's Tackle Shop, Llandrindod Wells (tel. 0597 2397).

50c Llanbadarn—Ithon River: mainly brown trout. Permits from Birmingham Anglers' Association (tel. 021 622 2904 or 1205). Fly only water.

50c Penybont—Ithon River: mainly brown trout, fly only. Permits from Birmingham Anglers' Association (tel. 021 622 2904 or 1025).

52a Twyni Bach. Shore: good flounder and bass. Very soft mud and strong tides so exercise extreme caution.

52b Aberdyfi. Shore and offshore: bass and numerous flatfish from channel and quay (spring, autumn and night only); flatfish, dogfish, occasional ray, skate and tope from estuary and bar.

52b Borth. Shore: monkfish (to 45 lbs) and occasional ray (summer) from the classic storm beach; flounders, dabs, bass and small turbot from rocks south of village.

52d Sarn Cynfelyn. Offshore: bass, small pollack, abundant black bream, good size thornback rays, dogfish, gurnards, tope (June to September) with porbeagle and some blue shark (July to September). Excellent area.

52d Aberystwyth. Shore: dogfish, dabs, whiting (winter), mackerel, small pollack, bass and mullet. Best marks are at Constitution Hill (channel and breakwater), Castle Rocks and the stone jetty in the harbour.
Offshore: large thornback rays, numerous small tope, big monkfish (to 56 lbs), plump black bream, plentiful whiting (September to January) with porbeagle and blue shark. Endeavour Deep Sea Angling Club based here.

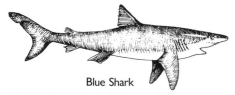
Blue Shark

52e Rheidol streams and rivers: salmon; sewin. Permits from Rosser's Tackle Shop, Aberystwyth (tel. 0970 617451) and Aber Gun Supplies, Terrace Road, Aberystwyth. Boats for hire from Rosser's Tackle Shop. Main run starts in July.

52f Penrhycoch Lakes (5 symbols north of A44): good quality trout. For permit details see 52e.

52f Lywernog—Llyn yr Oerfa: trout. For permit details see 52e.

52g Llanfarian—Ystwyth River: small salmon and numerous sewin. Permits from Rosser's Tackle Shop, Aberystwyth (tel. 0970 617451); Morfa Bychan Caravan Park, Llanfarian; Post Offices at Llanilar and Crosswood, Oak Inn, Llanfarian.

52h Ystwyth River: small salmon and numerous sewin. For permit details see 52e. Spate river, very clean and rocky as well as gravelly.

52i Trisant Lakes (3 symbols): trout. For permit details see 52e. (Frongoch Pool on Wednesdays, Saturdays and Sundays only). Boats available on all three lakes.

53c Llyn Clywedog: 625 acres of brown and rainbow trout. Permits from Travellers Rest Cafe, Llanidloes (tel. 055 12 2329). Boats from Evans, Dyffryn, Llanidloes (tel. 055 12 2129).

53d Nant-y-moch Reservoir: brown and rainbow trout (well-stocked with over 30,000). Permits from Ponterwyd Post Office and Aberystwyth Angling Association, Box 15, G.P.O., Aberystwyth, SY23 1AA.

53d Dinas Reservoir: 60 acres of brown and rainbow trout (1 April-30 September). Permits from Evans Garage, Ponterwyd.

53f Clywedog River: 3 miles of mainly brown trout, some late salmon. Permits from Llanidloes and District Angling Association (tel. 055 12 2644).

53i Elan Valley reservoirs. See 49c.

54a Afon Garno: trout. Permits from Bebb's Home Handicrafts, Newtown (tel. 0686 26917).

54b Fachwen Pool: 10 acres of brown and rainbow trout. Permits from Bebb's Home Handicrafts, Newtown (tel. 0792 26917).

54b Caersws—Trannon River, from Carnedd bridge to the Severn River: salmon, trout and coarse. Permits from Evans Jones, 2 Broneirion Cottages, Llandinam. Fly only during the game season.
Severn River, for 3½ miles east of Caersws: salmon and trout. Permits from Maesmawr Hotel, Caersws (tel. 068 684 255) or from Birmingham Anglers' Association (tel. 021 622 2904 or 1025).

54c Severn River (stretches at both symbols): salmon, trout and coarse. Permits from Birmingham Anglers' Association (tel. 021 622 2904 or 1025).

54d Morfodion—Severn River: brown and rainbow trout. Permits from Llanidloes and District Angling Association (tel. 055 12 2644).

56a Barmouth. Shore: bass, mullet, flatfish and sea trout (River Licence needed). Best marks at Ynys y Brawd and Penrhyn Point.
Offshore: skate, ray and pollack; mackerel bait is plentiful. Best mark near Barmouth Outer black buoy.

56d Aber Dysynni. Shore: shoaling bass. Fish from rocks around Sarn-y-bwch.

56d Dysynni River: 5 miles of salmon, sea trout, trout. Permits from J. J. Roberts, Trefellyn, Tywyn (tel. 0654 710697) and Sports Shop, Tywyn.

56e Dysynni River: 6-7 miles of trout. Permits from Rowlands Post Office, Abergynolwyn.

56f Tal-y-Llyn Lake: brown trout plus a few late salmon. Permits from Tynycornel Hotel, Tal-y-Llyn, nr. Tywyn (tel. 065 477 282). Limited number of permits.

56g Tywyn Sands. Shore: bass. Best mark ¼ mile below promenade when west wind blows.

56g Twyni Bach. See 52a.

56h Aberdyfi. See 52b.

57e Cwm Linau—Dovey River: large sea trout. Permits from Evans Garage, Cemmaes; Nat y Nest Stores, Dinas Mawddwy. 15 miles

58a Foel—Banwy River: trout and grayling, also salmon in lower stretch. Permits from Cann Office Hotel, Llangadfan (tel. 093 888 202).

58b Glan-y-rhyd—Vyrnwy River, for 3 miles from Vyrnwy Dam to the River Conwy: brown trout and rainbow trout. Permits from Lake Vyrnwy Hotel, Llanwddyn (tel. 069 173 244).

58b Vyrnwy River: trout, fly only during season. Permits from Birmingham Anglers' Association (tel. 021 622 2904 or 1025).

58f Banwy River: trout, fly only during season. Permits from Birmingham Anglers' Association (tel. 021 622 2904 or 1025).

58h Llyn-y-Tarw: 14 acres of American Brook trout (to 1½ lbs). Permits from Bebb's Home Handicrafts, Newton (tel. 0686 26917).

58h Afon Garno. See 54a.

58i Fachwen Pool. See 54b.

59a Cain River: trout (to 1 lb) and grayling. Permits from Cain Valley Hotel, Llanfyllin (tel. 069 184 366).

59a Meifod—Vyrnwy River: trout, fly only during season. Permits from Birmingham Anglers' Association (tel. 021 622 2904 or 1025).

59b Severn River: brown and rainbow trout. Permits from Birmingham Anglers' Association (tel. 021 622 2904 or 1025).

59c Severn River: brown and rainbow trout. Permits from Birmingham Anglers' Association (tel. 021 622 2904 or 1025).

59d Afon Rhiw: brown trout in flood. Permits from Bebb's Home Handicrafts, Newtown (tel. 0686 26917).

59d Severn River: trout. Permits from Birmingham Anglers' Association (tel. 021 622 2904 or 1025).

59e Severn River: trout. Permits from Birmingham Anglers' Association (tel. 021 622 2904 or 1025). Limited space.

59g Severn River: salmon and trout. Permits from Birmingham Anglers' Association (tel. 021 622 2904 or 1025).

60b Towyn and Porth Sgadan. Shore: bass is main quarry, also sizeable wrasse and pollack. Best marks are rock platforms between Porth Sgadan headland and Porth ychen.

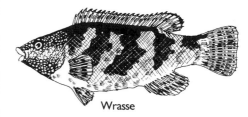
Wrasse

60c Porth Dinllaen to Nefyn. Shore; bass, flatfish and dogfish from beach at night; conger and mullet near lifeboat station.
Offshore: thornback ray, tope and voracious dogfish.

60d Porth Golmon. Shore: bass and tope.

60d Porth Oer. Shore: bass and tope. Popular beach, car park 400 yards from beach.

60d Aberdaron Sands. Shore: good bass. Popular with holidaymakers so fish mid-September to late April. Fishing trips bookable.

60e Porth Cadlan. Shore: daytime summer bass. Remote, idyllic beach.

60f Porth Neigwl (Hells Mouth). Shore: good bass (autumn to spring). This classic 3½ mile sand storm-beach is easily reached from a pull-in near Tai Morfa.

60f Abersoch. Shore: abundant whiting and dabs (winter); bass and plaice (autumn). Best marks by Sailing Club, small quay into river and beach north of town. Popular holiday beach best fished at night.
Offshore: plentiful small pollack, thornback rays (to 15 lbs), dogfish and bull huss around St Tudwals Island West (60i) and off Penrhyn Head. Launching from Abersoch only.

60g Bardsey Sound. Shore: good pollack, wrasse and bass abound. Fish from rock platforms facing Sound.
Offshore: excellent pollack, coalfish and bass (localised). Best mark is in shelter of the island and close in to mainland cliff wall.

60g Ynys Gwylan Fawr and Ynys Gwylan Fach islands. Offshore: Good mackerel and Pollack with bass in mid-summer. Islands are within dinghy distance in fine weather.

60i Porth Ceiriad and Trwyn Cilan. Shore: thornback ray, skate, dogfish, flounder and winter whiting. Both marks are less frequented by summer crowds.

61a Clogwyn—Erch River: 4 miles of salmon, sea trout and brown trout. Permits from D & E Hughes, Pwllheli (tel. 0758 3291).

61a Morfa Abererch. Shore: bass, plaice and flounder. Extensive beach only frequented in parts by holidaymakers from nearby Butlin's Camp (61b).

61a Bodegroes—Rhyd Hir River: salmon, sea-trout and brown trout. Permits from D & E Hughes, Pwllheli (tel. 0758 3291).

61a Pwllheli. Shore: bass and flounder from Carreg yr Ymbill (Gimblet Rock), limited and often crowded best fished September and late April; mullet and occasional bass from harbour mouth—free car park nearby.

    Offshore: bass and flounder between harbour's outer black buoy and Abererch beach; ray, flatfish, dogfish, small pollack, some tope (summer), monkfish (autumn) and whiting and codling (winter) from Gimblet Rock to Gimblet Shoals.

61b Pont Fechan. Shore: large bass. Vast deserted beach, difficult to fish.

61c Criccieth. Shore: bass, plaice. Beaches fishable only in late evening in summer.

61c Black Rock Sands. Shore: bass. Fish 2 hours before low water to well up the tide, early and late in the year.

61c Porthmadog Bay. Offshore: plump plaice, flounder, bass, dogfish, occasional rays, skate and tope. Constant 50 ft of water over wilderness of mud.

61d Carreg y Defaid. Shore: flounder, plaice and frequently bass. Carreg y Defaid is best mark, fished at night.

62a Pont Croesor—Glaslyn River: salmon, sea trout, brown trout. Permits from Pugh's, Portmadog (tel. 0766 2392).

62a Porthmadog Bay. See 61c.

62a Black Rock Sands. See 61c.

62a Ynys Cyngar. Shore: bass, plaice, flounder and dabs. Fish western side of channel leading into estuary.

62a Traeth Bach. Shore: abundant mullet, flounder and bass. Essential to always stay on the south bank of the main stream.

62c Dduallt—Cynfal and Goedol Rivers: salmon (to 16 lbs), sea trout, brown trout. Permits from Parry's Newsagents, Payne's Tackle Shop, Ffestiniog and Tackle Shop or Owen's Royal Stores, Blaenau Ffestiniog.

62c Llyn Trawsfynydd: 1,200 acres of all-year-round perch (in winter use warm water channel only). Permits from Lewis' Newsagent, Trawsfynydd (tel. 076 687 234)

62d Harlech Sands. Shore: bass, flatfish and tope easily caught from Harlech Point but involves 3 mile walk or bike ride to reach.

62d Mochras and Shell Island. Shore: bass, flounder and mullet invade lagoon on rising tide. Permit for south side of Artro estuary from G. G. Workman, Shell Island, Llanbedr (tel. 034 123 217).

62g Morfa Dyffryn. Offshore: bass, pollack, gurnard, monkfish, skate, plaice, dabs, tope and porbeagle. Launching from Artro estuary.

62g Talybont. Shore: bass and flatfish (late spring or autumn). 8 miles of uninterrupted sand storm-beach. Come armed with salted down or frozen razor fish and squid as bait is scarce.

62i Mawddach River: good quality salmon and sea trout. Permits from Dolmelynllyn Hall Hotel, Ganllwyd (tel. 034 140 273).

63a Llyn Morwynion: trout. Permits from Parry's Newsagents, Payne's Tackle Shop, Ffestiniog and Owen's Royal Stores, Blaenau Ffestiniog.

63b Llyn Celyn: 900 acres of brown trout (to 1½ lbs) and rainbow trout (to 1¼ lbs). Permits from Pugh's Tackle Shop, Bala (tel. 067 82 248). Fly and spinning only.

63c Dee River for 600 yards between the symbol and Bala Lake: trout only. Permits from Pugh's Tackle Shop, Bala (tel. 067 82 248).

63c Llyn Tegid (Bala Lake): 1,200 acres of brown trout and 13 species of coarse including roach, pike (to 20 lbs), perch, grayling, gudgeon and eels. Permits from Lake Warden's office, Bala (tel. 067 82 626). Boats for hire.

Brown Trout

64a Dee River. See 63c.

64d Hirnant River: trout only, 4 miles. Permits from Pugh's Tackle Shop, Bala (tel. 067 82 248).

64g Lake Vyrnwy: 1,100 acres of brown trout (to 3 lbs), rainbow trout (to 2 lbs). Permits for boat fishing only from Lake Vyrnwy Hotel, Llanwddyn (tel. 069 173 244). Bank fishing for residents only.

64h Vyrnwy River. See 58b.

65a Tregeiriog—Ceiriog River: brown trout only. Permits from West Arms, Llanarmon Dyffryn Ceiriog (tel. 069 176 665).

65b Cwmalis — Dee River. salmon (to 12 lbs), trout and coarse. Permits from J. Johnson, Maghull (tel. Liverpool 051 526 4083).

65c Froncysyllte — Dee River. 2 miles of mainly trout and coarse. Permits from Maelor Angling Association, Wrexham (tel. 097 881 2592).

65c Pentre—Dee River: 3 miles of trout and coarse. Permits from Newbridge Angling Society, Ruabon (tel. 097 881 2497).

65g Cain River. See 59a.

65h Llanymynech—Tanat River: trout and grayling. Permits from Bryn Tanat Hotel, Llansanffraid (tel. 069 181 259). Priority given to hotel residents.

65i Severn River. See 59c.

66c Aberffraw Bay. Shore: bass, best in September from beach.

    Offshore: tope, rays, dogfish, bull huss, plaice and winter whiting. Easy launching at Aberffraw.

66c Malltraeth Sands. Shore: bass and flounder. Requires 1 mile walk from Newborough Warren car park (67a).

66c Llanddwyn Island. Shore: bass, mullet, tope, ray, coalfish and the odd skate (summer); sizeable whiting, codling, flounder and dab (winter). Approached by foot from car park at Newborough Warren (67a).

66i Trefor. Shore: flatfish, dogfish and roaming bass. Cliff-bound quay is last easy access before Nefyn.

66i Porth-y-nant. Shore: bass, dogfish and flatfish, with plenty of mackerel and whiting in season. Steep descent to peaceful beach.

67a Menai Strait. Offshore: (north east of Abermenai Point) tope, bass, bull huss, thornback ray and specimen size flounders.

67a Abermenai Point and Traeth Melynog. Shore: good bass, excellent tope, prime flounders, dabs and whiting. Both over 2 miles walk from Newborough Warren car park.

67a Belan Point. Shore: tope, bass, dogfish, prime flounder and dabs.

67b Moel-y-don and Port Dinorwic. Shore: good bass, small conger, plaice and abundant mullet. Old quay wall and ferry crossing are good marks.

67b Caernarfon Ferodo Works. Shore: bass, flatfish—mainly flounders—and small eels.

67b Cae-mawr—Mermaid Inn. Shore: occasional good bass. Limited parking.

67b Seiont River: 5 miles of salmon and sea trout. Permits from Jones' Tackle Shop, Caernarfon (tel. 0286 3186).

67b Caernarfon. Shore: bass, abundant tope, flounders, mullet, small eels with good winter codling and whiting. Good marks by quay wall, along shore by golf course and swimming pool and between Ysgubor Isaf and Ty Calch. Fishing trips bookable.

67c Llyn Padarn: brown trout and char. Permits from Jones' Tackle Shop, Caernarfon (tel. 0286 3186) and West Gwynedd Water Division, Bron Castell, Bangor (tel. 0248 52881). Boats available at Llanberis.

67c Cwm-y-glo—Rhythallt River, from Llyn Padarn to the road bridge north east of Llanrug; salmon and sea trout. Permits from Jones' Tackle Shop, Caernarfon (tel. 0286 3186).

67d South Sands—Caernarfon Bar and Llanddwyn Bay (67a). Offshore: bass; troll with large red gills and rubber eels.

67d Dinas Dinlle. Shore: bass (late autumn is best). Good surfcasting beach.

67d Pont, Llyfni to Aberdesach. Shore: bass (late summer and throughout autumn).

67d Lleuer-fach—Llyfni River: 4 miles of salmon and sea trout. Permits from Roberts Newsagent Snowdon Street, Penygroes and Jones' Tackle Shop, Caernarfon (tel. 0286 3186).

67f Gwyrfai River: 3 miles of salmon and sea trout. Permits from Jones' Tackle Shop, Caernarfon (tel. 0286 3186) and Castell Cidwm Hotel, Betws Garmon (tel. Waunfawr 0286 243).

67f Llyn Cwellyn: sea and brown trout. Permits from Jones' Tackle Shop, Caernarfon (tel. 0286 3186) and Castell Cidwm Hotel, Betws Garmon (tel. Waunfawr 0286 243).

67f Llyn-y-Gader: brown trout. Permits from Jones' Tackle Shop, Caernarfon (tel. 0286 3186). Boat and bank fishing available.

67i Llyn Cwm-ystradllyn: 95 acres holding brown trout. Permits from the lake's treatment works, Gardolbenmaen (tel. 076 675 255).

68a Llyn Padarn. See 67c.

68a Gwyrfai River. See 67f.

68a Llyn Cwellyn. See 67f.

68b Llyn Idwal: brown trout. Permits from Buckley Wynn, Outfitters, Bethesda (tel. 0248 600020).

68c Llyn Ogwen: salmon, sea trout, brown trout. Permits from Buckley Wynn, Outfitters, Bethesda (tel. 0248 600020).

68c Llugwy River: brown trout. Permits from Bryn Tyrch Hotel, Capel Curig (tel. 0569 04 223) and Hughes Garage, Capel Curig.

68c Pen-y-Gwryd Lake: good brown and rainbow trout to 1¼ lbs. Permits from Pen-y-Gwryd Hotel, Nant Gwynant, Nr. Llanberis (tel. 028 682 211).

68d Llyn-y-Gader. See 67f.

68d Llyn Cwm-ystradllyn. See 67i.

68e Llyn Dinas: salmon and sea trout (to 6 lbs) and brown trout. Permits from Craflwyn Hall Hotel, Beddgelert (tel. 076 686 221). Boats for hire.

68e Craflwyn—Glaslyn River: salmon, sea trout and brown trout. Permits from Craflwyn Hall Hotel (tel. Beddgelert 076 686 221).

68f Barlwyd Lakes: brown trout. Permits from Parry's Newsagent, Payne's Tackle Shop, Ffestiniog and Owen's Royal Stores, Blaenau Ffestiniog. Beware soft peaty shore.

68f Llyn Cwmcorsiog: trout (up to 2 lbs). Access not easy, but worth the visit. Permits as for Barlwyd (68f).

68f Llyn Cwmorthin: brown trout. Well stocked. Permits as for Barlwyd (68f).

68f Llyn Dubach: brown trout. Dry fly suitable. Permits as for Barlwyd (68f).

68f Llyn-y-Maniod: trout. Permits as for Barlwyd (68f).

68f Tanygrisiau Reservoir: 95 acres of rainbow trout. Permits from power station reception centre, Blaenau Ffestiniog (tel. 076 681 465). *Season 6 March to 31 October.*

68g Black Rock Sands. See 61c.

68g Porthmadog Bay. See 61c.

68g Ynys Cyngar. See 62a.

68g Traeth Bach. See 62a.

68h Pont Croesor—Glaslyn River. See 62a.

68i Dduallt—Cynfal and Goedol Rivers. See 62c.

68i Llyn Trawsfynydd. See 62c.

69a Llyn Goddion-duon: salmon, sea trout and trout. Permits from Tan Lan Cafe, Betws-y-Coed (tel. 069 02 217).

69a Llugwy River: mainly trout. Permits from Gwydyr Hotel, Betws-y-Coed (tel. 069 02 217). Tickets are also for Llyn Elsi.

69a Llyn Elsi. See Llugwy River (above).

69d Conwy River: 7 miles of brown trout. Permits from National Trust, Dinas, Betws-y-Coed (tel. 069 02 312).

69d Gamallt Lakes: finest trout in Wales. Permits from Parry's Newsagent, Payne's Tackle Shop, Ffestiniog and Owen's Royal Stores, Blaenau Ffestiniog. 25 minute walk from road marked with white quartz stones.

69g Llyn Morwynion. See 63a.

69h Llyn Celyn. See 63b.

70a Brenig Reservoir: 919 acres of brown and rainbow trout (fly only). Permits from: Interpretation Centre (tel. 049 082 435). Boats (motor or rowing) bookable in advance.

70a Alwen Reservoir: mainly brown trout. Permits from Keeper's Office at site. Ground bait and maggot prohibited.

70e Craig Arthbry—Alwen River: 1 mile of mainly trout. Permits from Owain Glyndwr Hotel, Corwen (tel. 0490 2115).

70g Dee River. See 63c.

70g Llyn Tegid (Bala Lake). See 63c.

71d Dee River: salmon (to 20 lbs), sea trout and rainbow trout. Permits from Berwyn Arms Hotel, Glyndyfrwdy (tel. 049 083 210).

71e Dee River: 6 miles of salmon and trout with some coarse. Permits from Elbourne's Tackle Shop, Llangollen (tel. 0978 786055).

71g Tregeiriog—Ceiriog River. See 65a.

71h Cwmalis—Dee River. See 65b.

71i Froncysyllte—Dee River. See 65c.

71i Pentre—Dee River. See 65c.

72g Erbistock—Dee River: salmon, sea and brown trout. Permits from Boat Inn, Erbistock (tel. Overton-on-Dee 097 973 243).

74b Church Bay. Shore: bass, rays, plaice, dabs with cod and whiting very late in the year.

74c Ynys Badrig (Middle Mouse Island). Offshore: cod, coalfish, whiting, rays, tope and pollack.

74c Cemaes Bay. Shore: cod, wrasse, conger, dabs, flounders and pout whiting. Marks at National Trust headlands.

74c Cemlyn Bay. Shore: bass (autumn), sizeable pollack and coalfish. Best marks are along the strand enclosing lagoon and from rocks over the headland (very dangerous).

74d South Stack. Shore: bass spinning and wrasse float fishing.

74d Holyhead. Shore: conger, tope, ray, dogfish, bass, dab, whiting and cod. Permit needed for British Rail Mail Pier from BR booking office. Entry to breakwater is unrestricted.

74e Porth Penrhyn-mawr. Shore: good bass.

74e Penhros Beach. Shore: bass, flounders, dabs and mullet abound on flooding tide.

74f Alaw Reservoir: brown and rainbow trout. Permits from Fishing Office at site (tel. Bangor 0248 52881). Boats for hire.

74g Trearddu Bay. Shore: bass, tope, thornback ray, dogfish, mackerel and flatfish—mainly flounders.

74h Rhoscolyn and Cymmeran Bay. Shore: roving bass, flatfish and the occasional bass.

74h Rhosneigr. Shore: bass, dabs, flounders and occasional thornback ray and dogfish. Popular holiday area in summer so fish late evening or night.

75a Bull Bay. Offshore: cod, coalfish, whiting, rays, tope and pollack.

75a Amlwch (harbour and rocks). Shore: cod, wrasse, small conger, dabs, flounders and pout whiting.

75b Point Linas. Shore: conger, ray, dogfish, pout (summer); cod and whiting (late autumn, winter).

Offshore: skate, rays, conger, gurnard, dabs, coalfish and pollack (summer); pouting, whiting and cod (winter).

75e Moelfre. Shore and offshore: bass, tope, dabs and abundant mackerel; cod and whiting (winter).

75e Traeth Bychan. Shore: fish from each side of the bay for whiting and coalfish.

75e Benllech. Shore: abundant mackerel, flounder, dabs with occasional bass and conger; excellent cod and whiting in winter. Traditional all-the-year-round mark.

75f Red Wharf Bay. Shore and Offshore: flounder, dabs and the occasional bass and conger with abundant mackerel in summer, excellent winter cod and whiting. Best time is a rising tide in late evening.

75i Beaumaris. Shore: summer bass and plaice, autumn whiting and winter cod. Gallows Point, town pier and sea wall are most popular marks.

75i Bangor. Shore: bass, plaice, whiting, cod.

75i Menai Straits. Shore: large mullet, bass (6-8 lbs), conger, flounder, dogfish, whiting, wrasse and pollack. Best marks at Britannia Rail bridge, Ynys Llandysilio, Menai Bridge at water level and St Georges pier and slipway.

Offshore: cod, tope, conger, black bream, bass, plaice and pollack. Fish the Swellies and Pwll Fannogl Deeps.

76b Outer Road—Black Point, Priory Beach and Puffin Island. Shore: excellent bass, flatfish, pollack and mackerel. Point reached by private road (small charge).

Offshore: bass, tope, ray and coalfish.

76d Beaumaris. See 75i.

76d Bangor. Shore: bass, plaice, whiting, cod.

76e Tre-castell (Anglesey) — Aberlleiniog Beach. Shore: large bass and fat flounders.

76e 76f Llanfairfechan and Penmaenmawr. Shore: superb bass. Beware walking too far out on Lavan Sands.

76g Cwm-y-glo—Rhythallt River. See 67c.

76g Llyn Padarn. See 67c.

76h Ffynnon Laer: brown trout. Permits from Buckley Wyn, Outfitters, Bethesda (tel. 0248 600020).

76h Llyn Ogwen. See 68c.

77a Great Ormes Head. Offshore: small tope, thornback rays, flatfish, dogfish and excellent gurnard. Powerful engine and boat over 14 ft needed in this area.

77a Llandudno. Shore: large plaice, dabs and flounders with occasional bass; conger, wrasse and small pollack from rockier marks near Great Ormes Peninsula.

77a Little Orme Head. Shore: bass, plaice, flounder, dabs, whiting, codling. Marks from Villa Marina (rocky) to Arcadia Theatre (shingle).

77a Gogarth — Llandudno Black Rocks. Shore: noted spot for shoaling bass and dabs. Fishes best on evening tides in mid-autumn.

77a Conwy Bay. Offshore: big bass, plaice and flounders (summer) with codling, whiting and dabs (winter).

77a Conwy Marsh. Shore: bass, plaice, flounders.

77b Colwyn Bay. Shore: bass, mullet, plaice, flounders, conger, dabs, whiting and the odd ray. Good marks at Cayley Promenade, Bay of Colwyn Yacht Club, Rhos Point, Little Orme and Victoria Pier.

Offshore: gurnard, small rays and abundant small tope in summer with whiting and codling in winter. Area is very convenient for launching small craft.

77c Colwyn Bay and Kinmel Bay. Shore: bass, flounders, plaice, dabs, tope. Comparatively peaceful in summer.

77d Conwy Estuary. Offshore: bass, flounders and eels. Fishing trips bookable at Conwy.

77d Llansantffraid — Afon Garreg Ddu Lakes: 2 acres of rainbow trout (2-3 lbs). Permits from Pengwern Trout Farm, Glan Conwy (tel. 049 268 751). Small artificial lakes, well stocked.

77g Tal-y-bont—Conwy River: salmon (to 28 lbs), sea trout and brown trout. Permits from Dolgarrog Fishing Club (tel. 049 269 651).

77g Llyn Crafnant Reservoir: 60 acres of brown and rainbow trout. Permits from Lakeside Cafe (tel. Llanrwst 0492 640 818). Boats for hire.

77g Conwy River: salmon (to 30 lbs), sea and brown trout. Permits (weekly only) from The Library Tackle Shop, Llanrwst (tel. 0492 640 525).

78b Prestatyn. Shore: rich shoals of flounders, occasional plaice and dabs. Popular holiday area makes it untenable to daytime anglers.

78c Point of Ayr. Shore: silver eels, big bass, early season tope. Fish light as incoming tide is dangerous.

78c Mostyn Quay. Shore: dabs, whiting and occasional small bass. Beach is only lightly fished.

78d Elwy River: salmon, sea trout and trout. Permits from A. H. Fogerty, 29 Queen Street, Rhyl (tel. 0745 54765).

78e St Asaph — Elwy River: salmon (to 10 lbs) and sea trout (to 2 lbs). Permits from Foxon's Newsagents, Penrhewl, St Asaph (tel. 0745 583583) and Plas Elwy Hotel, St Asaph (tel. 0745 582263).

78e Clwyd River: salmon, sea trout and trout. Permits from A. H. Fogerty, 29 Queen Street, Rhyl (tel. 0745 54765).

78f Ysgeifiog Reservoir: 18 acres of brown and rainbow trout, fly only. Permits from Cambrian Fisheries, Afonwen, nr. Caerwys (tel. 035 282 389). Boats for hire.

78i Cilcain Reservoirs: 12 acres of brown trout in 5 small reservoirs. Permits from Cilcain Fly Fishing Association, 9 Maes Cilan, Cilcain, Mold.

Skiing Climbing

Rock climbing, mountaineering, severe hill walks and orienteering; ski centres, both mountain and artificial; also activity centres offering courses or tuition in these sports. (See page 14 for information about safety in the hills).

24e Cardiff: Skiing. Artificial slope at Cardiff Ski Centre (tel. 0222 561793). *Weekdays 1400-2200; weekends 1000-1300, 1400-1800.*

30b Ty-isaf Adventure Centre (tel. Warwick 0926 41961). Climbing, hill walking and orienteering holidays arranged. Most equipment supplied. ♣ ⚠ ☾

32c Pont-sticill: Rock Climbing. Easy 30 to 50 ft routes on rock crags in Taf-fechan Quarries.

33f Pontypool: Skiing. Two artificial slopes (170 yards and 20 yards) at The Sports Centre (tel. 049 55 56955). Toboggan run. Lessons given. Ski hire. Largest artificial ski centre in Wales. *Daily.* ☕

40i Ty Isaf Adventure Centre. See 30b.

43h Craig y Castell: Rock Climbing. About 2 miles of climbs on a 100 ft limestone escarpment on the north slopes of Mynydd Llangattwg. Severe routes at the east end.

49c Craig Foel: Rock Climbing. Cliffs and buttresses up to 100 ft long, mostly easy, on the north west bank of Caban Coch Reservoir. Also ½ mile north, on the west slopes of Y Foel, are about a dozen routes around 200 ft.

50a Gwastedyn Hill: Rock Climbing. Several routes of 100 ft or so on crags.

52b Aberdovey: Outward Bound (tel. 065 472 464 or London 01 491 1355). Extensive range of holidays arranged here include climbing and hiking. Unaccompanied boys over 14 accepted. ⚠

53i Pen Rhiw-wen: Rock Climbing. Scrambles and fairly easy 160 ft climbs on the north east slopes.

54g Pen Rhiw-wen. See 53i.

56c 56e Cader Idris: Rock Climbing. The symbols show points of easy access rather than actual climbing locations, which are many. Best areas are east and west of the summit, and on crags around Llyn Cau. Scrambles, gullies, buttresses, ridges and faces are available. Some experience necessary.

56h Aberdovey. See 52b.

57b Craig Cywarch: Rock Climbing. Over 50 climbs in a 1½ mile area, suitable for all standards and including a 400 ft main crag.

62a Portreuddyn Castle: Rock Climbing. Tremadoc Rocks stretch for 2½ miles on the north side of A498 and offer several dozen routes up to 300 ft long, all requiring previous experience. Easy access, but some slopes fall within nature reserve and permission is needed.

63h Craig Cywarch. See 57b.

66i Bwlch-yr-Eifl: Rock Climbing. Buttresses up to 800 ft on the northern slopes of The Rivals.

67f Craig Cwm-bychan: Rock Climbing. Many routes, up to 400 ft long and for all standards, but on poor rock.

67f Snowdon. See 68.

67f Trum-y-Ddysgl: Rock Climbing. Buttresses of up to 400 ft requiring some skill.

67h Garnedd-goch: Rock Climbing. Many routes, up to 400 ft in places and some with overhangs.

67i Beddgelert Forest: Orienteering. Course at forest campsite, used for international events. Compass and detailed map of route available on payment of returnable deposit. *Daily. Free.* ♣

68 Snowdon: Hill Walking. The symbols show the 6 main routes up the mountain. Starting near Hebron Station (68a) and going clockwise around the mountain, these are: Llanberis Path, the easiest route which is long but slow; Pen-y-Gwryd ('Pyg') Track, more interesting, but rough in places; Miners' Track, very wide and easy, also very popular (♣↓T); Watkin Path passes through marvellous scenery at its lower end, but requires agility and fitness at the top end; Beddgelert Track; and Ranger Path, which starts from the Youth Hostel. All routes take some time. Take waterproof and warm clothing even in fine weather.

Rock Climbing. Extensive all over the mountain, but some of the more interesting locations are listed here. At Llyn Du'r Arddu, above the Ranger Path, are buttresses which should be attempted only by experts; Cwm Glas, east of Rocky Valley Halt, has many climbs, some over 400 ft long, some also very hard; Clogwyn y Ddysgl, ½ mile north of the summit, is a rock spur with many medium routes up to 350 ft long on its west ridge–the east ridge is poor rock; Clogwyn y Person (the Parson's Nose), between Llyn Glas and Glaslyn lakes, is ideal for novices; Crib Goch buttress, west of Crib Goch summit, is a medium climb of 300 ft; Y Lliwedd, reached by Watkin Path, is a huge crag with many buttresses and gullies on its north face — it was the scene of the first recorded Welsh rock climb in 1883; Llechog, south west of the summit, has several long routes of medium standard up to 400 ft long; Clogwyn Du, above the two tiny lakes south of Llechog, offers several medium faces under 500 ft long; Clogwyn y Bustach, on the north face of Gallt-y-Wenallt, has an unusual semi-underground route called Lockwood's Chimney, together with several conventional climbs.

Mountain Rescue Posts, which are not shown, can be found at: Rhyd Ddu, junction of A4085/B4418 (68a); Nant Peris (68b); the Youth Hostel west of Llyn Ogwen on A5 (68b); Capel Curig, south west of A5 on A4086 (68c); Pen-y-Gwryd Hotel at junction of A498/A4086; Aberglaslyn (68e); and Blaeunau Ffestiniog (68f).

68a Craig Cwm-bychan. See 67f.

68b Pass of Llanberis: Rock Climbing. The north side of A4086 has three very steep buttresses offering severe 250 ft climbs; also climbs on wet black rocks. The south side of the road has many climbs for all levels of ability, especially on the northern ridge of Crib Goch, where there are short routes and some lasting 250 ft. The road offers good places to watch skilled climbers at work.

68c Tryfan: Rock Climbing. The north slopes offer a wide variety of climbs of all degrees of severity, including Monolith Crack. At the 10th milestone out of Bangor on A5 is Milestone Buttress, with many routes for novices. The east slopes of Tryfan have been in use since 1887 and offer routes for all standards.

Glyder Fach, about 1 mile south of Tryfan, offers numerous long (400 ft) climbs on good rock, especially on the northern slopes, where all standards are catered for.

Devils Kitchen, 1 mile west, has many cliff faces, but on poor rock. ↳

Llyn Idwal: the rocks above this lake are popular for their slab climbs, with hard routes on steep walls.

68c Capel Curig: Plas y Brenin (tel. 069 04 280). The Sport's Council's national centre for mountain activities, offering an extensive range of residential courses, including rock climbing, hill walking, orienteering and mountaineering. Skiing facilities include two artificial outdoor slopes and a 500 yard cross country track, all available daily when not in use for residential courses. Minimum age 15; Permanent staff. ⚠

68d Trum-y-Ddysgl: Rock Climbing. Buttresses of up to 400 ft requiring some skill.

68d Beddgelert Forest. See 67i.

68f Moelwyn Bach: Rock Climbing. Numerous slopes for all grades.

68g Portreuddyn Castle. See 62a.

69d Penmachno: Orienteering. Introductory 'wayfaring' course through mountain and woodland scenery. Maps from Penmachno Post Office, B4406.

74d South Stack: Rock Climbing. Extremely severe climbs on 500 ft cliffs and on the stack itself, pioneered in 1966 by Joe Brown and Pete Crewe. Not for amateurs. ♣ ↳ ✦ ☆

76e Llanfairfechan: The Towers Adventure Centre, Promenade (tel. 0248 680012). Holidays arranged for rock climbing, caving, winter mountaineering and skiing. Equipment supplied. Minimum age 8. Elementary courses available. ⚠ ☆

76h Cwm Llafar: Rock Climbing. Steep crags on the north west face of Carnedd Ddafydd; many difficult routes with overhangs.

76h Elidir Fawr: Rock Climbing. A detached rock pillar with several routes.

76h Craig-ddu: Rock Climbing. Several fairly hard climbs starting 300 ft above the Nant Ffrancon road. Also, 1 mile east, the south slopes of Carnedd Ddafydd offer buttresses of up to 300 ft, some easy.

76i Craig yr Ysfa: Rock Climbing. Whole range of routes around the ridge, including a gully with steep, 800 ft walls.

77a Great Ormes Head: Rock Climbing. Several hard, technical routes can be found around the Marine Drive.

Little Ormes Head: Rock Climbing. Several climbs similar to above, but slightly shorter.

Golf Courses

18

The location of all known courses is shown accurately, along with the relevant number of holes at each course. Because membership qualifications, tournament dates and rules vary so much, however, no details are given here.

Application to use any course should be made at the club house in person, or ask the nearest Tourist Information Office (see page 122) for details.

Riding and Pony Trekking

Includes riding schools, pony trekking and hacking centres, pony and donkey rides on beaches, race courses (flat and National Hunt). Always telephone the school or hire centre in advance for booking information. The figure at the end of most entries denotes the number of horses or ponies for hire.

20e Llangennith: Burrows Hall Hotel (tel. 044 127 221). Trekking; hacking. 24. *December to October.*

20f Parkmill: Woodlands Riding School, Vennaway Lane (tel. Bishopston 044 128 2704). Hacking; instruction. 25.

20f Southgate: Pennard Riding School (tel. Bishopston 044 128 3233). Hacking. 8. *March to October.*

21a Cwm Dulais Trekking Centre (tel. Pontardulais 0792 883351). Trekking; unaccompanied children. 10. *March to December.*

21d Mumbles: pony rides on the beach.

22b Goetre: L & A Holidays, The Riding Centre (tel. Port Talbot 063 96 5509). Trekking; hacking. 60.

22e Nottage Riding School.

22e Porthcawl: donkey rides.

24d Cardiff: Equitation and Riding Centre, Pontcanna Fields.

27f Island Farm Riding Stables, Devonshire Drive (tel. Saundersfoot 0834 813263). Trekking; hacking. 18.

27i St. Florence: East Tarr Farm Riding Stables (tel. Manorbier 083 482 274). Hacking; jumping. 15. *May to October.*

27i Norchard Farm Riding School (tel. Manorbier 083 482 242). Trekking; hacking; instruction. 28. *March to October.*

28d Island Farm. See 27f.

28g Tenby: pony and donkey rides.

29a Pant-yr-Athro Riding School.

29b Towy Castle (tel. Carmarthen 0267 6286). Trekking; hacking; trail riding; instruction; unaccompanied children. 8.

29h Llangennith. See 20e.

30b Ty-isaf Adventure Centre (tel. Warwick 0926 41961). Riding holidays for teenagers. ♣ ⚐ ▲

30b Glyn-hir Parc Stud & Stables, Glynhir Road (tel. Llandybie 0269 850664). Trekking; hacking; instruction. 14.

30e Cwm Dulais. See 21a.

31b Pen-y-cae: Pentre Pony Trekking Centre, Pentre Farm (tel. Abercrave 063 977 639). Trekking; unaccompanied children. 22. *April to October.*

31h Goetre. See 22b.

32d Ty-draw Farm (tel. Treherbert 044 389 711). Hacking; instruction. 20.

33c Llanwenarth: Pinegrove Stud.

34c Monmouth: pony treks.

35g Piercefield Park: Chepstow National Hunt and Flat Racecourse (tel. 029 12 2237).

37h Treffgarne: Bowling Riding Establishment (tel. 043 787 257). Trekking; hacking. 24.

38b Caerau: Trewidwal Farm Trekking Stables (tel. Moylgrove 023 986 211) Hacking; unaccompanied children. 7. *April to October.*

38b Ty-gwyn: Dyfed Riding Centre, Maes-y-Felin (tel. Cardigan 0239 2594). Trekking; hacking; instruction. 16. *Trekking April to September.*

38e Tre-fach Manor Pony Trekking Centre (tel. Hebron 099 47 457). Trekking; hacking. 12.

39c Pen-y-banc Pony Trekking & Field Centre (tel. Pencader 055 934 515). Trekking; hacking. 10.

39f Llanpumpsaint: Rhydganol Riding Centre (tel. 026 784 635). Hacking; unaccompanied children. 15.

40a Llanllwni: Bluewell Pony Trekking Centre (tel. Brechfa 026 789 274). Hacking. 17.

40b Rhyd-cymerau: 4 K's Riding Centre, Rhydyfallen-Ganol (tel. Pumpsaint 055 85 479). Trekking; trail riding; unaccompanied children. 12. *April to October.*

40c Pumpsaint: Dark Orchard Farm Guest House (tel. 055 85 224). Trekking; hacking; unaccompanied children. *April to October.*

40e Llanfynydd: Ponderosa Ranch, Bryndafydd (tel. Talley 055 83 497). Trail riding; unaccompanied children. 10. *April to September.*

40i Ty-isaf. See 30b.

41h Llanddeusant: Blaenau Farm (tel. Gwynfe 055 04 277). Trekking, trail riding. 30. *April to October.*

43b Velindre: Cadarn Trail Riding Farm (tel. Glasbury 049 74 327 or 303). Trail riding; instruction; unaccompanied children. 55. *March to November.*

43c Llanigon: Stables at 11 Digeddi Villas, Pen-y-Beacon (tel. Hay-on-Wye 049 72 689).

43c Tregoyd Trekking Centre (tel. Glasbury 049 74 351). Trekking; trail riding; unaccompanied children. 80. *April to October.*

43d Cantref Trekking Centre (tel. 087 486 223). Trekking; unaccompanied children. 45.

43e Rhyd-y-bont Farm: Welsh Horse Drawn Holidays (tel. Talgarth 087 481 346). Horse drawn caravans and pony traps. 15. *April to October.*

43e Pen-y-genffordd: Cwmfforest Riding Centre (tel. Talgarth 087 481 398). Trekking; hacking; instruction; unaccompanied children. 50. *April to November.*

43e Llangorse: Ellesmere Riding & Trekking Centre (tel. 087 484 252). Trekking; hacking; unaccompanied children. 14.

Llangorse Trekking Centre (tel. 087 484 280 or 272). Trekking; hacking; unaccompanied children. 200.

43f Capel-y-ffin: Grange Trekking Centre (tel. Crucorney 087 382 215). Trekking; unaccompanied children. 40. *March to November.*

43i The Wern Riding Centre (tel. Crickhowell 0873 810899). Trekking; hacking; trail riding; instruction; unaccompanied children. 40. *April to November.*

43i Crickhowell Riding Club (tel. 0873 810244). Trekking; hacking; instruction; unaccompanied children. 15.

43i Llangenny Trekking Centre, Penrhiw Cottage (tel. Crickhowell 0873 810175). Trekking; hacking; unaccompanied children. 15.

44d Capel-y-ffin. See 43f.

44d Neuadd-lwyd: Daren Farm Pony Trekking Centre (tel. Crucorney 087 382 306). Trekking; unaccompanied children. 24. *April to October.*

44g Neuadd Farm (tel. Crucorney 087 382 276). Trekking; hacking; unaccompanied children. 20. *April to November.*

44g Cwmyoy: Queens Head Pony Trekking Centre (tel. Crucorney 087 382 251).

44g Llanwenarth: Pinegrove Stud (tel. 0873 810228). 20.

46g Caerau. See 38b.

47i Gors goch: Llanybyther Horse Centre (tel. Brechfa 026 789 323).

48b Penuwch: Brynamlwg Pony Trekking Centre (tel. Llangeitho 097 423 629). Trekking; hacking. 16. *March to October.*

48f Tregaron: Tregaron Pony Trekking Association, Tanybryn (tel. 097 44 364). Trekking. *May to September.*

Tregaron Riding Centre, Blaenant (tel. 097 44 292).

48h Ffarmers: Cae-Iago Trekking Centre (tel. Pumpsaint 055 85 303). Trekking. 30.

49d Maes-glas Mountain Trekking Centre, Soary-Mynydd (tel. Tregaron 097 44 584). Trekking. 12. *May to September.*

49i Llanwrtyd Wells: Mid Wales Riding Centre (tel. 059 13 300). Hacking; trail riding; instruction; unaccompanied children. 30.

Llanwrtyd Wells Pony Trekking, Association, Beulah Road (tel. 059 13 239). Trekking; unaccompanied children. 50. *May to September.*

50a Rhayader: Overland Pony Treks, Ddole Farm, east of 'New House' (tel. 0597 810402). Trekking; trail riding; unaccompanied children. 25. *May to September.*

Lion Royal Hotel Pony Trekking Centre, Weir Street (tel. 0597 810202). Trekking unaccompanied children. 26. *May to October.*

Rhayader Pony Trekking Association, Nantserth House (tel. 0597 810298). Trekking; unaccompanied children. 40. *May to September.*

50a Blaen-y-cwm: Range Rides (tel. Rhayader 0597 810627). Trekking; trail riding; unaccompanied children. 20. *April to September.*

50e Pen-cerig Country House Hotel and Pony Trekking Centre (tel. Builth Wells 098 22 3226).

51c Norton: The Meeting House Riding Stables (tel. Presteigne 054 44 221). Trekking; hacking. 10.

51g Bryngwyn: Cwm Farm Riding and Trekking Centre (tel. Paincastle 049 75 661). Trekking; hacking; unaccompanied children. 20.

52b Borth Trekking Centre, Penlon (tel. Borth 097 081 278). Trekking; hacking. 25. *April to October.*

52e Glanrafon: Troedrhiwlas Riding Centre (tel. Capel Bangor 097 084 229). Hacking; instruction; unaccompanied children. 18.

52f Bont-goch: North Cardiganshire Trekking Centre, Plas Cefn gwn, north of village (tel. Talybont 097 086 413). Trekking; hacking; trail riding; instruction. 29.

54g Rhyader. See 50a.

56a Barmouth: pony and donkey rides on the beach.

56b Abergwynant Farm and Trekking Centre (tel. Dolgellau 0341 422377). Trekking. 30. *April to October.*

56i Pennal: Gwerniago Stables.

58e Llanerfyl: Craen Riding Centre (tel. Llangadfan 093 888 349). Trekking hacking; unaccompanied children. 20.

58e Cefn Coch Inn Pony Trekking Centre (tel. Llanfair Caereinion 093 882 247). Trekking; hacking; unaccompanied children. 20. *May to October.*

60f Bwlchtocyn Ponies for Hire (tel. Abersoch 075 881 2285). Hacking. 12.

61b Ty'n-lon Riding Centre (tel. Chwilog 076 688 618). Hacking; instruction; unaccompanied children. 10.

62d Dolbebin Riding & Trekking Centre & Nantcol Stud, Pen-y-bont (tel. Llanbedr 034 123 374). Trekking; hacking; instruction. 15.

62i Abergwynant. See 56b.

64a Tytandderwen Riding and Trekking Centre, off B4931 east of Bala (tel. Bala 067 82 273).

64f Tan-y-Ffridd Pony Trekking Centre, (tel. Llanrhaeadr-ym-Mochnant 069 189 349). Trekking; hacking. 20. *May to September.*

65a Ddol-hir Pony Trekking Farm (tel. Glyn Ceiriog 069 172 331). Trekking; hacking. 35.

65a Pont-y-meibion (tel. Glyn Ceiriog 069 172 358). Trekking; instruction. 14. *April to October.*

65b Tal-y-Garth Farm: Golden Pheasant Riding Centre, off B4500 (tel. Glyn Ceiriog 069 172 408). Trekking; hacking; trail riding. 12.

65e Rhydycroesau Riding Centre (tel. Oswestry 0691 3826). Trekking; hacking; instruction; unaccompanied children. 22. *April to October.*

67e Waunfawr: Snowdonia Riding Stables, Weirglodd Fawr (tel. 028 685 342). Trekking; hacking. 14. *April to November.*

68a Waunfawr. See 67e.

69a Pont-y-Pant: Dolmurgoch Pony Trekking Centre (tel. Dolwyddelan 069 06 286). Trekking; hacking; instruction. 13. *May to October.*

69d Penmachno: Ty Coch Riding Centre, Ty Coch Farm (tel. 069 03 248). Trekking; hacking; instruction. 17.

70c Pwll-glas: Evers Haflinger Riding Centre & Stud, Bonygraig (tel. Ruthin 082 42 2891). Hacking; unaccompanied children. 6.

70g Tytandderwen. See 64a.

71a Llanfair-Dyffryn-Clwyd: Brondyffryn Stables (tel. Ruthin 082 42 2074). Trekking; hacking; instruction. 10.

71c Llanfynydd: Clwyd Riding Centre, Tyn-y-Cyffion (tel. Pont y Bodkin 035 287 446). Hacking; instruction. 4.

71f Erddig Hall: Wrexham Riding Centre (tel. Wrexham 0978 57875). Trekking; hacking; instruction. 17. ✿ ⊞ ↓T

71f Pant Farm (tel. Wrexham 0978 840254). Trekking; hacking. 14.

71f Pen-y-bryn Farm: Llangollen Pony Trekking Centre (tel. Llangollen 0978 860642). Trekking; hacking. 12. *April to September.*

71h Ddol-hir. See 65a.

71h Tal-y-Garth Farm. See 65b.

71h Pont-y-meibion. See 65a.

72d Erbistock: Mill House (tel. Overton-on-Dee 097 873 373). Hacking. 9.

72d Erddig Hall. See 71f.

72e Bangor-on-Dee: National Hunt Racecourse (tel. 0978 780323).

72e Pandy: Springbank Riding Centre, Halghton

Lane Farm (tel. Hanmer 094 874 307). Hacking; instruction; unaccompanied children. 15.

74d Holyhead: Gors Wen Riding Stables and Farm (tel. 0407 2706). Trekking; instruction. 24.

75e Benllech: donkey and pony rides on beach.

76e Rhiwiau Riding Centre (tel. Llanfairfechan 0248 680094). Trekking; hacking; instruction. 17.

77a Llandudno: donkey rides on the beach.

77b Colwyn Bay: donkey and pony rides.

77c Pensarn: pony and donkey rides on the beach.

77d Conwy: Pinewood Riding Stables, Sychnant Pass Road (tel. 049 263 2256). Hacking. 40.

77f Garthewin: Pony Trekking Centre at the Farm (tel. Llanfair Talhaiarn 074 584 288). Trekking; instruction. 27. *March to November.* ⊞

78a Rhuddlan: Pegasus Riding School, Pentre Lane (tel. 0745 590561). Hacking. 8.

78e Bodfari: Bryn Derw Riding School (tel. 074 575 272). Hacking; instruction. 17.

79d Brynford: Glas-Llyn Riding Stables, Glan-Llyn Uchaf (tel. Holywell 0352 711561). Trekking; hacking; trail riding; instruction; unaccompanied children. 12.

79g Cefn Eurgain: Bryn Ffynnon Farm (tel. Northop 035 286 664). Trekking; hacking; unaccompanied children. 16. *March to October.*

79g Cilcain Riding Centre, 'Bronwylfa', Celyn Mali Road (tel. Hendre 035 283 847). Trekking; hacking; trail riding; instruction; unaccompanied children. 14.

North Wales Pony Treks (tel. 035 283 391). Trekking. 8.

Aviation
Motor Sport

Aviation entries include flying clubs, aircraft museums, popular gliding and hang gliding venues. Motor sport information includes permanent and temporary race tracks (for cars, karts and bikes); hill climb and sprint courses; stock car and speedway stadia.

Rallies. The forests of Wales, together with the military roads of the Epynt Ranges (42a, b) are used frequently for high-speed special stage events organised at local, national and international level. The major events are the Welsh International Rally (May) and the World Championship RAC Rally (November). For details contact South Wales Automobile Club at Llandow (tel. 0222 23912).

20e Llanmadog Hill: popular hang-gliding venue.

21d Swansea Airport: planes for hire, pleasure flights and flying instruction organised by Swansea and District Flying School and Club. *Pleasure flights at weekends.*

22b Mynydd Morgam: Gliding. Eastern slopes popular with gliders looking for lift.

23g Racing Circuit: Llandow Kart Track. Permanent oval circuit used for regular meetings organised by Cardiff Kart Club (Secretary tel. 0222 32439). *February to October: 1 Sunday each month (national meeting September).*

23h St Athan: RAF Historic Aircraft Museum (tel. Barry 044 65 3131 ext 312). Collection includes the Hawker Hunter prototype, two Spitfires and several captured German and Japanese World War II aircraft. *Open only on Battle of Britain Days or by arrangement:* Community Relations Office (ext 3356).

Motor Sport: sprint meetings organised by Welsh Counties Car Club (Secretary tel. Cardiff 0222 734361). *Two Sundays per year in August and October.*

23i Glamorgan Rhoose Airport: Wales Aircraft Museum, airport approach road (tel. 055 44 50563). Run by the South Wales Aircraft Preservation Society, it contains about 20 aircraft, including two Viscount airliners, Whirlwind, Gannets, Sea Hawks, Venom, Meteor, Super Sabre, Lockheed T-33, Hunter, Mystere, Hovercraft and some engines. Also photographs, models, historical items and an airport fire engine. *Sundays 1030 to dusk.* ☛

Cambrian Flying School (tel. Barry 0446 710336 or 710153). Superb training facilities, with Private Pilot's Licence and more advanced courses. Many new aircraft.

26b Talbenny: Motor Sport. Sprint course 2800 yds long used for meetings organised by Pembrokeshire Motor Club (Secretary tel. Haverfordwest 0437 5124 or 2149). *Two Sundays per year: club event in July; national championship meeting in September.*

Kart Racing. Temporary circuit used for meetings organised by New Pembrokeshire Kart Club (Secretary tel. 0437 5009). *March to December: 1 Sunday each month.*

27a Haverfordwest Airport: Gliding. Instruction and aircraft for hire.

29h Llanmadog Hill: popular hang-gliding venue.

30h Swansea Airport. See 21d.

37h Haverfordwest Airport: Gliding. Instruction and aircraft for hire.

31c Ton-y-ffildre: Gliding. The slopes in this area are popular for soaring.

43i Crickhowell: Welsh Hang Gliding Centre, New Road (tel. 0873 810019). 2, 4 and 6-day courses in the Black Mountains or Brecon Beacons, with instruction for novices and experienced fliers. Minimum age 16. Glider and equipment supplied. Gliders for hire for experienced pilots.

Birdman National Park Hang Gliding School, The Quay (tel. 0873 810681). 2, 4 and 6-day courses approved by the British Hang Gliding Association.

67a Belan Airfield (tel. Llanwda 0286 830220). Pleasure flights from private airfield. *Easter to September: daily 1000-1700.* ☛ ♨ ↓T

72d Llay: Birdman Hang Gliding School, 186 Bryn Place (tel. Gresford 097 883 2065). 2, 4 and 5-day courses for groups and individuals, with tuition and lectures for absolute novices. Minimum age 16. Glider, equipment and club membership included.

71a Ruthin: Hang Gliding: North Wales Branch of the Welsh Hang Gliding Centre, 17 Well Street (tel. 082 42 4568). For facilities see 43i Crickhowell.

76e Llanfairfechan: The Towers Adventure Centre, Promenade (tel. 0248 680012). Hang gliding holidays arranged for groups and families. No experience necessary; equipment supplied. ⚠ ⅄ ▲

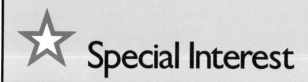

⭐ Special Interest

A potpourri of lighthouses, military training areas, caves, male voice choirs and other fascinations which simply could not be listed under any other heading.

23e Llantrisant: home of Britain's Royal Mint (tel. 0443 222111).

23g Nash Point: Lighthouse (tel. Llantwit Major 044 65 306). Superb views. *Monday to Saturday PM (not in fog). Free.* Nearby is a disused lighthouse.

24f Peterstone Wentlooge: 'Little Holland' of pastures below sea level, drained by iron doors in the sea wall. A plaque on the village church marks the height reached by the Great Flood of 1606 — 5 ft 9 in.

26e St Anne's Head: Lighthouse (tel. Dale 064 65 218). Good views of giant oil tankers to and from Milford Haven (26d). *Monday to Saturday PM (not in fog). Free.* ♥

27g Warren: Castlemartin Army Ranges (tel. 064 681 321). Tanks and other vehicles of the Royal Armoured Corps can be seen at exercise from a spectator area just off B4319. *Firing times displayed at Bosherton Post Office. Free.*

28b Pengawsai Fach: The Colinsdown Herd of Dairy Goats (tel. Whitland 099 44 659). Holidays on which one can learn all about goatkeeping. Own goats allowed. Unaccompanied children over 12 accepted. *Easter to October.*

28c Laugharne: The Boat House, Cliff Walk (tel. 099 421 420). Home for 16 years of the poet Dylan Thomas, who wrote much of his work in the garden shed. An exhibition of his life and work is now housed here; live reading of his poetry on summer evenings. *Easter to October: daily 1000-1800.* He lies buried in an annexe to the local churchyard.

28d Wiseman's Bridge: meeting place in 1943 of Eisenhower, Churchill and Montgomery for a full scale rehearsal of the D-Day landings on the nearby shingle and sand beaches.

28f Pendine Sands. Six miles of hard sand which during the 1920s were used for attempts on the World Land Speed Record. In 1924 Sir Malcolm Campbell achieved 146 mph in *Bluebird*; the Welshman J G Parry Thomas was killed while trying to surpass that at the wheel of *Babs* soon afterwards: in 1927 Campbell achieved the final record set at Pendine at 174.88 mph. In 1933, Amy Johnston took off from here for her successful solo trans-atlantic flight. All but the most western mile is now under military control and is used for test firing experimental rockets and shells. *Open unless MoD signs say otherwise.*

31b Dan-yr-Ogof Caves (tel. Abercrave 063 977 284). Spectacular limestone caverns stretching 1½ miles, with stalactites, stalagmites, underground lakes and weird rock formations, all impressively floodlit. Guided tours. Britain's largest showcaves. Dinosaur Park. *April to 31 October daily from 1000. Telephone for winter times.* ☕ ◼ ⌂

32h Llwynypia: Glyncornel Field Archery Centre (tel. Tonypandy 0443 432490). Fifty acres of woodland with 28 world championship field archery courses.

41i Dan-yr-Ogof Caves. See 31b.

43c Hay-on-Wye: Richard Booth Books. Reputedly the largest secondhand bookshop in the world, it occupies a whole network of buildings in the town centre, including the castle. Expensive. *Normal shop hours.* �m

46i Blaenannerch: Rocket Station. The airfield is occupied by a Ministry of Defence missile research establishment. Firing trials can be seen from the nearby cliff tops. *Base not open; firing when red flags fly.*

50b Llandrindod Wells: Rock Park Pump Room, Rock Park. Spa Waters, said to help alleviate gout and rheumatism, can still be taken here. At one time they helped draw 80,000 people a year to the town. Now undergoing restoration.

51h Hay-on-Wye. See 43c.

53g Devil's Bridge: Three Bridges. Built one above each other to span the River Mynach, the lowest was completed by local monks in 1087; the second span went up in 1708; both are now crossed by the modern steel bridge carrying A4120. ♣ 🚲

57d Llwyn-gwern: Centre for Alternative Technology (tel. Machynlleth 0654 2400). 'Village of the Future' with nature-powered equipment, etc.; also vegetable growing ideas, salad lunches in summer, electric vehicles, animals, crafts, books, steam engines, children's play area. *Daily 1000-1700 (dusk in winter).*

60d Porth Oer: Whistling Sands. When walked upon, the pale sands of this beach produce an odd squeaking noise, caused by the fine particles grinding together. 🏊 🚣

62a Porthmadog: *Garlandstone*. Sailing ketch which once worked the North Wales ports, first visiting Porthmadog in 1909. She is now moored at The Harbour, and her holds contain displays of local history as an extension of the Maritime Museum. *April to September daily 1000-1800.* ⚓

68f Blaenau Ffestiniog: Gloddfa Ganol Mountain Tourist Centre, A470 (tel. 076 681 664). The 'largest slate mine in the world' with over ½ mile of underground workings to visit. Conducted tours by Land Rover. Fairy grotto and children's play area. *Easter to October daily 1000-1730.* ☕ ◼ ⚓ 🚲

68g Porthmadog. See 62a.

71a Ruthin Castle (tel. 082 42 2664). Luxury hotel which recreates the atmosphere of mediaeval Wales with banquets cooked to Tudor recipes and served to Welsh harp and folk music. *Monday to Saturday nights.* ☕ 🏰

71f Rhosllanerchrugog: Choirs. The Rhos Male Choir and the Rhos Orpheus Choir are acknowledged to be two of the finest in Wales. Rehearsals can be visited at Ysgol y Wern. *Wednesdays 1930, Sundays 1130.*

74d South Stack: Lighthouse (tel. Holyhead 0407 2042). Although standing 200 ft above the sea, the tower is dominated by the surrounding cliffs, which are 500 ft high in places. To reach the island on which the light was built (in 1809), one must descend 400 steps to a narrow iron bridge. *Monday to Saturday PM (not in fog). Free.* ♣ ♥ 🚣 ▲

74d North Stack: 'The Parliament House'. A giant cavern with an arch 70 ft high, given its name for the constant chatter of thousands of birds which nest here in summer.

74d Breakwater: completed in 1873, this 1.87 mile breakwater is Britain's longest. It makes an excellent vantage point for watching RAF Air/Sea Rescue boats practising with helicopters from RAF Valley (74h). The lifeboat station on the other side of New Harbour can also be visited.

74h RAF Valley: training airfield, where interceptors and fighters can often be seen in low level formations; also the base for air/sea rescue helicopters. Parking available on the small road immediately north of the airfield.

75i Llanfairpwllgwyngyllgogerychwyrndrobwll-llantysiliogogoch. Britain's longest place name, which translates as "St Mary's Church in the hollow of the white hazel near a rapid whirlpool and the church of St Tysilio near the red cave". It can be seen (and photographed!) at the local garage, the newsagents and at the railway station, where you can buy the longest ticket in the world.

Llanfairpwll Tourist Centre contains 'the world's largest' model railway; also other railway items in a small museum. *Easter to October: daily 0900-1800.* ☕

77a Llandudno: Professor Codman's Wooden Headed Follies, near the pier entrance. A Punch and Judy show which has been run by the same family since 1864.

77b Colwyn Bay: Eirias Park, East Parade. Dinosaur World, plus many other amusements and rides for children; also crazy golf, bowling, tennis, trampolines and other sports.

77f Rhyd-y-Foel: Llandulas Male Voice Choir. The community centre here is used for rehearsals by this fine choir, who welcome visitors. *Wednesday and Sunday evenings. Free.*

77g Llanrwst: Encounter — The North Wales Museum of Wildlife, Fron Ganol, School Bank Road (tel. 0492 640664). The unusual craft of taxidermy can be seen, as future exhibits for display are prepared in the museum's own studios. *Easter to September: daily 1100-1600 (later in summer; other times by appointment).* ☕ ◼

78a Rhyl: Marine Lake Leisure Park, west end of Promenade. Splash Cats, pirate ships, Treasure Island competition, etc. for children.

Lifeboat Station. Launching point in 1962 of the first ever rescue of a hovercraft — a painting commemorates the event.

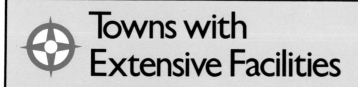

✦ Towns with Extensive Facilities

In order to qualify for this symbol, a town must offer a combination of good commercial facilities (shopping, accommodation, etc.) *and* a range of all-weather facilities. These may not be available out of season, and you should first check with the relevant Tourist Information Office (see page 122).

Tourist Information Offices

Including those run by the Wales Tourist Board, by local authorities and by such bodies as the National Trust. Accommodation enquiries can be handled only by offices in the larger towns. Those offices whose addresses are preceded by * are open only during the summer months (usually Easter to September)

21d The Mumbles: *Oystermouth Square (tel. 0792 61302).

21e Swansea: Guildhall Kiosk, Swansea (tel. 0792 50821); *Crymlyn Burrows, Jersey Marine (tel. 0792 462403 or 462498).

21f Aberavon: Afan District Council Offices (tel. Port Talbot 063 96 3141).

22a Aberavon. See 21f.

22e Porthcawl: *Old Police Station, John Street (tel. 065 671 6639).

24a Caerphilly: *Twyn Car Park (tel. 0222 863378).

24e Cardiff: Castle Street (tel. 0222 27281).

24g Barry: Vale of Glamorgan Borough Council, King Square (tel. 0446 730311).

24h Penarth: West House (tel. 0222 707201).

26c Broad Haven: *Car Park. Pembrokeshire Coast National Park Countryside Unit (tel. 043 783 412).

27a Haverfordwest: *40 High Street (tel. 0437 3110). Pembrokeshire Coast National Park information: Council Offices (tel. 0437 3708).

27h Pembroke: *Drill Hall, Main Street. Pembrokeshire Coast National Park centre (tel. 064 63 2148).

28d Kilgetty: *Kingsmoor Common (tel. 0834 813672 or 813673). Includes Pembrokeshire Coast National Park information.

28g Tenby: Guildhall, The Norton (local information tel. 0834 2402). Pembroke Coast National Park information (tel. 0834 3510). National Trust centre at Tudor Merchant's House, Quay Hill (tel. 0834 2279).

30i Swansea. See 21e.

31b Dan-y-Ogof Caves: *(tel. Abercraf 063 977 284).

31g Aberavon: see 21f.

32f Merthyr Tydfil. *Callers:* Merthyr Borough Council, Cyfartha Park. *Written enquiries:* John Stoker, Sports and Leisure Centre.

33c Abergavenny: *2 Lower Monk Street (tel. 0973 3254). Includes Brecon Beacons National Park information.

33i Cwmbran: Torfaen District Council, 42 Gwent Square (tel. 063 33 67411).

34a Abergavenny. See 33c.

34b Raglan: *Pen-y-Clawdd Service Area (tel. Dingestow 060 083 694).

34c Monmouth: *Nelson Museum (tel. 0600 3899).

34g Cwmbran. See 33i.

35d Tintern: *Abbey (tel. 029 18 431).

35g Chepstow: *The Gatehouse (tel. 029 12 3772).

36h St David's: *Car Park, High Street (tel. 043 788 747). Pembrokeshire Coast National Park Centre: City Hall (tel. 043 788 392).

37b Fishguard: *Town Hall (tel. 0348 873484). Includes Pembrokeshire Coast National Park information.

37h Treffgarne: *Nant-y-Coy Mill (tel. 043 787 671 or 686).

39i Carmarthen: Darkgate (tel. 0267 7557); *Old Bishop's Palace, Abergwili (tel. 0267 31557).

40g Abergwili: see 39i Carmarthen.

41b Llandovery: *Central Car Park, Broad Street. Brecon Beacons National Park centre (tel. 0550 20693).

41i Dan-y-Ogof Caves: *(tel. Abercraf 063 977 284).

42e Libanus: Brecon Beacons Mountain Centre, Cae Harn (tel. Brecon 0874 3366).

42f Brecon: *Market Car Park (tel. 0874 2485). Brecon Beacons National Park information: 7 Glamorgan Street (tel. 0874 4437).

43b Talgarth: Bruton House, High Street (tel. 087 481 586).

46h Cardigan: *3 Heathfield, Pendre (tel. 0239 3230).

47b Aberaeron: *Harbour Car Park, Market Street (tel. 0545 570602).

47d New Quay: *office near the harbour.

48f Tregaron: *The Square (tel. 087 44 415).

50a Rhayader: *West Street (tel. 0597 810591).

50b Llandrindod Wells: Town Hall Gardens (tel. 0597 2600).

50e Builth Wells: *Groe Car Park (tel. 098 22 3307).

52b Aberdovey: *The Wharf (tel. 065 472 321). Includes Snowdonia National Park information.

52d Aberystwyth: Eastgate (tel. 0970 612125).

52f Ponterwyd: *local information from Llywernog Silver Lead Mine (tel. 097 085 620).

53f Llanidloes: *Great Oak Street (tel. 055 12 2605).

54c Newtown: *Central Car Park (tel. 0686 25580).

54d Llanidloes. See 53f.

56a Barmouth: *The Promenade (tel. 0341 280787).

56c Dolgellau: *The Bridge (tel. 0341 422888). Includes Snowdonia National Park information.

56g Tywyn: *Publicity Office, Neptune Road (tel. 0654 710070).

56h Aberdovey. See 52b.

57b Dinas Mawddwy: *local information from Meirion Mill (tel. 065 04 311).

57g Machynlleth: Mid Wales Tourism Council, Owain Glyndwr Centre (tel. 0654 2401 or 2653). *Spring Bank Holiday to end August only:* for caravan pitches in mid-Wales, tel. 0654 2727).

59e Welshpool: Vicarage Garden Car Park (tel. 0938 2043).

62a Porthmadog: *High Street (tel. 0766 2981).

62b Maentwrog: Snowdonia National Park information (tel. 076 685 274). *Written enquiries only.*

62d Harlech: *Gwyddfor, High Street (tel. 076 673 658). Includes Snowdonia National Park information.

62f Pont Dolgefeilian: *Maesgwm Forestry Commission information centre (tel. Ganllwyd 034 140 210).

62h Barmouth. See 56a.

62i Dolgellau. See 56c.

63c Bala: *High Street (tel. 0678 520367). Includes Snowdonia National Park information.

64a Bala. See 63c.

65f Whittington: *Babbinswood, near Oswestry (tel. Whittington Castle 0691 62488).

67f Llanberis: (tel. 028682765). Includes Snowdonia National Park and Central Electricity Generating Board information.

67g Caernarfon: *Slate Quay (tel. 0286 2232).

68f Blaenau Ffestiniog: *High Street (tel. 076 681 360). Includes Snowdonia National Park information.

68g Porthmadog. See 62a.

68i Maentwrog. See 62b.

69b Betwys-y-Coed: *Waterloo Complex (tel. 069 02 426).

69d Penmachno: Activity maps from the Post Office, B4406.

69i Bala. See 63c.

70a Llyn Brenig: Welsh Water Authority Visitor Centre (tel. Cerrigydrudion 049 082 463).

70g Bala. See 63c.

71e Llangollen: *Town Hall (tel. 0978 860828).

72d Wrexham: *Guildhall Car Park, Town Centre (tel. 0978 578459).

74d Holyhead: *Marine Square, Salt Island Approach (tel. 0407 2622).

75i Menai Bridge: Isle of Anglesey Tourist Association, Coed Cyrnol (tel. 0248 712626).

75i Bangor: *Bron Castell (tel. 0248 52786).

76d Menai Bridge. See 75i.

76d Bangor. See 75i.

77a Llandudno: Chapel Street (tel. 0492 76413); kiosk on North Promenade (*July and August only* tel. 0492 76572); Arcadia Theatre (*July and August only* tel. 0492 76413 ext 264).

77b Colwyn Bay: *Prince of Wales Theatre (tel. 0492 30478); *Colwyn Bay Hotels and Guest Houses Association (tel. 0492 55719).

77d Conwy: *Castle Street (tel. 049 263 2248) Includes Snowdonia National Park information.

77g Llanrwst: Glan-y-Borth, Snowdonia National Park Countryside Centre (tel. 0492 640604).

77g Gwydyr: *Forest Information Centre (tel. Llanrwst 0492 640578).

78a Rhyl: *Information Bureau, Promenade (tel. 0745 55068); Town Hall (tel. 0745 31515).

78b Prestatyn: *Publicity Office, c/o Council Offices, Nant Hall Road (tel. 074 56 2484).

79d Holywell: (tel. 0352 780144).

Index

Abbreviations

B.	Bay	Mts.	Mountains
C.	Cape	Pen.	Peninsula
Hd.	Head	Pt.	Point
I.	Island	R.	River
Is.	Islands	Res.	Reservoir
L.	Lake, Loch	Sd., sd.	Sound
Mt.	Mountain	St.	Saint

Gwyn	*Gwynedd*
Mid Glam.	*Mid Glamorgan*
S. Glam.	*South Glamorgan*
W. Glam	*West Glamorgan*

Bryn-crug Gwyn 56d
Bryn Crugog Powys 54a
Bryn Du Powys 42b
Bryn Garw Powys 49b
Bryn-gobaith Dyfed 39a
Bryn-gwyn Powys 51g
Bryn Gydfa Powys 54f
Bryn-Hoffnant Dyfed 47g
Bryn Nichol Dyfed 49h
Bryn Rhyd Dyfed 48f
Bryn Rhudd Dyfed 48f
Bryn-Siencyn Gwyn 67b
Bryn Titley Powys 53i
Bryn-y-Fedwen, Mt. Powys 53b
Bryn-yr-Oerfa, Mt. Powys 53c
Bryn-y-Tail Powys 53c
Brynteg Gwyn 75e
Brynog Dyfed 48d
Brynmawr Powys 33b
Bryngwyn Gwent 34b
Bryngwran Gwyn 74i
Brynford Clwyd 79d
Bryncroes Gwyn 60e
Bryncir Gwyn 67h
Bryr Garw Dyfed 53g
Buckley Clwyd 79h
Buckspool Dyfed 27g
Bugeilyn, L. Powys 53b
Builth Wells Powys 50e
Bull Bay Gwyn 75a
Burry R. Dyfed 20b
Burry Holms W. Glam. 20d
Burry Inlet Dyfed 20b
Burry Port Dyfed 20b
Burton Dyfed 27e
Burwen Gwyn 75a
Buttington Powys 59e
Bwlch Powys 43h
Bwlch Cerig Duon Powys 42g
Bwlch-clawdd Dyfed 39b
Bwlch-gwyn Clwyd 71c
Bwlch-newydd Dyfed 39h
Bwlch y-Cibau Powys 59a
Bwlch-y-ddar Clwyd 65g
Bwlch-y-Eign, Mt. Gwyn 57a
Bwlch y-ffridd Powys 54b
Bwlch-y-groes Dyfed 38f
Bwlch-y-Rhiw Gwyn 60e
Bwlch-y-Sarnau Powys 54h
Bwlchllan Dyfed 48d
Bylchau Clwyd 78g
Bynea Dyfed 20c

Caban-Coch Res. Powys 49c
Cadair Benllyn, Mt.Gwyn 69f
Cadair Berwyn, Mt. Clwyd 64
Cader Fawr, Mt. Mid Glam. 32b
Cader Idris Gwyn 56c
Cadole Clwyd 79g
Cadoxton S. Glam. 24g
Caeathro Gwyn 67b
Caerau Mid Glam. 31i
Caerau S. Glam. 24d
Caer-Ian Powys 31b
Caer-geiliog Gwyn 74e
Caer Farchell Dyfed 36i
Caer Deon Gwyn 56b
Caergwrle Clwyd 71c
Caerhun Gwyn 77d
Caerleon Gwent 34g
Caernarfon Gwyn 67b
Caernarfon B. Gwyn 66b
Caerphilly Mid Glam. 24a
Caersws Powys 54b
Caerwent Gwent 34i
Caerwys Clwyd 78f
Caio Dyfed 41a
Caldicot Gwent 34i
Caldicot Level Gwent 25b
Caldy I. Dyfed 28g
Caldy Sound Dyfed 28g
Camlad, R. Powys 55c
Camllo Hill Powys 54h
Camrose Dyfed 27a
Canaston Bridge Dyfed 27c
Canton S. Glam. 24d
Cantreff Res. Powys 32b
Capel-bangor Dyfed 52e
Capel Coch Gwyn 75d
Capel Curig Gwyn 68c
Capel Dewi Dyfed 39c
Capel Dewi Dyfed 52e
Capel Dewi-uchaf Dyfed 40g
Capel Garmon Gwyn 69b
Capel Gwynfe Dyfed 41g
Capel Hendre Dyfed 30b
Capel-Ifan Dyfed 39a
Capel Llanilltern Mid Glam. 23f
Capel-St. Silin Dyfed 47i
Capel Seion Dyfed 52e
Capel-Uchaf Gwyn 67g
Capel-y-ffin Powys 44d
Capellan-dyry Dyfed 20a
Capelulo Gwyn 76f
Carcwm, Mt. Powys 49i
Cardiff S. Glam. 24e
Cardigan Dyfed 46h
Cardigan I. Dyfed 46g
Careg Wasted Pt. Dyfed 37b
Careg-y-Fran Powys 57c
Carew Dyfed 27f
Carew Cheriton Dyfed 27f
Carmarthen Dyfed 39i
Carmarthen B. Dyfed 28/29
Carmel Clwyd 78f
Carmel Gwyn 67e
Carmel Dyfed 30b
Carmel Head Gwyn 74b
Carnedd Dafydd, Mt. Gwyn 76i
Carnedd Llwelyn, Mt. Gwyn 76h
Carnedd y-Filiast Gwyn 69f
Carn Fadryn Gwyn 60c
Carn Gron Dyfed 49a
Carn Nant-yr-ast Dyfed 48i
Carneddau Powys 50e
Carno Powys 58g
Carrog Clwyd 70f
Carway Dyfed 29f
Cascob Powys 51b
Castell Caereinion Powys 59d
Castell-gorfod Dyfed 39g
Castell-howell Dyfed 47h
Catell Madoc Powys 42c
Castellau Mid Glam. 23b
Castle Morris Dyfed 37d
Castle Vale Powys 54i
Castleblythe Dyfed 37f
Castlemartin Dyfed 27g
Castlemartin Brook Dyfed 26i
Castleton Gwent 24c
Cathedine Powys 43e
Cefn-brith Clwyd 70d
Cefn Bryn W. Glam. 20f
Cefn-caer-Fech Gwyn 61b
Cefn Cantref Powys 42f
Cefn Cenarth Powys 54g
Cefn Clawdd Powys 42c
Cefn Cnwe Dyfed 49d
Cefn Coch Clwyd 64b
Cefn Coch, Mt. Powys 49e
Cefn Coed y-Cymmer Mid Glam. 32b
Cefn Cribwr Mid Glam. 22f
Cefn Crin Powys 48h
Cefn Crug, Mt. Powys 49e
Cefn-Cul Powys 42g
Cefn Cyff Powys 42i
Cefn-ddwysarn Gwyn 64a
Cefn Drum W. Glam. 30e
Cefn-eithin Dyfed 30a
Cefn Fanog, Mt. Powys 49e
Cefn-gorwydd Powys 49i
Cefn Grug, Mt. W. Glam. 31f
Cefn Gwenffrwd Dyfed 49g
Cefn Gwrhyd W. Glam. 31a
Cefn-gwyn Powys 55a
Cefn Gwyngul Mid Glam. 32h
Cefn Hirgoed Mid Glam. 23d
Cefn Llechyd Powys 42e
Cefen Llwydlo Powys 49h
Cefn Mably Mid Glam. 24b
Cefn Manmoel Gwent 33d
Cefn-mawr Clwyd 71f
Cefn Meriadog Clwyd 78d
Cefn Morfydd W. Glam. 31h
Cefn Pennar Mid Glam. 32e
Cefn-Rhudd Gwyn 69b
Cefn Sidan Sands Dyfed 29d
Cefn Tyle Brych W. Glam. 31f
Cefn-y bedd Clwyd 72a
Cefn-y-coed Powys 55a
Cefn Ynysowen Merthyr Mid Glam. 32f
Cefn-y Rhondda Mid Glam. 32g
Cefn-yr-Ystrad, Mt. Powys 32c
Cefnhir Fynydd Clwyd 65d
Cefni Res. Gwyn 75d
Ceiriog, R. Clwyd 65b
Cellan Dyfed 48h
Cemaes Gwyn 74c
Cemaes B. Gwyn 74c
Cemaes Hd. Dyfed 46g
Cemmaes Powys 57e
Cemmaes Road Powys 57e
Cenarth Dyfed 39a
Cerrigceinwen Gwyn 75g
Cerrigydrudion Clwyd 70d
Chapel Hill Gwent 35d
Chepstow Gwent 35g
Chepstow Park Wood Gwent 34f
Chequer, The Clwyd 72i
Cheriton W. Glam. 20e
Cheriton or Stackpole Elidor Dyfed 27h
Chirk Clwyd 65c
Christchurch Gwent 34g
Church Bay Gwyn 74b
Church Stoke Powys 55b
Church Village Mid Glam. 23c
Chwefru, R. Powys 50d
Chwilog Gwyn 61b
Cilcain Clwyd 79g
Cilcennin Dyfed 47f
Cilfaesty Hill Powys 54f
Cilfynydd Mid Glam. 23c
Cilgerran Dyfed 38b
Cilgwyn Dyfed 38d
Cilgwyn Dyfed 41e
Ciliau-Aeron Dyfed 47f
Cilmery Powys 50d
Cilrhedyn Dyfed 39d
Cil-y-bebyll W. Glam. 31d
Cilycwm Dyfed 41b
Cilycwm Fforest Dyfed 41b
Claerwen Res. Powys 49b
Clarbeston Dyfed 37i
Clarbeston Road Dyfed 37i
Clatter Powys 54a
Clawdd Newydd Clwyd 70c
Cledan, R. Powys 49i
Clegyrnant Powys 57f
Clemenstone S. Glam. 23g
Clettwr, R. Dyfed 52c
Clettwr Fawr Dyfed 47h
Cliff Dyfed 29a
Clocaenog Dyfed 70c
Clochnant R. Clwyd 64b
Clunderwen Dyfed 28a
Clwt-y-bont Gwyn 67c
Clwyd, R. Clwyd 78a
Clwyd, Vale of Clwyd 78e
Clwydian Range Clwyd 78i
Clydach Powys 33b
Clydach W. Glam. 30f
Clydach Vale Mid Glam. 32g
Clyn Dyfed 38e
Clyne Common W. Glam. 21d
Clynnog-fawr Gwyn 67g
Clyro Powys 51h
Clyro Hill Powys 51g
Clytha Hill Gwent 34b
Clywedog, R. Powys 53f
Clywedog, R. Clwyd 72d
Cnewr Powys 42g
Cnwch-coch Dyfed 52i
Coalbrookvale Gwent 33b
Cockett W. Glam. 21d
Coed Morgan Gwent 34a
Coed-poeth Clwyd 71c
Coed-y Gaer Powys 54e
Coed-y-paen Gwent 34d
Coed-yr-ynys Powys 43h
Coedana Gwyn 75d
Coelbren Powys 31c
Cogan S. Glam. 24h
Coity Mid Glam. 23d
Coity Mt. Gwent 33b
Cold Blow Dyfed 28a
Colva Powys 51d
Colva Hill Powys 51d
Colwinston S. Glam. 23d
Colwyn Bay Clwyd 77b
Commercial Dyfed 28a
Commins-coch Powys 57e
Connah's Quay Clwyd 79e
Conwy Gwyn 77d
Conwy, R. Gwyn 77d
Conwy, Vale of Gwyn 77g
Conwy B. Gwyn 76e
Conwy Sands Gwyn 77a
Corlan Fraith, Mt. Gwyn 56g
Corndon Hill Powys 59i
Corn Du Powys 42i
Corngafallt Powys 50a
Corntown Mid Glam. 23d
Corris Powys 57d
Cors Fochno Dyfed 52b
Cors Goch Glanteifi Dyfed 48c
Corwen Clwyd 70f
Cosheston Dyfed 27e
Cowbridge S. Glam. 23h
Coychurch Mid Glam. 23d
Coytra-hen Mid Glam. 22c
Craig-bron-banog Clwyd 70b
Craig-cefn-parc W. Glam. 30f
Craig Fan-ddu Powys 42i
Craig-fawr W. Glam. 30e
Craig-goch Res. Powys 53i
Craig-tre-branos W. Glam. 21c
Craig Twrch Dyfed 48i
Craig y Ffynnon, Mt. Gwyn 63h
Craig-y-Llyn, Mt. W. Glam. 31f
Craig-y-Llyn Gwyn 56b
Craig-y-nos Powys 31b
Craiglyn Dyfi Gwyn 63h
Crawcwellt Gwyn 62f
Creffta Mid Glam. 23f
Cregrina Powys 50f
Cresselly Dyfed 27f
Cresswell Dyfed 27f
Cresswell R. Dyfed 27e
Cribyn Dyfed 47i
Criccieth Gwyn 61c
Crick Gwent 34i
Crickadarn Powys 43a
Crickhowell Powys 43i
Criggion Powys 65i
Crincoed Pt. Dyfed 37b
Crinow Dyfed 28a
Croes Hywel Gwent 34a
Croes-y-ceiliog Gwent 34g
Croes-y-mwyalch Gwent 34g
Croes-yn-y-pant Gwent 33f
Croeserw W. Glam. 31i
Croesgoch Dyfed 36f
Croesyceilog Dyfed 29b
Cross Ash Gwent 44i
Cross Gates Powys 50c
Cross Hands Dyfed 30a
Cross Inn Dyfed 48a
Crossway Powys 50e
Crug Powys 55g
Crug Mawr Powys 44g
Crug Siaris Dyfed 48i
Crumlin Gwent 33h
Crundale Dyfed 27a
Crunwear Dyfed 28a
Crwbin Dyfed 29c
Crymlyn Gwyn 76e
Crymych Dyfed 38e
Crynant W. Glam. 31e
Cwm Gwent 33e
Cwm Clwyd 78b
Cwm Afan, R. W. Glam. 31h
Cwm Amman, R. Dyfed 30c
Cwm-bach Powys 43b
Cwm-bach Mid Glam. 32e
Cwm-bach Dyfed 39g
Cwm-bach Powys 50e
Cwm-belan Powys 53f
Cwm-brwyno Dyfed 52f
Cwm-carn Gwent 33h
Cwm Clydach, R. W. Glam. 30
Cwm-du Powys 43h
Cwm Dulas Powys 49f
Cwm-felin-boeth Dyfed 28b
Cwm-felin-fach Gwent 24b
Cwm-felin-mynach Dyfed 38i
Cwm-ffrwd Dyfed 29b
Cwm-giedd Powys 31b
Cwm Hirnant, R. Gwyn 64d
Cwm Llinau Powys 57e
Cwm Llwyd, R. Powys 58g
Cwm-llyfrau Dyfed 29a
Cwm-Morgan Dyfed 39d
Cwm Owen Inn Powys 50h
Cwm-parc Mid Glam. 32g
Cwm-pencraig Dyfed 39b
Cwm-sychbant Dyfed 47i
Cwm-symlog, L. Dyfed 52f
Cwm Taf Mid Glam. 32b
Cwm-tillery Gwent 33e
Cwm-y-glo Gwyn 67c
Cwmaman Mid Glam. 32e
Cwmaran, R. Powys 50c
Cwmavon W. Glam. 31g
Cwmbran Gwent 33i
Cwmcoy Dyfed 39a
Cwmcarvan Gwent 34c
Cwmdar Mid Glam. 32e
Cwmduad Dyfed 39e
Cwmgorse Dyfed 30c
Cwmllynfell W. Glam. 31a
Cwmyoy Gwent 44g
Cwmystwyth Dyfed 53g
Cwrt Gwyn 56f
Cwrt-newydd Dyfed 47i
Cyffylliog Clwyd 70c
Cyfnwy, L. Clwyd 71b
Cymmer Mid Glam. 31i
Cymmeran B. Gwyn 74h
Cynfal, R. Gwyn 62c
Cynghardy Dyfed 41c
Cynwyd Clwyd 64b
Cynwyl Elfed Dyfed 39e
Cyrn-y brain Clwyd 71e
Cyrnau Bach Dyfed 53g
Cyrniau Nod, Mt. Gwyn 64d

Dafen Dyfed 20c
Dale Dyfed 26e
Dale Pt. Dyfed 26e
Darowen Powys 57h
David's Well Powys 54e
Ddyle Powys 54h
Defynnog Powys 42e
Dee, R. Clwyd 79a
Degannwy Gwyn 77a
Deiniolen Gwyn 67c
Denbigh Clwyd 78h
Deri Mid Glam. 33d
Deri Gwent 44g
Derwen Clwyd 70f
Derwen-las Powys 56i
Dethenydd Powys 54e
Deunant Clwyd 78g
Devauden Gwent 34f
Devils Bridge Dyfed 53g
Dewi Fawr Dyfed 39g
Dibyn Du Dyfed 49a
Diffwys, Mt. Gwyn 62h
Dihewyd Dyfed 47f
Dinas Dyfed 39d
Dinas Dyfed 37c
Dinas Gwyn 60b
Dinas Gwyn 67e
Dinas Powys 43d
Dinas Fawr Hd. Dyfed 36i
Dinas Head Dyfed 37c
Dinas I. Dyfed 37c
Dinas Mawddwy Gwyn 57b
Dinas Powis S. Glam. 24g
Dingestow Gwent 34c
Dinorwig Gwyn 76g
Discoed Powys 51b
Disgwylfa Fawr, Mt. Dyfed 52f
Disserth Powys 50e
Doethie Fach R. Dyfed 49d
Dolanog Powys 58b
Dolbenmaen Gwyn 61c
Dolfach Powys 53i
Dol-fawr Powys 57e
Dolfor Powys 54c
Dol-goch Gwyn 56e
Dolgarrog Gwyn 77g
Dolgellau Gwyn 56c
Dolwen Clwyd 77e
Dolwyddelan Gwyn 69a
Doly-bont Dyfed 52b
Dol-y-garreg Dyfed 41e
Dol-yr-onen Powys 57h
Dol-y-wern Clwyd 65b
Dolyhir Powys 51e
Dovey, R. Powys 56i
Dovey Valley Powys 56i
Dowlais Mid Glam. 32c
Dreenhill Dyfed 27a
Dre-fach Dyfed 47i
Dre-fach Dyfed 30a
Dre-fach Dyfed 39b
Dre-felin Dyfed 39b
Drosgol, Mt. Dyfed 53a
Drosgol, Mt. Gwyn 76h
Druid Clwyd 70e
Drum, Mt. Gwyn 76f
Drum Ddu, Mt. Powys 50g
Drum Ddu, Mt. Powys 50a
Drum Peithant, Mt. Dyfed 53d
Drum yr Eira, Mt. Powys 49e
Drury Clwyd 79h
Drygran Fawr Powys 49e
Dryslwyn Dyfed 40h
Dudwell Mt. Dyfed 37g
Dubestown Gwent 33a
Dulais, R. W. Glam. 31e
Dulas, R. Clwyd 77c
Dulas, R. Powys 50b
Dulas, R. Powys 50d
Dulas Bay Gwyn 75b
Dulyn Resr. Gwyn 76i
Dunvant W. Glam. 21d
Dutlas Powys 55d
Dwygyfylchi Gwyn 76f
Dwyran Gwyn 67a
Dyffryn Mid Glam. 31i
Dyffryn W. Glam. 31h
Dyffryn Gwyn 62g
Dyffryn Dyfed 37b
Dyffryn-castell Dyfed 53d
Dyffryn Crawnan Powys 43g
Dyffryn Edeirnion Clwyd 64b
Dylife Powys 53b
Dyrysgol Powys 54g
Dyserth Clwyd 78b

Earlswood Common Gwent 34i
East. Aberthaw S. Glam. 23h
East Williamston Dyfed 28d
Eastern Cleddau Dyfed 27b
Ebbw R. Gwent 24c
Ebbw Vale Gwent 33a
Ebbw Valley Gwent 33e
Edern Gwyn 60c
Edwinsford Dyfed 40c
Efail-isaf Mid Glam. 23c
Efail-newydd Gwyn 61a
Efenechtyd Clwyd 70c
Egbwys Fach Dyfed 56i
Eglwys-bach Gwyn 77d
Eglwys Cross Clwyd 72i
Eglwyseg Mountain Clwyd 71e
Eglwyswrw Dyfed 38b
Egremont Dyfed 38g
Eisingrug Gwyn 62b
Eisteddfa Gurig Powys 53d
Elidir Fawr, Mt. Gwyn 76h
Ely S. Glam. 24d
Ely, R. S. Glam. 23f
Ely Valley Mid Glam. 23b
Erbistock Clwyd 72d
Erch, R. Gwyn 61a
Erwood Powys 43a
Eryrys Clwyd 71b
Esclusham Mountain Clwyd 71e
Esgair Dyfed 39e
Esgair Cerig Dyfed 49d
Esgair Elan Dyfed 53h
Esgair Garthen Powys 49b
Esgair-geiliog Ceinws Powys 57d
Esgair Llethr Dyfed 48f
Esgair Nantau Powys 51a
Eunant Powys 64g
Evenjobb Powys 51b
Ewenny Mid Glam. 22f
Ewloe Clwyd 79h
Ewng Dyfed 49h
Eyton Clwyd 72d

Fairbourne Gwyn 56a
Fairyhill W. Glam. 20e
Fan Hill Powys 53c
Fanagoed, R. Dyfed 48i
Fan Bwlch Clwyth Powys 42g
Fan Fawr Powys 42h
Fan Frynach Powys 42h
Fan Gihirych Powys 42g
Fan Hir Powys 41i
Fan Llia Powys 42h
Fan Nedd Powys 42g
Fedw Ddu Powys 53b
Felindre Dyfed 41d
Felindre Dyfed 40h
Felindre W. Glam. 30f
Felindre Powys 55d

Felin-foel *Dyfed* 20c
Felin-gwm-uchaf *Dyfed* 40g
Fenns Moss *Clwyd* 72i
Fenton Brook *Dyfed* 27a
Ferndale *Mid Glam.* 32h
Ferryside *Dyfed* 29a
Ffair-fach *Dyfed* 40i
Ffair-rhos *Dyfed* 49a
Ffarmers *Dyfed* 48h
Ffestiniog *Gwyn* 62c
Ffestiniog, Vale of *Gwyn* 62c
Fforest Fach *Powys* 42d
Fforest-fach *W. Glam.* 21d
Ffostrasol *Dyfed* 47g
Ffos Trosol *Dyfed* 53h
Ffos-y ffin *Dyfed* 47e
Ffridd Trawscoed *Gwyn* 63e
Ffrith *Clwyd* 71c
Ffrwdgrech *Powys* 42f
Ffwyddog *Powys* 43i
Ffynnon-ddrain *Dyfed* 39i
Ffynnongroyw *Clwyd* 78c
Fishguard *Dyfed* 37b
Fishguard B. *Dyfed* 37b
Five Roads *Dyfed* 20c
Flat Holme, I. *Gwent* 24i
Flemingston *S. Glam.* 23h
Flint *Clwyd* 79d
Flint Mountain *Clwyd* 79e
Fochrhiw *Mid Glam.* 32f
Foel *Clwyd* 65a
Foel Bendin, Mt. *Gwyn* 57b
Foel Cwm-cerwyn *Dyfed* 38d
Foel Dolu *Gwyn* 63e
Foel Drych *Dyfed* 38e
Foel Dugoed, Mt. *Gwyn* 57b
Foel Eryr *Dyfed* 38d
Foel Fraith *Dyfed* 41h
Foel Fras, Mt. *Gwyn* 76h
Foel Goch *Dyfed* 52c
Foel Goch, Mt. *Gwyn* 64a
Foel Grach, Mt. *Gwyn* 76h
Foel Lus *Gwyn* 76f
Foel Mynyddau *W. Glam.* 31h
Foel Rudd, Mt. *Gwyn* 63i
Foel Wyllt *Gwyn* 56e
Foel y Geifr, Mt. *Gwyn* 64c
Foel-y-Geifr, Mt. *Gwyn* 56f
Folly *Dyfed* 37h
Forden *Powys* 59h
Foryd Bay *Gwyn* 67d
Four Crosses *Powys* 59b
Four Crosses *Clwyd* 70e
Four Mile Bridge *Gwyn* 74e
Four Roads *Dyfed* 29c
Freni Fawr *Dyfed* 38f
Freshwater West *Dyfed* 26i
Freystrop Cross *Dyfed* 27a
Friog *Gwyn* 56b
Frochas *Powys* 59e
Fron *Dyfed* 41e
Fron *Powys* 59e
Fron *Powys* 59g
Fron *Powys* 50c
Fron Cysyllte *Clwyd* 65b
Fron-goch *Gwyn* 63c

Gamalt *Powys* 54g
Garden City *Clwyd* 79f
Gareg-Goch, Mt. *Powys* 31b
Garland Stone *Dyfed* 26d
Garn Boduan *Gwyn* 60e
Garn Caws *Powys* 43h
Garn Dolbenmaen *Gwyn* 67i
Garn Ddu *Mid Glam.* 32b
Garn Prys *Clwyd* 69f
Garnant *Dyfed* 30c
Garneddwen, Mt. *Clwyd* 64f
Garneddwen *Gwyn* 57d
Garreg *Gwyn* 62b
Garreg-ddu Res. *Powys* 49c
Garreg-las *Dyfed* 41h
Garreg-lwyd *Dyfed* 41h
Garth *Mid Glam.* 32c
Garth *Powys* 50g
Garth *Clwyd* 71f
Garth *Mid Glam.* 22c
Garthmyl *Powys* 59g
Garthbrengi *Powys* 42f
Gartheli *Dyfed* 48d
Garthynty *Dyfed* 48i
Gateholm, I. *Dyfed* 26e
Gaufron *Powys* 50a
Gell *Gwyn* 61c
Gelligaer *Mid Glam.* 33g
Gelli-wen *Dyfed* 39g
Gelly *Dyfed* 27c
George Town *Gwent* 33a
Gerlan *Gwyn* 76h
Gernos *Dyfed* 47g
Geufron *Powys* 53e
Geuffordd *Powys* 59a
Gileston *S. Glam.* 23h
Gilfach *Mid Glam.* 33d
Gilfach Goch *Mid Glam.* 23a
Giltar Point *Dyfed* 28g
Gilwern *Gwent* 33c
Gilwern Hill *Powys* 50f
Ginst Point *Dyfed* 29d
Gladestry *Powys* 51e
Glais *W. Glam.* 21c
Glamorgan, Vale of *S. Glam.* 23g
Glan Adda *Gwyn* 76d
Glan Bran *Dyfed* 41c
Glan-Brydan Park *Dyfed* 41d
Glan-dwr *Dyfed* 38f
Glan-hafon, Mt. *Powys* 64f
Glan Honddu *Powys* 42f
Glan-llynfi *Mid Glam.* 22c
Glan-rhyd *Dyfed* 38b
Glan-Sefin *Dyfed* 41e
Glanaman *Dyfed* 30c
Glangrwyne *Powys* 33b
Glanwye *Powys* 50h
Glanyllyn *Mid Glam.* 24a
Glasbury *Powys* 43b
Glascoed *Gwent* 34d
Glascwm *Powys* 51d
Glasfryn *Clwyd* 69f
Glasinfryn *Gwyn* 76g
Glaslyn, L. *Gwyn* 68b
Glaslyn, L. *Powys* 53b
Glaspant *Dyfed* 39a
Glaspwll *Dyfed* 56i
Glenarthen *Dyfed* 47g
Glôg Hill *Powys* 55g
Glyder-fach, Mt. *Gwyn* 68c
Glyder Fawr, Mt. *Gwyn* 68b
Glyn-Ceiriog *Clwyd* 71h
Glyn-hir *Dyfed* 30b
Glyn Neath *W. Glam.* 31f
Glyn Taff *Mid Glam.* 23c
Glyncorrwg *W. Glam.* 31f
Glyn Dyfrdwy *Clwyd* 71d
Godor *Powys* 59a
Godrer-graig *W. Glam.* 31d
Gogarth *Gwyn* 77a
Goginan *Dyfed* 52f
Goldcliff *Gwent* 25d
Goodwick *Dyfed* 37b
Gorllwyn, Mt. *Powys* 49f
Gorllwyn *Dyfed* 39e
Gorsedd *Clwyd* 78d
Gorseinon *W. Glam.* 21a
Gors-gôch *Dyfed* 47i
Gors-las *Dyfed* 30b
Gowerton *W. Glam.* 21d
Graig *Clwyd* 77d
Graig Goch, Mt. *Gwyn* 56f
Graig Syfyrddin *Gwent* 44i
Graig Wen, Mt. *Gwyn* 63a
Grangetown *S. Glam.* 24e
Granston *Dyfed* 37d
Greatoak *Gwent* 34b
Gt. Ormes Head *Gwyn* 77a
Gt. Rhos, Mt. *Powys* 51a
Greenfield *Clwyd* 79d
Green Scar I. *Dyfed* 36i
Gresford *Clwyd* 72a
Griffithstown *Gwent* 33f
Groes *Clwyd* 78g
Groes faen *Mid Glam.* 23f
Groes-llwyd *Powys* 59a
Groesffordd *Gwyn* 60i
Gronant *Clwyd* 78b
Grosmont *Gwent* 44f
Groves End *W. Glam.* 21a
Grwyne Fawr R. *Powys* 44d
Grwyne Fechan *Powys* 43f
Guilsfield *Powys* 59b
Gumfreston *Dyfed* 28d
Gurnos *Powys* 31a
Gwaelod-y-garth *Mid Glam.* 23c
Gwaen Nant-ddu *Powys* 42i
Gwaithla *Powys* 51d
Gwalchmai *Gwyn* 74i
Gwastadros *Gwyn* 63c
Gwastedyn Hill *Powys* 50a
Gwaun-cae-gurwen *W. Glam.* 31a
Gwaun-ceste Hill *Powys* 51d
Gwann-leision *W. Glam.* 30c
Gwbert on Sea *Dyfed* 46g
Gwenddwr *Powys* 50h
Gwendraeth, R. *Dyfed* 29e
Gwendraeth Fach *Dyfed* 29c
Gwendraeth Fawr *Dyfed* 29f
Gwenlas, R. *Dyfed* 41b
Gwernaffield *Clwyd* 79g
Gwernesney *Gwent* 34e
Gwern-y-mynydd *Clwyd* 79g
Gweryd, L. *Clwyd* 71a
Gwespyr *Clwyd* 78c
Gwmann *Dyfed* 48g
Gwrhyd, Mt. *Powys* 42b
Gwyddelwern *Clwyd* 70f
Gwyddgrug *Dyfed* 39c
Gwynfryn *Gwyn* 62e
Gwystre *Powys* 50b
Gwytherin *Clwyd* 77h
Gyfelia *Clwyd* 72d
Gyffin *Gwyn* 77d
Gyrn Moelfre *Clwyd* 65d

Hafod Br. *Dyfed* 41a
Halfway *Dyfed* 40f
Halfway *Dyfed/Powys* 41f
Halghton Mill *Clwyd* 72d
Halkyn *Clwyd* 79d
Halkyn Mountain *Clwyd* 79d
Hanmer *Clwyd* 72i
Happy Valley *Gwyn* 56g
Harlech *Gwyn* 62d
Haroldston West *Dyfed* 26c
Hasguard *Dyfed* 26f
Haverfordwest *Dyfed* 27a
Hawarden *Clwyd* 79i
Hawen *Dyfed* 47g
Hay Bluff, Mt. *Powys* 43c
Hay-on-Wye *Powys* 43c
Hayscastle *Dyfed* 37g
Hayscastle Cross *Dyfed* 37g
Head, The *Dyfed* 26d
Heartsease *Powys* 55i
Hebron *Dyfed* 38e
Henbwell R. *Gwyn* 57c
Heneglwys *Gwyn* 75g
Hengoed *Mid Glam.* 33g
Henllan *Clwyd* 78g
Henllan *Dyfed* 39b
Henllys *Gwent* 24c
Henllys *Dyfed* 41b
Henrys Moat *Dyfed* 37i
Heol-ddu *Dyfed* 30a
Heol-llygoden *Powys* 43e
Heol Senni *Powys* 42h
Herbrandston *Dyfed* 26f
Hermon *Gwyn* 66c
Hermon *Dyfed* 38f
Highmead *Dyfed* 40a
Hill *Dyfed* 28d
Hill Mountain *Dyfed* 27e
Hirddau Fawr *Powys* 64g
Hirfynydd *W. Glam.* 31e
Hirnant *Powys* 64h
Hirwaen *Clwyd* 78i
Hirwaun *Mid Glam.* 32d
Hirwaun Common *Mid Glam.* 32d
Hirwaun Common *Mid. Glam* 23d
Hodgeston *Dyfed* 27h
Hodley *Powys* 55a
Hoel-galed *Dyfed* 40f
Holt *Clwyd* 72b
Holy Island *Gwyn* 74b
Holyhead *Gwyn* 74d
Holyhead B. *Gwyn* 74e
Holyhead Mountain *Gwyn* 74d
Holywell *Clwyd* 79d
Honddu R. *Powys* 42c
Honeyborough *Dyfed* 27d
Hooper's Point *Dyfed* 26e
Hope *Clwyd* 72a
Hopkinstown *Mid Glam.* 32i
Horeb *Dyfed* 20c
Horeb *Dyfed* 39b
Horton *W. Glam.* 20h
Houghton *Dyfed* 27e
Howey *Powys* 50e
Hugmore *Clwyd* 72d
Hundleton *Dyfed* 27g
Hundred House *Powys* 50f
Hyssington *Powys* 55c

Ifton *Gwent* 25c
Ilston *W. Glam.* 30g
Innage *Gwent* 35g
Irfon, R. *Powys* 50r
Is-coed *Dyfed* 29b
Ithon, R. *Powys* 54i
Ithon, R. *Powys* 50c
Itton *Gwent* 34i

Jameston *Dyfed* 27i
Jeffreston *Dyfed* 27f
Johns Town *Dyfed* 39i
Johnston *Dyfed* 27d
Johnstown *Clwyd* 72d
Jordanston *Dyfed* 37d

Keeston *Dyfed* 26c
Keeston Bridge *Dyfed* 26c
Keeston Hill *Dyfed* 26c
Kell, The *Dyfed* 37h
Kemeys Inferior *Gwent* 34h
Kenfig *Mid Glam.* 22e
Kenfig Hill *Mid Glam.* 22e
Kenfig Pool *Mid Glam.* 22e
Kerry *Powys* 54c
Kerry Hill *Powys* 54f
Kidwelly *Dyfed* 29e
Kilgetty *Dyfed* 28d
Killay *W. Glam.* 21d
Kilvey Hill *W. Glam.* 30i
Kingcoed *Gwent* 34e
Kingsfold *Dyfed* 27h
Kingsland *Gwyn* 74d
Kingswood *Powys* 59e
Kinnerton *Powys* 51b
Knelston *W. Glam.* 20e
Knighton *Powys* 55h
Knucklas *Powys* 55h

Laleston *Mid Glam.* 22f
Lambston *Dyfed* 26c
Lampeter *Dyfed* 48g
Lampster-Velfrey *Dyfed* 28a
Lamphey *Dyfed* 27h
Lan Ystenn *Powys* 50d
Landore *W. Glam.* 30i
Landshipping *Dyfed* 27b
Langland Bay *W. Glam.* 21g
Laugharne *Dyfed* 28c
Laugharne Burrows *Dyfed* 28f
Laugharne Sands *Dyfed* 28f
Lavernock *S. Glam.* 24h
Lavernock Pt. *S. Glam.* 24h
Lavan Sands *Gwyn* 76e
Lavister *Clwyd* 72b
Lawrenny *Dyfed* 27e
Leckwith *S. Glam.* 24g
Leighton *Powys* 59e
Letterston *Dyfed* 37e
Libanus *Powys* 42f
Lightwood Green *Clwyd* 72h
Linney Hd. *Dyfed* 26i
Lis Werry *Gwent* 25a
Lisvane *S. Glam.* 24e
Little Hill *Powys* 50f
Little Newcastle *Dyfed* 37e
Little Ormes Head *Gwyn* 77a
Lixwm *Clwyd* 78f
Llain-goch *Gwyn* 74d
Llaithddu *Powys* 54e
Llanaber *Gwyn* 56a
Llanaelhaearn *Gwyn* 66i
Llanafan *Dyfed* 52i
Llanafan-fawr *Powys* 50d
Llanafan-fechan *Powys* 50g
Llanallgo *Gwyn* 75e
Llanarmon *Gwyn* 61b
Llanarmon Dyffryn Ceiriog *Clwyd* 65a
Llanarmon-yn-Iâl *Clwyd* 71a
Llanarth *Gwent* 34b
Llanarth *Dyfed* 47e
Llanrthney *Dyfed* 40h
Llanasa *Clwyd* 78c
Llanayron *Dyfed* 47f
Llanbabo *Gwyn* 74f
Llanbadarn-Fawr *Dyfed* 52d
Llanbadarnfynydd *Powys* 54f
Llanbadarn Garreg *Powys* 50i
Llanbadoc *Gwent* 34e
Llanbedr *Gwyn* 62d
Llanbedr *Powys* 50i
Llanbedr *Powys* 43i
Llanbedr-goch *Gwyn* 75e
Llanbedr Hill *Powys* 50i
Llanbedrog *Gwyn* 60f
Llanbedr-y-Cennin 77d
Llanberis *Gwyn* 68a
Llanberis, Pass of *Gwyn* 68b
Llanberthy *S. Glam.* 23h
Llanbister *Powys* 54i
Llanblethian *S. Glam.* 23h
Llanboidy *Dyfed* 38i
Llanbradach *Mid Glam.* 24a
Llanbrynmair *Powys* 57f
Llancarfan *S. Glam.* 23h
Llancayo *Gwent* 34e
Llandaf *S. Glam.* 24d
Llan-dafal *Gwent* 33e
Llandanwg *Gwyn* 62d
Llandawke *Dyfed* 28c
Llanddaniel Fab *Gwyn* 75h
Llanddarog *Dyfed* 29c
Llanddeinial *Dyfed* 52g
Llanddeiniolen *Gwyn* 67c
Llandderfel *Gwyn* 64a
Llanddeusant *Gwyn* 74f
Llanddeusant *Dyfed* 41h
Llanddew *Powys* 43d
Llanddewi *W. Glam.* 20e
Llanddewir Cwm *Powys* 50h
Llanddewi Rhydderch *Gwent* 34a
Llanddewi Ystradenny *Powys* 54i
Llanddewibrefi *Dyfed* 48f
Llanddoged *Gwyn* 77g
Llanddona *Gwyn* 75f
Llanddwyn Bay *Gwyn* 67a
Llanddwyn Island *Gwyn* 66c
Llanddwywe *Gwyn* 62g
Llandefalle *Powys* 43a
Llandefalle Hill *Powys* 43a
Llandefaelog Fach *Powys* 42f
Llandegai *Gwyn* 76d
Llandegfan *Gwyn* 75i
Llandegfedd Res. *Gwent* 34a
Llandegla *Clwyd* 71b
Llandegley *Powys* 50c
Llandegley Rhos *Powys* 50c
Llandeilo *Dyfed* 40i
Llandeilo-graban *Powys* 50i
Llandeilo Hill *Powys* 50i
Llandeilor Fan *Powys* 42a
Llandeloy *Dyfed* 37g
Llandenny *Gwent* 34e
Llandevenny *Gwent* 25b
Llandilo Abercowyn *Dyfed* 29a
Llandimore *W. Glam.* 20e
Llandinan *Powys* 54b
Llandogo *Gwent* 35d
Llandough *S. Glam.* 23h
Llandovery *Dyfed* 41b
Llandow *S. Glam.* 23g
Llandowror *Dyfed* 28c
Llandre *Dyfed* 52e
Llandre *Dyfed* 41a
Llandrillo *Clwyd* 64b
Llandrillo yn Rhos *Gwyn* 77b
Llandrindod Wells *Powys* 50b
Llandrinio *Powys* 59b
Llandudno *Gwyn* 77a
Llandulas *Clwyd* 77c
Llandwrog *Gwyn* 67d
Llandybie *Dyfed* 30b
Llandyfaelog *Dyfed* 29b
Llandyfodwg *Mid Glam.* 23a
Llandyfriog *Dyfed* 39b
Llandyfrydog *Gwyn* 75d
Llandygwydd *Dyfed* 38c
Llandyrnog *Clwyd* 78i
Llandysilio *Dyfed* 38h
Llandysilio *Powys* 59b
Llandyssil *Powys* 55a
Llandyssul *Dyfed* 39c
Llanedeyrn *S. Glam.* 24e
Llanegryn *Gwyn* 56d
Llanelian-yn-Rhos *Clwyd* 77e
Llanelidan *Clwyd* 70f
Llanelieu *Powys* 43b
Llanellen *Gwent* 33c
Llanelli *Powys* 33b
Llanelli *Dyfed* 20c
Llanelltyd *Gwyn* 62i
Llanelwedd *Powys* 50e
Llanenddwyn *Gwyn* 62g
Llanengan *Gwyn* 60f
Llanerchymedd *Gwyn* 75d
Llanerch-y-mor *Clwyd* 79a
Llanerch-yrfa *Powys* 49e
Llanerfyl *Powys* 58b
Llanfachraeth *Gwyn* 74e
Llanfachreth *Gwyn* 63g
Llanfaelog *Gwyn* 74i
Llanfaelrhys *Gwyn* 60e
Llanfaes *Gwyn* 75d
Llanfaes *Gwyn* 76d
Llanfaethlu *Gwyn* 74e
Llanfaglan *Gwyn* 67e
Llanfair *Gwyn* 62d
Llanfair-ar-y-bryn *Dyfed* 41c
Llanfair Caereinion *Powys* 58f
Llanfair Clydogau *Dyfed* 48h
Llanfair Dyffryn Clwyd *Clwyd* 78i
Llanfair Dylfryn Clwyd *Clwyd* 71a
Llanfairfechan *Gwyn* 76f
Llanfair-Nant Gwyn *Dyfed* 38b
Llanfair Orllwyn *Dyfed* 39b
Llanfair-pwllgwyngyll *Gwyn* 75h
Llanfair Talhaiarn *Clwyd* 77f
Llanfairynghornwy *Gwyn* 74b
Llanfair yn neubwll *Gwyn* 74h
Llanfaredd *Powys* 50e
Llanfarian *Dyfed* 52g
Llanfechain *Powys* 65g
Llanfechell *Gwyn* 74c
Llanferres *Clwyd* 79g
Llanfihangel Aberbythych *Dyfed* 40i
Llanfihangel Abercowin *Dyfed* 28c
Llanfihangel-ar-arth *Dyfed* 39c
Llanfihangel Bryn Pabuan *Powys* 50d
Llanfihangel Glyn Myfyr *Clwyd* 70e
Llanfihangel helygen *Powys* 50b
Llanfihangel Nant Bran *Powys* 42b
Llanfihangel nant Melan *Powys* 51d
Llanfihangel Rhydithon *Powys* 51a
Llanfihangel Tal-y-llyn *Powys* 43d
Llanfihangel-y-Creuddyn *Dyfed* 52h
Llanfihangel-yng-Ngwynfa *Powys* 58c
Llanfihangel yn-nhowyn *Gwyn* 74l
Llanfihangel-y-Pennant *Gwyn* 56e
Llanfihangel Ystern-Llewern *Gwyn* 34b
Llanfihangel-Ystrad *Dyfed* 47f
Llanfihangel-y-traethau *Gwyn* 62a
Llanfillo *Powys* 43e
Llanfoist *Gwyn* 33c
Llanfor *Gwyn* 63c
Llanfrecha *Gwyn* 34g
Llanfrynach *Powys* 43d
Llanfwrog *Gwyn* 74e
Llanfyllin *Powys* 65g
Llanfyrnach *Dyfed* 38f
Llanfynydd *Dyfed* 40e
Llanfynydd *Clwyd* 71c
Llangadfan *Powys* 58a
Llangadog *Dyfed* 41d
Llangadwaladr *Gwyn* 66c
Llangaffo *Gwyn* 67a
Llangallen, Vale of *Clwyd* 71e
Llangammarch Wells *Powys* 50g
Llan-gan *S. Glam.* 23d
Llangar *Clwyd* 70f
Llangathen *Dyfed* 40i
Llangattock *Powys* 43i

KEY TO MAP SECTION

1:100,000
MAP COVERAGE

Motorway

Through Routes

National & County
Boundaries

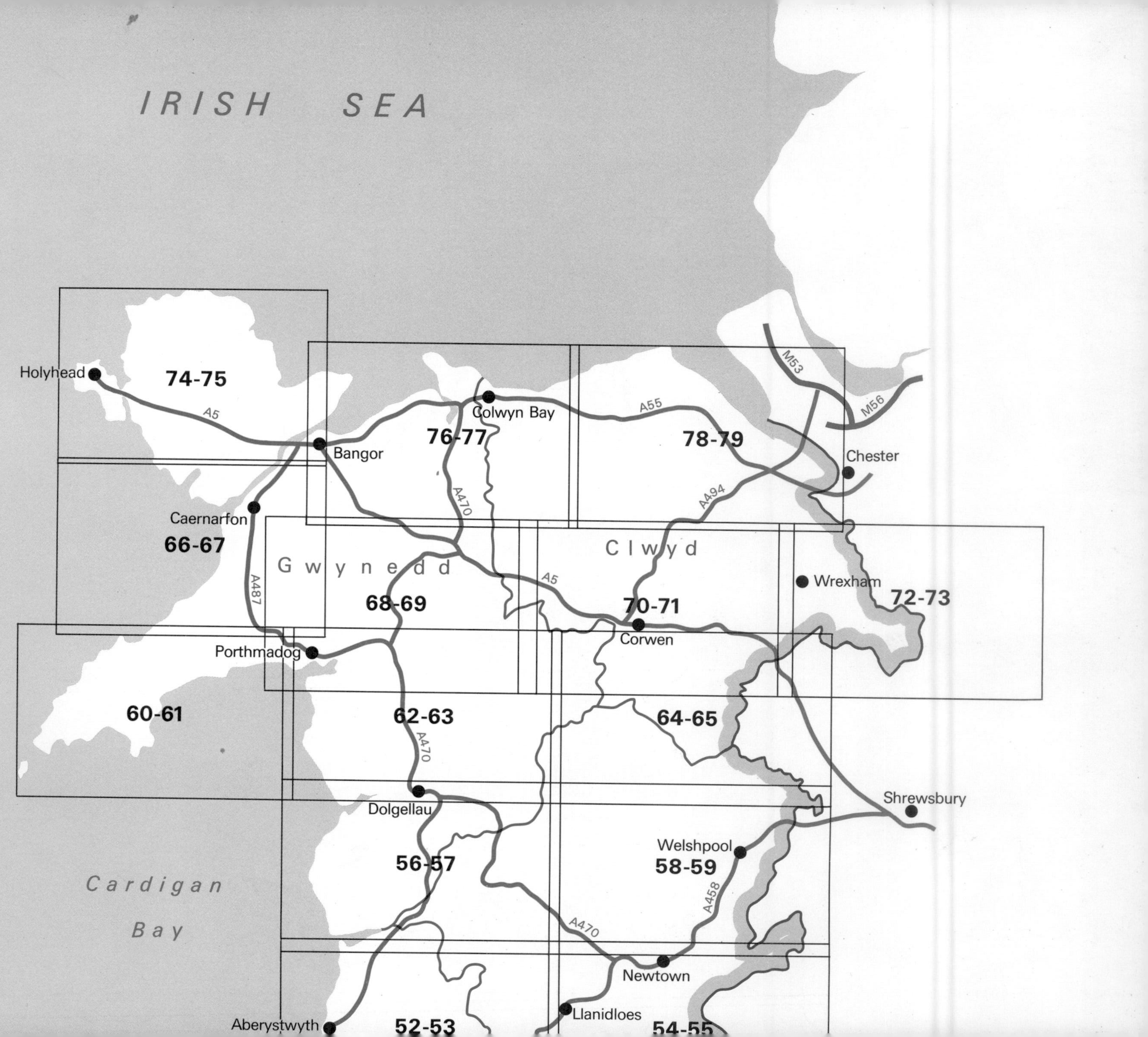

M4

A470

IRISH SEA

Cardigan

Bay

Gwynedd

Clwyd

M56

M53

Chester

Wrexham

Shrewsbury

Welshpool

Newtown

Llanidloes

Corwen

A55

A494

A5

A470

A487

A458

Colwyn Bay

Bangor

Caernarfon

Holyhead

Porthmadog

Dolgellau

Aberystwyth

72-73

78-79

70-71

64-65

58-59

54-55

76-77

68-69

62-63

56-57

52-53

74-75

66-67

60-61